CROSSBILL GUIDES

Madeira
PORTUGAL

Crossbill Guides: Madeira – Portugal
First print: 2019

Initiative, text and research: Dirk Hilbers, Kees Woutersen
Additional text: Albert Vliegenthart (insects and invertebrates)
Editing: John Cantelo, Brian Clews, Kim Lotterman, Gino Smeulders
Illustrations: Horst Wolter
Type and image setting: Oscar Lourens
Print: Drukkerij Tienkamp, Groningen

ISBN 978 94 91648 17 5
© 2019 Crossbill Guides Foundation, Arnhem, The Netherlands

This book is produced with best practice methods ensuring lowest possible environmental impact, using waterless offset, vegetable based inks and FSC-certified paper.

All rights reserved. No part of this book may be reproduced in any form by print, photocopy, microfilm or any other means without the written permission of the Crossbill Guides Foundation.
The Crossbill Guides Foundation and its authors have done their utmost to provide accurate and current information and describe only routes, trails and tracks that are safe to explore. However, things do change and readers are strongly urged to check locally for current conditions and for any changes in circumstances. Neither the Crossbill Guides Foundation nor its authors or publishers can accept responsibillity for any loss, injury or inconveniences sustained by readers as a result of the information provided in this guide.

www.crossbillguides.org
www.knnvpublishing.nl
www.saxifraga.nl

KNNV Publishing

CROSSBILL GUIDES FOUNDATION

This guidebook is a product of the non-profit foundation Crossbill Guides. By publishing these books we want to introduce more people to the joys of Europe's beautiful natural heritage and to increase the understanding of the ecological values that underlie conservation efforts. Most of this heritage is protected for ecological reasons and we want to provide insight into these reasons to the public at large. By doing so we hope that more people support the ideas behind nature conservation.
For more information about us and our guides you can visit our website at:

WWW.CROSSBILLGUIDES.ORG

Highlights of Madeira

1 Pull on your walking boots and explore Madeira's magnificent laurel cloud forests – the largest forests of this kind are found on Madeira and they contain a wealth of endemic wildflowers, birds and butterflies.

2 Get up early and walk at sunrise to the tip of the São Lourenço Peninsula, Madeira's dry eastern point with its magnificent cliffs and rare vegetation.

3 Visit the leafy gardens of Funchal and enjoy the colonial atmosphere of the town, marvel at the rich flora of both native and foreign plants and enjoy the Monarch butterflies and the local bird species.

4 Walk the spectacular trail from Pico do Areeiro to Pico Ruivo with its steep cliffs and dazzling native flora.

HIGHLIGHTS OF MADEIRA

5 Take the ferry and be chaperoned by dolphins and seabirds to the island of Porto Santo. Stroll along its the sun-drenched beach, go birdwatching (to see several species you won't find on Madeira) or walk the amazing trail to the Pico Branco.

6 The uninhabited sawblade islands of the Desertas can be visited on a guided tour that combines seabird and dolphin-watching, some snorkelling, a visit to the sea caves where Monk Seals are sometimes seen, with a visit to one of the wildest islands of Europe.

7 Take a gentle trip along the green and wild north coast and visit the paradisiacal *fajãs*, enjoy the traditional villages with their Madeira wine vineyards and sugar cane plots.

8 Explore the ocean on one of the many excellent excursions – snorkelling (with or without dolphins), go whale-watching or take a specialised trip to see the shearwaters, petrels and other seabirds.

About this guide

 boat trip or ferry crossing

 car route

 bicycle route

 walking route

 beautiful scenery

 interesting history

 interesting geology

This guide is meant for all those who enjoy being in and learning about nature, whether you already know all about it or not. It is set up a little differently from most guides. We focus on explaining the natural and ecological features of an area rather than merely describing the site. We choose this approach because the nature of an area is more interesting, enjoyable and valuable when seen in the context of its complex relationships. The interplay of different species with each other and with their environment is simply mind-blowing. The clever tricks and gimmicks that are put to use to beat life's challenges are as fascinating as they are countless.

Take our namesake the Crossbill: at first glance it's just a big finch with an awkward bill. But there is more to the Crossbill than meets the eye. This bill is beautifully adapted for life in coniferous forests. It is used like a scissor to cut open pinecones and eat the seeds that are unobtainable for other birds. In the Scandinavian countries where pine and spruce take up the greater part of the forests, several Crossbill species have each managed to answer two of life's most pressing questions: how to get food and how to avoid direct competition. By evolving crossed bills, each differing subtly, they have secured a monopoly of the seeds produced by cones of varying sizes. So complex is this relationship that scientists are still debating exactly how many different species of Crossbill actually exist. Now this should heighten the appreciation of what at first glance was merely a plump bird with a beak that doesn't seem to fit properly. Once its interrelationships are seen, nature comes alive, wherever you are.

To some, impressed by the 'virtual' familiarity that television has granted to the wilderness of the Amazon, the vastness of the Serengeti or the sublimity of Yellowstone, European nature may seem a puny surrogate, good merely for the casual stroll. In short, the argument seems to be that if you haven't seen some impressive predator, be it a Jaguar, Lion or Grizzly Bear, then you haven't seen the 'real thing'. Nonsense, of course.

But where to go? And how? What is there to see? That is where this guide comes in. We describe the how, the why, the when, the where and the how come of Europe's most beautiful areas. In clear and accessible language, we explain the nature of the Madeiran archipelago and refer extensively to routes where the area's features can be observed best. We try to make Madeira come alive. We hope that we succeed.

How to use this guide

This guidebook contains a descriptive and a practical section.
The descriptive part comes first and gives you insight into the most striking and interesting natural features of the area. It provides an understanding of what you will see when you go out exploring. The descriptive part consists of a landscape section (marked with a red bar), describing the habitats, the history and the landscape in general, and of a flora and fauna section (marked with a green bar), which discusses the plants and animals that occur in the region.
The second part offers the practical information (marked with a purple bar). A series of routes (walks) is carefully selected to give you a good flavour of all the habitats, flora and fauna that Madeira has to offer. At the start of each route description, a number of icons give a quick overview of the characteristics of each route. These icons are explained in the margin of this page. The final part of the book (marked with blue squares) provides some basic tourist information and some tips on finding plants, birds and other animals.
There is no need to read the book from cover to cover. Instead, each small chapter stands on its own and refers to the routes most suitable for viewing the particular features described in it. Conversely, descriptions of each route refer to the chapters that explain more in depth the most typical features that can be seen along the way.
We have tried to keep the number of technical terms to a minimum. If using one is unavoidable, we explain it in the glossary at the end of the guide. There we have also included a list of all the mentioned plant and animal species, with their scientific names and translations into German and Dutch.
Some species names have an asterisk (*) following them. This indicates that there is no official English name for this species and that we have taken the liberty of coining one. For the sake of readability we have decided to translate the scientific name, or, when this made no sense, we gave a name that best describes the species' appearance or distribution. Please note that we do not want to claim these as the official names. We merely want to make the text easier to follow for those not familiar with scientific names. When a new vernacular name was invented, we've also added the scientific name.
An overview of the area described in this book is given on the map on page 12 and 13. For your convenience we have also turned the inner side of the back flap into a map of the area indicating all the described routes. Descriptions in the explanatory text refer to these routes.

 interesting flora

 interesting invertebrate life

 interesting reptile and amphibian life

 interesting mammals

 interesting birdlife

 site for snorkelling

 interesting for whales and dolphins

 visualising the ecological contexts described in this guide

Table of contents

Landscape	**11**
Geographical overview	12
Geology	20
Climate	27
Evolution	28
Habitats	34
The marine habitat	36
Dry scrubland and coastal cliffs	40
Urbanised areas and non-native forest	42
Laurel cloud forest	45
The high mountains	52
History	55
Nature conservation	63
Flora and Fauna	**69**
Flora	72
Mammals	90
Birds	94
Reptiles and amphibians	106
Insects and other invertebrates	108
Practical Part	**117**
Route 1: The Funchal area	118
Route 2: Machico to Ponta de São Lourenço	122
Route 3: Ponta de São Lourenço	127
Route 4: The northeast coast	130
Route 5: Madeira's wild west coast	134
Route 6: Ribeiro Frio	138
Route 7: Levada do Furado	141
Route 8: Rabaçal	144
Route 9: Ribeira da Janela and Fanal	148
Route 10: Paúl da Serra plateau	152
Route 11: The valley of the Lily-of-the-Valley Tree	155
Route 12: Pico do Areeiro to Pico Ruivo	158
Route 13: Pico Ruivo	162
Route 14: Queimadas and Caldeirão Verde	165
Route 15: Porto Santo daytrip	168
Route 16: The Pico Branco	173
Additional sites	176
A – Lugar de Baixo	176

TABLE OF CONTENTS

B – Cabo Girão and Fajã dos Padres	177
C – Seawatching from Funchal	177
D – Rocha Alta	178
E – Quinta do Palheiro	179
F – Miradoura Curral das Freiras	179
G – Funchal ecological park	180
H – Pico do Areeiro	180
I – Ponta Garajau	181
J – Fajã da Nogueira	182
K – Seixal and Chão da Ribeira valley	183
L – Porto Moniz	183
M – Levada de Ribeiro Janela	185
N – The crest route	185
Excursions	186
1 – Whalewatching and dolphin watching	187
2 – Trip to the Desertas Islands	188
3 – Pelagic birdwatching tour	190
4 – Zino's Petrel night excursion	191
5 – Land birdwatching	192
6 – Cruise to the Selvagens Islands	193
Tourist information and observation tips	**195**
Acknowledgements	**213**
Picture and illustration credits	**214**
Species list and translation	**215**

List of Text boxes

Wildlife of Porto Santo	17
Wildlife of the Desertas	17
Wildlife of the Selvagens	19
19th Century naturalists on Madeira	56
What makes Madeira so important in Portuguese history?	62
Life projects	67
Extreme rarities	84
Whale hunting and the Whale conservation	93
Downfall and recovery of the Trocaz Pigeon	100
Re-discovery of the Zino´s Petrel	102
Insecta Maderensia, discoveries by the 19th Century naturalist Wollaston	111

LANDSCAPE

In a riot of green, Madeira rises out of the Atlantic. From top to bottom the island is formed from volcanic rock. Midway up its flanks a sheet of cloud slices across the slopes, so that on some days it almost looks like a blade has decapitated the island. However, far from being an executioner, it is what nurtures Madeira's main natural wonder: the moist laurel forest with its unique flora and fauna. In an almost permanent state of dampness, thick layers of ferns, mosses, lichens and liverworts thrive, carpeting the rocks and evergreen trees and completing the image of an emerald jungle. There is water everywhere, moistening the air, dripping from branches to the ground where it forms rivulets which stream down steep slopes. The water gathers in Madeira's contour-hugging *levadas* (the island's characteristic irrigation channels), which transport it to where it's needed.

Further down the slopes and on the southern half of the island are the towns and villages. Some of them still exude a colonial atmosphere, not in the least because of their fine gardens and parks, where hundreds of tropical and subtropical trees and flowers were planted reflecting Portugal's imperial past.

But that's not all. Madeira is an archipelago. The nearby island of Porto Santo and the Islas Desertas are quite different. They have a dry climate and arid landscape with their own natural attractions.

The surrounding ocean is rich in marine life. Dolphins, whales and turtles come close to shore. The archipelago is of international importance for its breeding seabirds.

All of this can be enjoyed to the fullest. With over 2,170 km of walking trails, many of which following the levadas, you have easy access even to the wildest and steepest part of the mountains. Boat excursions to the other islands not only enable you to visit them, but also offer excellent opportunities to get a taste of the marine life *en route*.

All in all, Madeira is a place to visit and visit again. This book helps you discover the best sites, walk the most beautiful routes and above all, shows you the flora and fauna that makes the island unique.

The green north coast of Madeira is wild and spectacular (route 4).

Geographical overview

The area described in this book comprises Madeira, the much smaller inhabited island of Porto Santo and the uninhabited Desertas Islands which together form the Madeiran archipelago. This book also briefly describes the small Selvagens Islands, which belong to Portugal but lie much further south.

The Madeiran archipelago lies 560 kms east of Morocco and 860 kms southwest of Lisbon. The distance to the Canary Islands is less than 500 kms and the nearest island of the Azores is 840 kms. In other words, it is in a pretty isolated position in the Atlantic.

Biologically speaking, Madeira is most akin to the Canary Islands. Like these, Madeira has laurel forests and succulent scrub at low altitudes, a foggy north slope and an overall sunny south. Like the Canaries, Madeira has a unique flora and fauna with many endemic species, many of which are related to those found on the Canaries.

Overview of the Atlantic or *Macaronesian* islands (top), the Madeira archipelago (bottom) and the island of Madeira (facing page).
The numbers in the white squares refer to the routes that are described on page 118 and further. The letters are a reference to the sites described on page 176 and further, while the purple letters pertain to the guided excursions described on page 190 and onwards.

GEOGRAPHICAL OVERVIEW

The islands in figures

	surface	max. altitude	inhabitants
Madeira	740.7 km2	1861 m	262,456 (2011)
Porto Santo	42.6 km2	516 m	5,483 (2011)
Desertas	14.2 km2	442 m	0
Selvagens	2.7 km2	163 m	0

Another striking feature these island groups share, is that Madeira is completely of volcanic origin and has never been part of any continent, making it a splendid place to watch evolution in action.

But there are differences too. The climate of Madeira is more temperate, due to its northern location. It is wetter and greener. Whereas an island like Tenerife was originally inhabited only on the north slopes because the south was too dry, Madeira has its towns on the south, which has a more benign climate. Furthermore, Madeira lies much further out in the ocean and is thus more isolated than the Canaries.

Brief overview of Madeira

Although Madeira is the biggest island of the archipelago, it is still a rather small island. All but one of the major Canary Islands are larger. A little under 270,000 people live on the island (2011 figures) to which a yearly total of more than a million

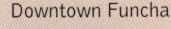
Downtown Funchal

LANDSCAPE

GEOGRAPHICAL OVERVIEW

View on Funchal from the ferry to Porto Santo.

tourists should be added. The island's capital is Funchal. Situated around a beautiful and lively marina, Funchal has beautiful, historic centre and abundant gardens and parks. With 150,000 permanent inhabitants, over half of the Madeirans live in the greater Funchal area.

Most other towns and villages on the island are close to the coast, forming a ring around the wild and largely deserted interior. Especially on the west coast, the steep and heavily eroded coastline makes living close to the sea impossible. Villages are situated on top of cliffs from which steep trails run down to small and isolated coastal plains known as *fajãs*. Not so long ago, many of these villages had no road connection to the outside world. Now, a very good, EU-funded ring road connects them. It pierces through the mountains in a network of tunnels, allowing you to cross beneath the rugged terrain unhindered.

East of Funchal lies a series of coastal villages like Santa Cruz, Machico and Caniçal on relatively gentle slopes, which is also the reason that the airport was built here. The southeast is also the sunniest part of the island. The eastern tip of the island is a spectacular elongated peninsula that juts out into the ocean and has a much drier climate.

West of Funchal lies Camara de Lobos, Ribeira Brava and Ponta do Sol. This is the region where lots of bananas are cultivated and where Madeira's highest cliff is situated, the Cabo Girão (page 177). As you travel further west, the land becomes more rugged and less populated.

GEOGRAPHICAL OVERVIEW

Madeira's northern slopes are even steeper than those in the south, and therefore much more sparsely populated. The wildest coastal area is perhaps the northwest, where the main villages, Porto Moniz and Seixal, are situated on recent lava flows close to the coast.

The northeast has many pretty, historic coastal villages such as São Vicente, Santana and Ponta Delgada. Here, fishermen still go out onto the unpredictable ocean and surrounding fields are cultivated with grapes for the Madeira wine.

Central Madeira is steep and wild. On the higher south slopes, much of the original forest made way to ugly, non-native Eucalyptus and pine forests, but in the north the slopes are clad in the unique laurel forest and the ravines are full of mysterious, dark forests. This is hikers' country, with a myriad of the trails following the small water channels (*levadas*), which ensure that even on the steepest slopes many routes are undemanding.

More walking trails are situated along the central mountain ridge which is so high that on most days, it pierces through the cloud cover. The central ridge consists of two parts, divided by the main north-south valley that runs from Ribeira Brava in the south over the Encumeadas pass to São Vicente in the north. West of this natural divide, the highest mountains are rounded hills on the odd, almost un-Madeiran highland plateau of Paúl da Serra. The eastern massif has the highest mountains, and these are extraordinary steep and wild. At 1,862, the Pico Ruivo is Madeira's highest mountain.

The system of water channels or *levadas* offer a unique trail network that provides easy access to even the steepest parts of Madeira. This is what gives the island its status of a ramblers paradise.

LANDSCAPE

GEOGRAPHICAL OVERVIEW

Portuguese words that you will find on the map

Chão level ground where you can walk.
Fajã a flat area on the coast formed by accumulation of gravel, sand and debris fallen down from erosion on a beach, a river side or a river mouth.
Farol light house
Jardim garden
Ilhéu island
Levada mini-canal that carry water from the mountains to lower areas, especially for agriculture
Lombo mountain ridge
Miradouro view point
Monte mountain or part of a mountain
Paragem bus stop
Pico mountain top
Ponta headland
Porto port, harbour
Ribeira river, riverside
Serra mountain range

Brief overview of Porto Santo

The small island of Porto Santo lies only 43 km to the northeast of Madeira, but is very different from its big neighbour. It is less mountainous (although there are still five peaks of around 500 m) and most slopes are gentle. Porto Santo enjoys a dry and sunny climate and the vegetation is grassy or bushy. On the north side, Porto Santo has some rugged cliffs, but on the south the land slopes gently towards a sandy bay with a wonderful beach, which is together with the sun, the main attraction for visitors. As beautiful as Madeira is, it can be overcast and dreary at times, so both tourists and residents escape to Porto Santo for some beach time. No wonder that Porto Santo's economy runs on tourism.

Only 5,500 people live on Porto Santo (2011 figures), nearly all in the main village of Vila Baleira, which lies right beside the beach. For naturalists, the birdlife of dry arable land of the interior and the cliff flora in the north form the greatest attractions of the island.

Brief overview of the Desertas

The uninhabited Desertas islands are situated about 25 kilometres to the southeast of Madeira. The jagged crest is a landmark that can be seen from just about anywhere in the southeastern part of Madeira. Long ago, the Desertas were a part of the main island and under water, the range continues and connects with the São Lourenço Peninsula of Madeira.

Traditional windmill on Porto Santo.

GEOGRAPHICAL OVERVIEW

> **Wildlife of Porto Santo**
> In terms of wildlife, Porto Santo is in most respects a small, dry version of Madeira. The diversity is much lower, but Porto Santo has a number of species you won't find on Madeira (like Spanish Sparrow and Kentish Plover) or in much higher numbers (Linnet, Hoopoe, Rock Sparrow). Porto Santo also has a number of wildflowers that are either absent from or very rare on Madeira.

The Desertas consist of three long and narrow islands. From north to south these are Ilhéu Chão, Deserta Grande and Bugio. Chão is the smallest, 1,600 m in length and up to 500 m wide. Chão means level ground, which is fitting as it is basically a square, flat-topped block of lava, around 100 metres high. Desertas Grande in the middle is the biggest island, 12 km long, measuring less than 2 kms across on its widest point and with multiple peaks, the highest being 479 m. Along its coast are numerous caves and crags and in the interior are deep valleys. The southern Bugio is the narrowest and most irregular shaped island, 7,500 m in length, up to 700 m width, with a maximum height of 388 m.

The Rock Sparrow is one of the birds of dry lands that is easier to see on Porto Santo than on Madeira.

> **Wildlife of the Desertas**
> The most emblematic mammal species of the Desertas is the extremely rare and threatened Mediterranean Monk Seal. There is a colony of about 25 animals on Deserta Grande (see page 92). Furthermore, the islands support one of the most important seabird colonies of the north Atlantic with Cory's Shearwater, Macaronesian Shearwater, Bulwer's Petrel, Madeiran Storm-petrel, Common Tern and Yellow-legged Gull. Amongst these is a rare seabird that vies with the seal as the islands' most emblematic species, the Desertas Petrel (sometimes called Fea's Petrel; see page 102). Equally emblematic, if of more limited appeal, are the endangered hand-sized Desertas Tarantula and the 16 endemic terrestrial molluscs. Land birds on the Desertas are Buzzard, Kestrel, Barn Owl, Canary and Berthelot's Pipit. Other animals include Madeira Wall Lizard.

LANDSCAPE

GEOGRAPHICAL OVERVIEW

All three are rather barren, with only cliff-dwelling plants and some scrub scattered over the yellow, brown and blackish lava. Arid and with an impoverished flora and fauna, *Deserta* lives up to its name since, apart from a single warden's house where a small team of guards is stationed, there are no people on the islands. There are no roads, few paths and there is hardly any fresh water. For a long time, the Desertas were private property of two English families. The Portuguese State bought them in 1971 and declared them a Nature Reserve. Access is only possible with an organised trip (see page 188).

Brief overview of the Selvagens Islands

The uninhabited Savage Islands or Selvagens Islands form their own archipelago – a tiny one, with a total land surface of only 2.73 square kms. They are situated far away from the other islands, 300 kilometres south of Madeira, but 'only' 150 kms from the Canaries. Nevertheless the Selvagens are Portuguese territory. There are no boat or air services to the islands, making them about the most isolated place in Europe (if you can call it European, but that's a different discussion).

Selvagem Grande, perhaps the remotest and least visited part of Europe.

GEOGRAPHICAL OVERVIEW

The small, uninhabited islands are divided into two groups 15 kilometres apart. Each has one major island and several satellite islets, which are no more than chunks of rock emerging from the ocean. Salvagem Grande is a plateau of 245 hectares ringed by sea-cliffs; Salvagem Pequena is no larger than 20 hectares.

Both islands are very dry, without surface water and with just a scant vegetation. They are famous for their seabird colonies. There is a biological station with permanent wardens, who must have about the loneliest job in the European Union.

During centuries, the Selvagens have been economically exploited by families who had obtained the property rights. Lichens (to make red dye), weed, shells and molluscs were collected, and introduced goats and rabbits were hunted. In 1971 the Portuguese government bought the islands and declared them to be a nature reserve. Access is only possible with an organised trip (see page 193).

The White-faced Storm-petrel is the most numerous breeding bird on the Selvagens Islands.

Wildlife of the Selvagens

The Selvagens Islands are a seabird paradise. With more than 5,000 pairs of Bulwer's Petrel, the islands host the species' largest colony in the Atlantic and probably in the world. Cory´s Shearwater breed with an estimated 19,000 pairs, and there are 1,500 and 2,000 pairs of respectively Madeiran Storm-petrel and Macaronesian Shearwaters. The most common bird however is the White-faced Storm-petrel. No less than 36,000 pairs breed on Salvagem Grande and around 25,000 on Salvagem Pequena. In addition, there are small colonies of Yellow-legged Gull, Common Tern and Roseate Tern. These seabirds are only present during the breeding season.

Believe it or not, there are even populations of land birds: Berthelot´s Pipit and Kestrel. The latter feeds on the Madeira Wall Lizard, and the local Selvagens Island Gecko.

LANDSCAPE

Geology

Madeira is the kind of island that makes geologists of us all. The terrain is so rugged that much of it is inaccessible. The rock formations are spectacular, with shapes and forms that demand an explanation. The island is also geologically variable, with steep areas that suddenly give way to almost level plains that then, in turn, plunge into an abyss.

In spite of all of this, Madeira's geology is not that complicated. Its bedrock is almost entirely of volcanic origin and most of its awe-inspiring shapes are the result of the erosive force of waves, wind and rain.

From a distance you can see that Madeira is one large Shield volcano.

In geography class we've been taught that old mountains, subject to erosion, have smoothened forms. Every rock or pinnacle that sticks out its head is subjected to erosive rain and wind much more fiercely than the rest of the mountain. So over time, anything that sticks its head up is relentlessly ground down.

But that's just part of the story. More precisely, it's the end of it. Before erosion smoothens the shape of the mountains, wind and water first create cliffs and pinnacles, in particular in volcanic areas like Madeira, which has so many different strata. Volcanic eruptions produce a plethora of different rocks and sediments. There are coarse, sharp lava fields, soft smooth lava, extremely dense and resistant rock types and brittle layers of volcanic ash, each with its own specific background (as we will discuss a bit further on). In particular the ash and tuff stone, resulting from violent eruptions cover the island in layers that cover the sharp basalts. Geologists call tuff *pyroclastic* – 'pyro' referring to fire of the volcano and 'clastic' meaning that it is built up from small pieces.

The subsequent erosion does the opposite. It nibbles on the softer rocks, uncovering the harder rock types, which remain as rocks, pinnacles, walls and cliffs. On the ocean side, the action of the waves does the same, with steep cliffs as the result.

Wind, sea and rainfall are strongest on the north slope of the island. Hence this is where you find the most extreme landscape with the deepest gorges and most precipitous coastline.

GEOLOGY

The genesis of an island
Most geologists agree that, like the Canary Islands, Madeira formed above a *hotspot* – an area where, due to tectonic forces, the Earth's mantle is thinner than elsewhere. As a result, the magma chambers (reservoirs of molten rock) lie closer to the surface. Periodic ruptures of the crust, either the result of tectonic forces or by increased pressure in the magma chamber, cause hot lava to flow into the ocean. A less widely accepted rival theory based on the structure of submarine mountains, suggests that a series of tectonic faults through which the magma leaks, is the cause of the formation of Madeira and its submarine mountains.

It is not hard to imagine that when a huge mass of hot, molten rock, is suddenly exposed to cold water, it causes a violent reaction. However, as the seafloor is 3,000 metres below the surface, the explosive result is concealed from view. The massive pressure of the ocean's water contains the eruptions, pushing the lava out to all sides and creating a massive, flat shield volcano.

With each eruption, 'proto-Madeira' rose and came closer to the surface. Without the same weight of water above, the constricting water pressure lessened and each new eruption became more violent than the previous one, until, roughly between five and seven million years ago, the young island we call Madeira lifted its head up out of the water.

Madeira's steep slopes are the result of erosion.

LANDSCAPE

GEOLOGY

All over the islands, you can encounter beautiful rock formations, such as columnar basalt (below; route 9), weathered basalts know as onion skins (top right; route 3), soft, yellowish tuff stone (centre right; route 12) and volcanic dykes (below right; praia de Garajau; page 181).

An underwater archipelago

Madeira is the highest mountain of a large, submarine range. The other mountains were formed in a similar way but most of them stopped growing long before they reached the surface. As the tectonic forces push the marine floor, complete with its islands, away from the hotspot (which is anchored deeper in the Earth's mantle), the budding island is robbed of its magma source and remains as an underwater mountain. With a new part of the Earth's crust now above the hotspot, the process starts all over again. A look at the underwater maps of the coast between Madeira and Portugal shows an elongated mountain range from Madeira to roughly 300 kms off the coast of Lisbon, with several lateral ranges.

So the seafloor around Madeira is extremely mountainous. There are areas not far from the island where the sea is deeper than 3,000 metres, but counterintuitively, much further out into the ocean, there are entire areas where the submarine peaks create shallows of just several tens or hundreds of metres deep. These underwater ranges are extremely rich in submarine life (see page 36).

Madeira island

Madeira rose above the surface as a wide, dome-shaped island, a shield volcano. Typical of this sort of volcano, there is not a single vent. Rather, lava oozed out through many fissures in the bedrock, some positioned laterally on the slopes. Most of the eruption sites are not visible anymore. There are just two exceptions, one of which is the crater lake at Fanal (route 9).

In the shallow waters around the island large coral reefs formed. As the island was pushed up (by still little understood tectonic forces), the reefs were lifted up too. Some of them are still found in fossilized form in the Madeiran mountains and on the São Lourenço Peninsula. They constitute the only non-volcanic rocks of the island.

Since the island's birth, there have been five distinct phases of increased volcanic activity, separated by more tranquil intervals. Each of these phases produced

GEOLOGY

massive amounts of new material that mostly covered the previous layers. In the valleys and along the coastal cliffs however, wind and water erosion cut deep in this layered cake, exposing the older strata at the base of the mountains.

There is a remarkable diversity of volcanic rocks on Madeira. There are the black, shiny rocks known as **basalt** which originate from liquid lava that solidified on the surface. As it cools down, basalt shrinks and cracks in angular columns that can be tens, even hundreds of metres long. In some places they tower above the surface looking like angular 'organ pipes' or, where you can stand on top of them, like a maze of random polygonal steps. **Old columnar basalt** weathers into odd, **'onion-skin' rocks**.

In more violent eruptions, massive amounts of fine volcanic ash are ejected, sometimes together with a coarser material the size of cat litter (grains between 2mm and 64mm in diameter) which is known as **lapilli**. Compressed layers of ash form the very soft **tuffstone**, which forms thick belts further away from the eruption vents.

Basically anywhere on the archipelago you can see odd seams in the rock of cliffs. It looks like streaky bacon, only the streaks are often vertically positioned and usually darker than the surrounding rock. These

LANDSCAPE

GEOLOGY

Most fajãs can only be reached via steep walking trails or with a cable car (route 5).

are **volcanic dykes**, made of hardy basalt that filled the small channels in lava and tuff.

All in all, Madeira consists of a potpourri of different rock types. Each of these reacts differently to the forces of erosion. Wind and water sculpt tuff stone easily, but where dykes lace the bedrock, it forms resistant formations. This is most splendidly visible around Pico do Areeiro (route 12), where vertical walls of solid rock (the dykes) form the backbone of the softer tuff formations. In places, the dykes are almost like the walls of an ancient ruin. On Paúl da Serra, a hard, resistant basalt layer is positioned horizontally, protecting the softer bedrock beneath. Hence erosion has made little progress on the massif, which retains its flat form. Similarly, Chão, the northernmost of Desertas Islands, which is also formed from horizontal basalt layers has a curious, block-shaped appearance.

The rough Atlantic Ocean was (and still is) Madeira's most important sculptor. The island is attacked by waves from all sides – relentlessly and ceaselessly. Faced with softer strata, the waves easily erode the coastline, leaving massive cliffs. The highest and most impressive is doubtlessly

Cabo Girão, but all over the island, in particular in the exposed western half, there are many impressive cliffs.

The formation of cliffs is not a gradual process. Rather, the waves attack the base of the rocks, where they create caves and undermine the whole edifice. At some point an entire area of cliff collapses. The rocks tumble to the shore, where the sea further erodes the stones until a small coastal plain is all that remains. These plains are known as *fajãs* – wonderful, fertile, secluded and subtropical places, ideal for small-scale farming but extremely isolated at the base of the cliffs. Historically, access to the fajãs was only possible by perilous and steep footpaths or by boat. The entire village of Paúl do Mar is situated on such a fajã, and was before the construction of the ring road (in the final decades of the 20th century) only accessible by boat (route 5).

Today, there are cable cars, used by tourists and farmers alike, that take you down to the fajãs. A visit to such a secluded plain is a wonderful experience (see routes 4 and 5).

In the mountains, it is the rain and the rivers that sculpt the valleys. The north slope in particular receives so much precipitation, that the erosive force of rivers is very strong. Some of the most spectacular chasms and clefts were cut out by water. It is in these remote and impossible to reach spots that the laurel forest is in its most original form.

The exception is Chão da Ribeira near Seixal in the northwest (site K on page 183). This valley is not like a gorge, but wide and U-shaped, almost like the glacial valleys in Scotland and Scandinavia. But it was neither ice nor water that gave the Chão its characteristic form but a relatively recent lava flow (between 100,000 and 200,000 years old) that shaped the valley floor.

Porto Santo

The island of Porto Santo is much older than Madeira. It reached the surface around 14 million years ago. Again, reef formations were brought to the surface when the island appeared. Thanks to eruptions the island continued to grow until about 8 million years ago. Since then, the volcanic activities ceased (note, that's at least one million years before Madeira emerged).

Its greater age and the subsequently longer period of erosion makes Porto Santo a much less dramatic island. The island lacks the steep canyons and only on the north slope there are cliffs of significance.

What makes Porto Santo completely different from Madeira is the long sandy beach on the southern shore. It is a natural beach, consisting largely of debris of ancient reefs and shells. In the weathering process,

GEOLOGY

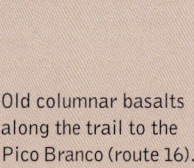

Old columnar basalts along the trail to the Pico Branco (route 16).

dissolved minerals cemented the grains together to form 'concretions' – a brittle type of calcareous sandstone that easily disintegrates into a fine-grained type of sand. Erosion by rain sculpts these concretions into spectacular shapes that you can find on the edge of the beach.

In these sands you can find on Porto Santo and on the São Lourenço Peninsula another geological oddity: fossilised roots. Prehistoric forests that grew in these places had extensive root systems, in which the concretions formed a firmer type of cemented sandstone, like a mould to cast metals.

Geological features and where you can see them

Dykes: Visible in many places on the islands. Most noticeable at Ponta São Lourenço (route 3), Pico do Areeiro (route 12), beach of Garajau (site I on page 181).
Tuff stone: Around Pico do Areeiro (route 12), island off Porto Moniz (site L on page 183).
Basalts and Onion-skins: Ponta São Lourenço (route 3), Porto Santo (route 15), Ribeira Janela (route 9).
Reefs and petrified roots: Ponta São Lourenço (route 2), Porto Santo (route 15).
Fajãs: North and west coasts (route 4 and 5), Cabo Girão (site B on page 177).
Most spectacular cliffs: Cabo Girão (site B on page 177), São Lourenço (route 3), Ponta Pargo (route 5).

Climate

One of the reasons Madeira became a popular tourist destination is that it enjoys mild temperatures year-round. This is the result of being surrounded by the ocean so that, from whichever direction the wind blows, it always crosses the sea. Cold winter winds warm up during their journey overseas, while the hot summer air is cooled. From January to April the sea temperature is about 17 °C and climbs to 23 °C in late summer.

This small fluctuation is reflected in the temperatures on land. January is the coldest month and even then average temperatures during the day in Funchal on the south coast rise to a comfortable 19 °C. At night, it doesn't get much colder than 13 °C. In August, the hottest month, it varies from 25 °C at midday to 18 °C at night.

Whereas temperatures don't change much during the year at any given spot, they vary wildly from one place to another on the island. Whereas the average temperature in Funchal is 18.8 °C, it drops to only 9.7 °C on the Pico do Areeiro (1,610 m). On the north coast temperatures are on average just a bit lower, but because there is less sunshine and more rain, it feels much colder. Average annual rainfall ranges from 553 mm in Funchal to 1,182 mm in Ponta Delgada and 3,084 mm in Pico do Areeiro. Overall, the wettest period is from November to January, while from May to October there is little rainfall. It is not unusual for the highest peaks to see a bit of snow in winter.

The wettest parts of the island are at middle altitude (500-1,500 metres) on the north slopes, particularly in the ravines. The trade winds from the north, full of vapour from having travelled over the ocean are forced to rise when they hit the island. The vapour turns into clouds as the air cools down, which happens mostly in this altitude range. In winter particularly, the clouds can stay for days on end. Vice versa, days when no fog is formed in this area are rare. Unsurprisingly, this is the zone where the mossy laurel cloud forest is best developed.

In complete contrast, the low eastern point of Madeira, where no high mountains block the trade winds, is arid and has a lot of sunshine.

This holds true even more for the island of Porto Santo and the Desertas. Porto Santo has a semi-desert climate. It has many more hours of sunshine than Funchal, and although the average temperatures are similar, Porto Santo feels a lot warmer. Between April to September, rain is exceptional and in some winters, precipitation is disturbingly low.

The climate on the Desertas is similar to that of Porto Santo – sunny, warm and with little precipitation.

EVOLUTION

Evolution

There are two reasons why the remote Galapagos Islands were so important for Charles Darwin's theory of evolution: isolation and simplicity. On the isolated islands there were unique life forms, seen nowhere else on the globe. That needed explanation. The ecosystem (a word that was only coined a hundred years later) was also much simpler. There were few species that interacted visibly and fulfilled very defined roles. That had to have a cause as well.

In the face of this comprehensible yet strange world of the Galapagos Islands, the pieces of the puzzle came together and the rest is history, written down in the book that changed biology forever: On the Origin of Species.

The processes Darwin discovered on the Galapagos, he could have witnessed on Madeira as well. For Madeira is like the Galapagos – an isolated and simple island, with large numbers of unique (endemic) species. It is the belonging-to-a-different-world and at the same time the readability of it all that makes Madeira such a joy to explore.

Isolation – a world within the world

Madeira lies 600 kms from the nearest coast, a daunting distance if you had to reach it under your own steam. And that is assuming you already knew where Madeira is and flew the shortest distance to it. Most plants and animals surely travelled a much greater distance before ending up on the island.

Evolution on islands tends to push large species towards dwarfs and small species towards giants. The native Canary Buttercup (*Ranunculus canariensis*) is clearly an example of island gigantism.

CROSSBILL GUIDES • MADEIRA

EVOLUTION

Madeira is completely volcanic, like the Galapagos, the Canary Islands and the Azores. Being the result of volcanic eruptions, it was never part of any continent, like for example Great Britain, Corsica or Crete. On Madeira, every land-based organism had to arrive by air or by sea, crossing many hundreds of kilometres of hostile ocean.

So how did life get to Madeira? Well, in part, it simply didn't. No land mammals set foot on the island (before being introduced by people). Nor any salt intolerant amphibians like frogs, newts or toads. Only a limited suite of birds arrived. No tits, treecreepers or woodpeckers inhabit the forests of Madeira.

Indeed, if you read through the flora and fauna chapters of this book, the absence of species is as least as striking their presence. Those that made it consists largely of species that are strong flyers, like pigeons, some dragonflies and butterflies, bats and lots of seabirds. Among the flora, there are species with small seeds that easily drift on the air currents, and those that travel as cargo in the gut of birds. Small insects and spiders arrived largely by air, floating on the wind. For a long time, the presence of this group that clearly couldn't actively fly across, was controversial. In a large research project in and around Hawaii (even more isolated than Madeira) scientists investigated the arrival of small bugs by the use of large nets. It turned out that there is a constant fallout of diminutive critters even thousands of kilometres away from the mainland. Spiders are picked up with web and all and as on a magic carpet, float on air currents high across the sea.

Pigeons, being strong flyers, frequently colonise remote islands and evolve into new species. The Wood Pigeon colonised Madeira at least twice. One early colonisation led to evolution of the Trocaz Pigeon (left). Much later the Wood Pigeon arrived again and established a population of what became the Madeiran Wood Pigeon. It went extinct in the 20th century and all that remains is a stuffed specimen in the botanical garden of Funchal (right).

LANDSCAPE

EVOLUTION

The arrival of some other animals, such as the lizards, is a bit harder to imagine. It is precisely this group of small, land-dwelling animals that is almost completely absent on the islands. Most probably, it is chance rather than anything else that caused this small group of animals to end up on Madeira. Perhaps it was driftwood that carried lizards from the continent to the island. The chances of any particular bit of driftwood, not least one laden with lizards, making it to Madeira are very small but there's a lot of driftwood and millions of years for the unlikely to become quite possible.

In contrast to most mammals and all reptiles, migrant birds are adept at flying great distances. The challenge of finding (and for some, settling on) Madeira is much less.

Simplicity – just a few species and a few genes

The hard and sad truth is that most plants and animals that inadvertently wound up over the ocean perished in the waves. The majority of those that did reach Madeira, most likely died sooner rather than later, due to lack of food or suitable habitat. Those odd individual animals that did survive mostly left no mark because they had no mate with whom to have offspring. Species have to arrive in a flock or carry eggs in order to become established. Settling on Madeira is a draw in a very unfair lottery. The very few winners have a grand prize – an entire island almost completely for themselves.

The rules for surviving in this new world, though, were completely different. The Trocaz Pigeon for example, evolved from a predecessor of the familiar Wood Pigeon. Once on Madeira, it had no natural predators anymore. The Goshawks, the crows, the martens, the rats, the cats and the foxes that had pigeons or their chicks and eggs on the menu, never settled on Madeira. Nor did some of its native food plants. So some traits that were vital to its survival, the pigeon didn't need anymore in his new environment, while others suddenly became important. The pigeon had to re-adapt, like Darwin's famous finches.

The natural lack of voles and mice forced Madeiran Kestrels to seek an alternative prey, which it found in the abundance of Madeira Wall Lizards...

EVOLUTION

For plants, there is a clear direction in which this adaption heads. Once the bigger laurel trees took root, the once open land soon became a forest. Only the steep slopes (of which there fortunately were a lot) kept receiving sunlight. Many of the herbs had to adapt. All the defence against herbivores was unnecessary in the new world, but what was important was the struggle for a bit of sunlight. Therefore, many herbs turned into bushes – the local globularias, foxgloves, sow-thistles, spurges, viper's-buglosses are not the familiar herbs from the continent, but tall bushes and in some cases even trees.

How did these plants manage to adapt? It is the genetic make-up (the genome) of that first and foremost dictates whether it is able to adapt. In new colonisations, something happens with the genome that speeds up the pace of evolution – a process called genetic drift. If you look at the genetic make-up of a large population of plants or animals, some genes (and by extension, some ecological traits) are much more common than others. However, if you focus on an individual, each will lack a few of the common traits and a lot of the rare ones, but it will also carry a few rare genes that most others lack. After all, each individual is unique. When an island is colonised by just a few individuals and the entire new population grows from these organisms (plants, lizards, birds, etc.) so that within a single generation, the genetic make-up of the new population will be different. A few of the common traits of the ancestor will suddenly have disappeared, while some rare traits are all of a sudden common. Blind chance determines the limited available gene pool and it is this that causes genetic change, hence the term genetic drift. Together with the radically different environment, evolution launches the population on the way to become a new species.

...The Madeira Wall Lizard in turn also display an odd behaviour that you won't observe on the continent. It frequently climbs in flower stalks and feeds on the nectar. It is thought that lizards actually play a role of importance in the pollinisation of certain native plant species.

The Madeiran archipelago has a large diversity of endemic snails (meaning snails that occur nowhere else in the world but here).

LANDSCAPE

EVOLUTION

Macaronesia – the wider context

In isolation, populations easily evolve into new species, which are unique to that particular island. They become endemics, occurring nowhere else in the world. Madeira has many endemics, although quite a few of them are shared with the Desertas Islands and Porto Santo. Logically so as the distance between these islands is so small that animals and plant seeds easily travel from one to the other. Many species are unique to the archipelago rather than to Madeira alone.

Widening the circle a bit more, the archipelago shares also quite a few species with the other Macaronesian islands, the Selvagens, Canaries and the Azores. They are considered Macaronesian endemics. Good examples are the Canary and the Berthelot's Pipit, the Canary Red Admiral and the Dragon Tree.

Macaronesia is considered a different biogeographical region thanks to its characteristic flora and fauna. Madeira is in the centre of this region, which includes the archipelagos of Cape Verde, Canaries, Selvagens, Madeira and Azores. In total it compromises 39 islands bigger than 1 km2 and more than 100 islets.

Even though the distances between the Macaronesian islands are considerable (the Canary Islands are 420 kms from Madeira and the Azores 840 kms) they have a lot in common: they are all of volcanic origin and most islands have a zone with temperate, moist and cloudy slopes, where laurel forests grow. Since there is an entire mountainscape beneath the surface of the ocean, it is thought that there may

Number of endemic species on Macaronesian Archipelagos

	Cabo Verde	Canaries	Selvagens	Madeira	Azores
Fungi and lichens	8	134	0	48	12
Non-vascular plants	6	10	0	11	9
Spore plants	1	3	0	8	7
Seed plants	64	636	7	131	61
Arthropods	435	3085	44	935	267
Molluscs	10	211	1	209	49
Vertebrates	15	72	2	11	13
Total endemics	540	4151	54	1355	420
% of all species	9.1%	27.0%	0.9%	22.8%	7.1%

from: The islands of Macaronesia, J.M. Fernández-Palacios. In Terrestial Arthropods of Macaronesia, 2010).

EVOLUTION

have been more islands in the area in the past, which could have served as stepping stones for colonisation. On the Canary Islands, genetic research on the different endemic Marguerite species has shown that older now collapsed mountain tops were once inhabited by marguerites which went on to settle on new islands.

Madeira extinctions

It is important not to forget the species that went extinct on Madeira and its adjacent islands. There are quite a few of them on record. Given the rigorous changes the island went through after the Portuguese settled in the early 15th century (see page 57), it is quite likely that many more extinctions happened unnoticed.

Fossil evidence confirms that the archipelago was inhabited by endemic birds of which we have no written records. Probably, at least three species of flightless rails, two quails, a scops owl and several passerines disappeared shortly after people arrived. The Madeiran Scops Owl (*Otus mauli*) was described in 2012 and its appearance reconstructed. It probably had a ground dwelling life-style and the causes of extinction are thought to be alteration of its habitat.

There are also more recent extinctions. The Madeira Wood Pigeon was a subspecies of the European Wood Pigeon. It was already rare in the 19th Century when they were seen on the north of the island in the same habitat as Trocaz Pigeons. It was seen (and collected) as late as 1904 (see page 100).

The Madeira Large White has not been found since the 1980s and is now considered extinct. Its decline was sudden – in the 1960s it was still considered a common butterfly. The extinction coincides with the introduction of a congener from the mainland, the Small White. It is assumed that the latter infected the native white with a virus that wiped out the endemic population. Fossil records show that nine terrestrial molluscs disappeared since human colonization. Many arthropod species have not been recorded since they were found and described in the 19th Century.

The genus of the marguerites is unique to the Atlantic Islands. The Canary Islands have the highest diversity. On Madeira there are 3 species, 2 of which are very rare. The third is widespread and occurs in two very different-looking varieties. This is one of these, the Mandon's Marguerite (*Argyranthemum pinnatifidum ssp succulentum*).

LANDSCAPE

Habitats

On Madeira you'll find a large variety of habitats in a relatively small area. With peaks of over 1,800 metres, the altitude plays an important role in creating this diversity. The temperatures on the high slopes and peaks are much lower than on the almost subtropical coast, and the precipitation is much higher. Furthermore, the east-west position of the main mountain ridge divides the island in a south-facing and a north-facing slope, with the latter catching the lion's share of the clouds that form around the island. As a result, the north-facing slopes are much cooler and much wetter than the south-facing ones on the same latitude.

High mountains (p. 52)

Laurel forests (p. 45)

Non-native forests (p. 42)

Urbanised areas (p. 42)

Dry scrublands and coastal cliffs (p. 40)

The marine habitat (p. 36)

HABITATS

This chops up the island in neat vegetation zones, each with its own peculiar habitats and its own selection of flora and fauna. The main habitats of Madeira are the dry and warm scrublands near the coast, the laurel forests higher up and the dry scrublands and grassy areas in the high mountains. Between these three are large areas of transitional vegetation. Originally, between the coastal scrubland and the laurel forest was a large area with a mixture of laurel forest and scrubland species, but this zone has been almost completely replaced by housing, agriculture and forestry. This zone has become its own habitat type, which we describe as urbanised areas. The transition between laurel forest and high mountain vegetation is quite intact and consists of dense tangles of Tree Heath, mixed with some of the hardier species of laurel forest.

A very important and attractive habitat, if very hard to explore, are Madeira's coastal waters. Few places in Europe have such numbers of whales, dolphins, sea turtles and seabirds as Madeira. This is the first of the habitats we'll look at on the following pages.

LANDSCAPE

THE MARINE HABITAT

The marine habitat

> The excursions on the ocean are excellent for spotting seabirds, whales and dolphins, plus there are chances on seeing sea turtles, flying fish and other marine species. For a description of these trips, see page 186. Route 15 also brings you on open sea, but on a large ferry. Sea life on the coastal cliffs can be explored on routes 1, 2, 4 and 5. Seixal (site L) and Porto Moniz (site M – with sea aquarium) are also attractive to explore the marine habitat.

The ocean surrounding Madeira and its satellite islands is brimming with life. It is one of Europe's richest marine areas. Cold and warm currents collide, the first coming from the west and north Atlantic and the latter from tropical Africa. Cetaceans (whales and dolphins) follow the currents and feed in the waters around Madeira (see page 91). They find plenty of food here. Underneath the surface lies an entire submarine mountain range, rising from the ocean floor that lies 3,000 – 4,000 metres beneath. The mountains force the water to rise, bringing nutrients to the surface, where cetaceans and seabirds await.

Not only is there plenty of food for seabirds, suitable nesting spots are abundant too. For the establishment of colonies, the availability of land without predators is indispensable and the Madeira archipelago has it in abundance. Sadly, cats and rats, introduced by people take their toll on the main islands, but on the smaller ones and on steep slopes where these predators can't reach, there are still massive seabird colonies.

The deep sea

Exploring the marine habitat without specialised diving equipment is next to impossible. Beneath what appears to be a uniform surface, is a diverse, stratified submarine landscape. Water temperature and light both play an important role in the submarine ecosystem.

Even the harbour in downtown Funchal is rich in fish, crabs and other marine life.

THE MARINE HABITAT

First temperature. There is little fluctuation in seawater temperature during the year and the transition over time is always gradual. The average minimum lies around 17.8 °C in March and the average maximum is 23.7 °C in September. The deeper you go, the smaller these annual differences become.

Typical of deeper waters is the separation of water layers based on temperature. As you descend, the water temperature doesn't drop gradually but in leaps. Below 2,000 m, there is a constant temperature of 4 °C.

Light is the second factor that determines life. The physical qualities of water are such that light is easily absorbed, first the red spectrum, and last the blue light. Below the 500 – 1,000 m the ocean is entombed in permanent darkness.

This has an enormous effect on the marine life. Photosynthesis is not possible in the deep zone, so there is no primary production. In other words, all life depends on organic matter that sinks down from the higher levels, mostly dead plankton and other animals. Molluscs, worms, squids and others spend their life on the bottom of the ocean, feeding on this so-called 'marine snow'. These animals attract predators. Many of the deep sea fish are predators and some sea mammals dive deep in search of food.

Deep sea fish are almost impossible to see. One exception is found on the market in Funchal – the Black Scabbard Fish with its large eyes and frightening dental work. It lives at a depth of 1,200 metres, but rises to 200 metres at night.

The top layer

At the higher levels there is light. With the upwelling currents, there are plenty of nutrients in the water too. Microscopic phytoplankton simply floats freely in the water, soaking up the sunlight and scooping up nutrients. This is the easy life – being submerged in the organic soup that sustains your every need. Phytoplankton flourishes. Zooplankton forms another group of microscopic life. It consists of animal cell types and feeds on phytoplankton or other species of zooplankton. Another step up the food chain are small crustaceans, jellyfish, worms and young fish that live on plankton. They are food for larger life forms, of which the baleen whales are the biggest.

Around Madeira there are about 550 different fish species, from small ones in the coastal waters to big game species in the deep ocean. Sharks,

LANDSCAPE

THE MARINE HABITAT

dolphins and toothed whales are the top predators of the sea.

Since the phytoplankton in the top layer is at the base of the marine food chain, the bulk of the fish community is found here too – conveniently within reach for seabirds. The waters of Madeira lack the typical northern seabirds like cormorants, gannets and auks. Instead, the cake is all icing, since the area has a great variety of 'tubenoses' – shearwaters and storm-petrels. These enigmatic and much sought-after birds are a great prize for visiting birdwatchers. Often, these seabirds follow cetaceans and predatory fish which bring prey to the surface as well as offal, which they pick up with their strong sense of smell. Birdwatching tours take advantage of that sense of smell and attract seabirds by putting out 'bait' or 'chum' (see page 190).

Although most marine life stays hidden underneath the water, there are some spectacular creatures to be seen on trips out on the ocean. The Cory's Shearwater (top) is perhaps the most common, but you may just as well be lucky and stumble upon a school of Flying Fish (bottom).

Submarine slopes

A large submarine community is found on or near the seabed, especially near the coast. This 'benthic fauna' as it is called, contains familiar animals like crabs, lobsters, starfish, corals, sponges, shellfish and a large variety of fish.

It is in this zone that divers and snorkelers are most richly rewarded. The waters of Madeira are not warm enough to sustain complete coral reefs, but cold water corals are scattered over the rocks and some of the colourful fish associated with warm seas are also present.

The tide line

Along the tideline, life changes again. The crashing waves wash away everything that isn't strongly fixed to the substrate. Red Algae of the genus *Corralina* and *Lythophyllum* form dense and quite hard layers. Seaweeds such as the long-fronded Bladder Wrack (*Fucus vesiculosus*; also common on European coasts) grow along the coastline of the archipelago. Limpets and barnacles attach themselves to the rocks. Limpets

THE MARINE HABITAT

are herbivores that abrasively graze rock surfaces whilst barnacles hold out their feathery legs at high tide to capture passing plankton. The barnacle here is a warm water species, Poli's Stellate Barnacle, which lives on exposed rocks and is also common in southwest England.

The tidal pools are unique environments – quiet, shallow and warm when the tide is low, turbulent and cool when the water level rises and replenish the water. It is a good place for Snakelocks Anemones (*Anemonia sulcata*) and a brown algea known as Peacock Tail (*Padina pavonia*). One of the creatures in the pools is the tiny and transparent Rockpool Shrimp (*Palaemon elegans*) that will pluck pieces of dead skin from your feet if you rest them in the water.

Several crabs, limpets and other sea snails that live on the tide line seek protection against the crashing waves in the pools. Shorebirds find a rich bounty in them. Although Madeira is quite far out into the ocean, quite a few waders wind up here. These tidal pools is where they feed. Dunlins, Sanderlings and Turnstones are basically present throughout the year, as are Little Egrets. Most other European species are seen regularly (see page 101 and 211).

Exploring the tideline can be a fascinating activity. Easiest access to the tideline zone are pebble beaches and harbours.

The Mediterranean Monk Seal is the rarest seal in the world. There is a small but increasing population in marine caves of the Desertas Islands.

LANDSCAPE

Dry scrubland and coastal cliffs

> Dry scrublands and coastal cliffs feature prominently on routes 2, 3, 4, 5, 9, 15 and 16, plus sites B, D and I on pages 177 to 181.

Madeira is known for its verdant lushness, its flowers and spectacular, mossy cloud forest. Therefore, the dry scrubland may come as a surprise. This landscape is about the sharpest possible contrast with the north slope cloud forests.
Desert scrubland grows in places that are beyond the influence of the cloud misted mountains. On Madeira itself, that is basically the far eastern peninsula and the lowest rim on the south coast. On Porto Santo, however, this vegetation dominates and on the Desertas, it is the only terrestrial habitat.
The scrublands' recognition as a special natural habitat is recent. Only in 2015 were sizeable areas of dry scrub protected within the Natura 2000 network. Previously, the scrub was seen as merely a degenerate stage of the laurel forests.
This attention to the scrublands was just in time. The first protected areas are also the last remaining examples of this unique habitat – the rest is swallowed up by the construction of houses, allotments and agriculture.
What makes this scrubland special? First, it is the vegetation itself – a mix of low, evergreen bushes and small trees, mixed with grassy patches and rock gardens. The latter take a prominent place, literally, as this vegetation persists only on the steepest, rockiest and most hard-to-cultivate slopes.
The plant species here are quite simply spectacular. Some of the rarest endemics are found in this vegetation zone, with the highest diversity on cliffs. The gentler slopes are covered in bushes of Spear-leaved Spurge* (*Euphorbia piscatoria*). If you've been on one of the Canary Islands, you will probably find these typical, dome-shaped bushes with their greyish leaves and thick stems familiar. Similar spurges grow on dry slopes there, but this Spear-leaved Spurge is endemic to Madeira.
Much rarer are the trees and bushes of this vegetation zone, the Madeiran Olive Tree and the Dragon Tree. Of the latter there is only one plant left in the wild (but Dragon Trees are widely planted as ornamental trees; see page 83).
As an ecosystem, the dry scrub is rather simple. Due to a combination of wind and drought, the steepness of the terrain and sparse plant

DRY SCRUBLAND AND COASTAL CLIFFS

One of the few remaining natural dry scrublands on Madeira. The grey bushes are Spear-leaved Spurges (Rocha Alta; site D on page 178).

cover, there is hardly any fertile soil. The bushes root in the cracks in the porous rocks, which retain water and accumulate nutrients. These cracks also play an important role for the fauna by providing shelter for insects and lizards. Any visitor will notice that the Madeira Wall Lizard, present all over the island, is especially numerous in these warm and sunny scrublands.

The lizards are bulk food for Buzzards and Kestrels, which specialise in tracking them down. Other typical birds are Canaries and Berthelot's Pipit, both unique to the arid lands of the Macaronesian Islands. Locally, there are Hoopoes, Spanish Sparrows and Linnets, particularly in places where there is a bit of dryland farming.

The best places for this are on Porto Santo, though, and some of these birds are restricted to that island (see page 98). On Madeira, it is the São Lourenço Peninsular where you'll find the most beautiful examples of dry scrubland.

LANDSCAPE

URBANISED AREAS AND NON-NATIVE FOREST

Urbanised areas and non-native forest

> The park-like nature of urbanised areas are prominently present on routes 1, 2, 3, 4, 9 and 15, plus sites E, I, K and L on pages 179 to 183.

Much of the south-facing slopes of Madeira are a mix of housing, arable land, parks, vegetable gardens, waste places, scrubland and plantations, laced with canyons and valleys. It is a bit of an odd pot-pourri – there are scenic places and decidedly tacky ones, and everything in between.

The area doesn't really qualify as a natural habitat of its own, but it does have some typical features and it is extensive and sufficiently different to warrant a description of its own. Besides, most hotels and services are situated in this zone, so you will spend quite some time here. That isn't necessarily a bad thing, as there is a lot going for the urbanised areas from a naturalist's point-of-view.

The Monarch, Queen of the city Parks.

The urbanised slopes reflect the landscape history of Madeira. Apart from a few local centres, the slopes were farmed. Steep as they are, the settlements are not the tight cores of whitewashed houses in the middle of arable land, as is typical of mainland Portugal. Rather it is a continuous scatter of houses with small areas of farmland around them.

In many places, the terrain is so rugged that cultivation is impossible. Here ribbons of more natural vegetation persist, following steep-sided river courses (although often half overgrown by invasive exotic plants). Even in the heart of Funchal, these *ribeiras* slice up the old town with linear growths of riverside vegetation and cliffs.

Madeira has long been used as a hub between Portugal and its colonies. Lots of different plant species were brought here and thrived in the mild climate. Many of them are still planted for ornamental reasons, whilst others invaded the surrounding countryside. That is another key feature of the urbanised areas: the presence of large numbers of often beautiful, exotic plants.

The exotic vegetation is more than just a collection of plants that went rogue. It is a budding novel ecosystem, in which step by step, new species enter that depend on these non-native species. The Monarch butterfly

URBANISED AREAS AND NON-NATIVE FOREST

is the best example. The caterpillars feed on an American species of milkweed, one of the invasive plants. The butterfly is a strong flyer and long distance migrant in America, and it is quite likely that it arrived on Madeira unassisted. It must have done before the settlers came to Madeira, but without the milkweed the Portuguese introduced, it had no chance of colonising. Only after people cultivated Madeira, there was a place for Monarchs, which currently have a strong population and can be seen flying near flowerbeds in parks all over Madeira.

The Monarch is just one example. Lang's Short-tailed Blue, Speckled Wood (not the endemic Madeiran one, but the 'European') are typical butterflies of urbanised areas. Among the birds, the Collared Doves and Waxbills are good examples, and among the reptiles, the geckos are recent arrivals that thrive on warm, south-facing walls.

Some native species do well too. Visit the city park in Funchal (route 1) on a warm sunny day, and you can't say the native Madeira Wall Lizard has a hard time coping in man-made environments. Canaries, Madeiran Chaffinches, Blackcaps, Robins, Grey Wagtails, Plain Swifts and Yellow-legged Gulls are all native birds that seem to do just fine in urban environments. Even Trocaz Pigeon seems to be staging a comeback.

All of these species have one thing in common – they are opportunists that adapt and disperse easily. The butterflies mentioned are strong flyers, as are some of the birds. Many other species most definitely arrived on Madeira by boat and were inadvertently introduced. They are species that are used to living in urban environments such as harbours. Otherwise they would never have made it onto the ship in the first place.

So all things considered, the urban environment including the parks and more natural fragments, are quite an exciting area for naturalists. You are able to see species here that you won't find elsewhere. Most of them are cosmopolitan species, some of which are spectacular in their

The beautiful parks hand you the commoner wildlife of Madeira on a platter. This is the city garden in downtown Funchal.

URBANISED AREAS AND NON-NATIVE FOREST

The rural landscape of the north coast (top). Canaries occur here in abundance (bottom).

appearance (Monarch!), but only very few are special in that typical island sense – endemic, specialised, mysterious and uniquely Madeiran. If you do find such a rarity in or close to the city (such as Yellow Musschia at Garajau for example) you are sure to have stumbled on a remnant piece of original vegetation.

We can't end this chapter without a brief mention of another man-made vegetation; one that does have nothing to offer to naturalists. We're talking about the Eucalyptus plague that infests the higher reaches of the housing zone and broods over Madeira like an unwanted party guest.

In the Eucalyptus forests nothing native and hardly anything non-native is able to grow. The trees ruthlessly draw moisture from the soil and the toxic chemical composition of the leaves make the forest about as welcoming as freshly poured concrete. However, that's not the biggest danger of the Eucalyptus forest. The problem is its combustive quality. Nothing burns better than Eucalyptus. Well, almost nothing. The Acacia trees, another introduced species that invades the Eucalyptus stands, are said to be even more volatile.

In some parts of the island, particularly in the west and south, there are extensive pine forests. These trees were introduced too and form much the same poor environments as the Eucalyptus forests.

Laurel cloud forest

> Laurel forests feature prominently on routes 6, 7, 8, 9, 11 and 14, plus sites F, J, L and N.

The laurel forest is the emerald jewel in the crown of Madeira's ecosystems. It is a leafy, green and moist jungle, spectacular in its scenery and unique in its species composition. It is a place to visit over and again. The moss-clad rock faces, the tall ferns, the subtle sprinkle of endemic wildflowers that grow up the gnarled tree trunks and the mysterious, enveloping clouds never cease to amaze.

Madeira's *Laurisilva* (as the laurel forest is called in Portuguese) is part of a larger ecosystem, the Macaronesian laurel forest. This forest type is unique to the western Canary Islands, the Azores and Madeira. Within this small range, the largest swathes are found on Madeira. The forest is absent from Porto Santo and the Desertas.

Besides scenic, the forest is very interesting from a biological perspective. It combines within it two things that at first glance seem to exclude one another: on the one hand it is a unique, endemic ecosystem, exclusive to the Atlantic islands, and on the other hand it is a relict of a forest that was once much larger.

The laurel cloud forest or *Laurisilva* forms a spectacular backdrop for long walks.

LAUREL CLOUD FOREST

To start with the latter: in the Tertiary era, before a series of cold and dry ice ages wrought ecological havoc in the northern hemisphere, damp subtropical laurel forests covered much of Europe, North Africa and Asia. The series of ice ages that swept over the earth after the Tertiary wiped out that huge expanse of laurel forest. Only in the far eastern periphery and on the Macaronesian islands this once the mighty forest persisted. Here the combination of a stable, warm-temperate maritime climate and the perpetual fog and rain from the trade winds maintained the perfect growing condition for the laurel trees.

The Madeiran version of the Tertiary forest was quite different from that of the mainland. It was a cloudy, volcanic island variety, where many of the trees and plants that were present on the continent, did not occur. Those that did, have evolved in isolation into varieties and species that are unique to the islands, some even to Madeira proper (see page 28). Broadly speaking, the laurel cloud forests you're visiting on Madeira are the last remaining stands of a prehistoric forest that covered much of Europe (e.g. there are fossilized remnants found the Czech Republic and France). If you look more closely at the Madeiran version of the forest, you soon realise that, having evolved in isolation from a limited range of common species, it must always have been different from the mainland forests.

At the far eastern end of its original range, in southern China and Japan, there are also relicts of laurel forests, as there are in various places in the southern hemisphere. What all the forests have in common is the dominance of trees belonging to the laurel family. However, the species are very different from those found on Madeira, the Canaries and Azores, as is the ecology, flora and fauna.

The Madeiran cloud forest grows in a broad zone between 300 and 1,300 metres on the north slope and between 700 and 1,200 on the south slope. This is the wettest zone, under almost permanent influence of the moist trade winds (see page 28). A glance at the map will tell you that the largest part of the island falls within this zone, yet today, most of this forest is degraded or has

The driver of the laurel forest ecosystem is the 'horizontal rain': the vegetation filters droplets out of the fog layers that blanket the slopes so frequently. The droplets run down to the tip of the leaf from where they fall to the ground, creating a perpetual drip even when it isn't actually raining (top).
Ferns and liverworts thrive on the shady, wet forest floor (bottom).

Ferns, mosses and liverworts frequently grow on tree trunks as epiphytes.

disappeared. Of the original cloud forests, only 10% -20% remains (and yet it is still the largest Macaronesian cloud forest on the planet!).
Fog and rain are at the base of the forest life. Leaves and mosses are shaped in such a way that they catch the fog droplets in the air. As the moisture accumulates to form larger drops, the water flows down the specially shaped leaves to their tip from where it eventually drops to the forest floor. The forest is its own rain-maker, transforming the grey ghost of mist to a perpetual soft dripping underneath the canopy. The forest is the opposite of an umbrella – even when not actually raining above the trees, it does so beneath the canopy. If the forest is sufficiently large, as is the case on Madeira, it forms its own dark and damp biosphere – amazing if you realise that at the same latitude some 1500 kms east, you're on the edge of the Sahara desert!

Flora and fauna of the laurel forest

The main tall trees of the forest are Canary Laurel (*Laurus novocanariensis*), Madeira Mahogany (*Persea indica*), Stink Laurel (*Ocotea foetens*) and Laurel Barbusano* (*Apollonia barbujana*). All four of them are members of the laurel family and not easy to tell apart (see box on page 49). Note that the familiar Bay Laurel you use in the kitchen, is not among them. It doesn't occur on the island. Locally, there are some Pedunculate Oak, Beech, Chestnut, Plane, Walnuts and pines with the laurel trees, but none of these are native to Madeira. You'll find them mostly near forest clearings and settlements.

LAUREL CLOUD FOREST

There is a large variety of smaller trees and bushes native to the laurel forest. Interestingly none of these belong to the laurel family either. Instead, they are all relatives to familiar European and African plants. Typical species are the Candleberry Myrtle (a bush of about 8 metres high, related to the familiar Bog Myrtle of temperate Europe), Besom and Tree Heath (both widespread in the Mediterranean), the beautifully flowering Lily-of-the-Valley Tree (*Clethra arborea*; endemic to Madeira and belonging to a genus of tropical origin), Honey Spurge (*Euphorbia mellifera*, the only tree-sized spurge in Europe), Picconia (relative to the olives), Madeiran Blueberry (*Vaccinium padifolium*, growing up to six metres and endemic to Madeira) and more familiar-looking species like Madeiran Elder (*Sambucus lanceolata*) and Canary Willow.

The fungus *Laurobasidium lauri* grows exclusively on Canary Laurels, making it a convenient feature to identify this tree from the other laurel species (top). Blackbirds on Madeira have a slightly different song than the European Blackbirds (bottom).

Deeper down in the understorey there are tall species of ferns, bush-sized sow-thistles, huge buttercups and large crane's-bills. Some of the more striking plants are portrayed on pages 78-83. Dense tangles of moss, lichens and liverworts occupy the trunks of bushes and trees, so that every spot is occupied with some sort of plant. Adding to the jungle feel is the presence of epiphytes – plants growing on other plants. Various species of ferns grow on tree trunks, Navelwort and houseleeks root in deep crevices of barks and vines climb up the trunks of other plants. All this gives the appearance of a tropical forest, where epiphytes constitute a large part of the biodiversity. On Madeira, the epiphytic species (mostly Hare's-foot Fern, Macaronesian Polypody, Navelwort and the houseleeks Hairy and Glabrous Aichryson) are all species that grow just as easily on wet rocks.

The deep laurel forest has a surprisingly poor birdlife. Almost none of the familiar forest birds of Europe occur on Madeira. There are no tits,

LAUREL CLOUD FOREST

Telling apart the four laurel trees

The four laurel trees are very similar in appearance. It takes a while to tell them apart.

< Canary Laurel
(*Laurus novocanariensis*) The most common of the laurels. Leaves with brown tufts of hairs all along the central vein. Smooth stem with white patches of lichens. The easiest way to recognise this species is by the antler-like fungus that grows on the bark.

Stink Laurel >
(*Ocotea foetens*) Like Canary Laurel but with wider leaves with brown tufts only at the base of the leaves. As a solitary tree it grows a wide crown. Mostly found in the upper part of the forest zone.

< Barbusano
(*Apollonias barbujana*) Glossier leaves than the previous trees, often infected with galls that show as swellings on the upper side of the leaf. Grows on rocky soils and often on dry sites.

Madeira Mahogany >
(*Persea indica*) Much larger and more elongated leaves. The leaves on the top of the twig are reddish.

LANDSCAPE

LAUREL CLOUD FOREST

treecreepers, nuthatches or woodpeckers. There are Blackbirds (the only thrush), Robins, Blackcaps, Chaffinches (a distinct Madeiran race) and two endemic species, the Madeira Goldcrest and the Trocaz Pigeon. All of these are fairly easy to find if you spend some time in the woods. Much harder to find are two very secretive birds of the interior forest – the Woodcock and the Sparrowhawk. Both are rare residents that live deep inside the forest.

Levadas, cliffs and river gorges

The levadas are one of the unique features of the island. These water channels were created to bring water from the ever-moist cloud forests to the villages on the south slopes and, as they usually have paths alongside them, they create wonderful passageways into the laurel forest for hikers.

The levadas run alongside damp cliffs which, with the narrow trail beside them, create a zone just wide enough for a bit more light to reach the forest floor, making the levadas hotspots for flora and wildlife. Here are many more ferns, the stout Madeira Marsh-orchid and several other wildflowers (see page 74). Such sunny spots also attract the modest butterfly fauna of the laurel forest, of which Canary Speckled Wood and Madeira Brimstone, both endemic to the island, are the key species.

The north-facing gorges are where the best sections of the laurisilva are preserved. These spots are so inaccessible that neither loggers nor the

Beautiful old specimens of Besom Heath arch over the trail at Rabaçal (route 8).

LAUREL CLOUD FOREST

acrobatic goats were able to do much damage to the forest. Even before Man and goat arrived on Madeira, the gorges must have been the heartland of the laurel forest as it is here that the shade is deepest and the rivers that tumble down create a permanently moist environment – the ideal growing conditions for many plants of the laurel forest. Some of the rarest plants of the Madeiran forest grow exclusively in these gorges, such as the endemic Wollaston's Musschia (a 3 metre tall relative of the bellfowers; page 84 and 157) and the extremely rare endemic orchid the Madeiran Lady's-tresses (page 84).

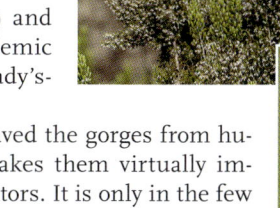

The inaccessibility that saved the gorges from human interference also makes them virtually impossible to explore for visitors. It is only in the few places that the levadas cross them that you have the chance of obtaining a glimpse of their special flora.

Tree heath vegetation

The cloud layer that sustains the laurel forest is not fixed. In summer it sits a bit higher and is generally a lot thinner. It is not present every day nor all day. On average, it wears thinner above 800 metres. This is where the Tree Heath starts to take a prominent place in the vegetation.

Tree Heath scrub (top) is the haunt of the Madeira Firecrest (bottom).

Whereas the familiar heathlands in northern Europe are covered by dwarf shrubs, the Tree Heath on Madeira is typically 3-5 metres tall, in places even higher. Tree Heath is not only found at this altitude, but it is only between 700 and 1300 metres above sea level that it dominates the vegetation. A number of other, similar sized trees are common here, particularly the *Faya* or Candleberry Myrtle (a relative of the Bog Myrtle). When not too dense, there may be a number of attractive wildflowers growing beneath the Tree Heath, such as Canary Buttercups, Dense-flowered and Madeiran Marsh-orchids. The common birds of the laurel forest may be found in the Tree Heath as well, but only the Madeira Goldcrest shows a clear preference for this vegetation.

LANDSCAPE

The high mountains

> Routes 10, 12 and 13 and sites H and N on pages 180 and 185 explore the high mountains.

Majestically, the jagged peaks of Madeira pierce through the steaming ceiling of clouds. They are covered in wildflowers. Butterflies dart all around and large flocks of Plain Swifts dash over the highest peaks. If heaven is indeed situated in the clouds, this could well be it.

Madeira's roof is like an island on top of an island. If you reach over about 1,300 metres, you reach a different kind of shoreline – the one that borders the cloud layer. Under normal weather conditions, you can dip your toes into the clouds almost like you'd do on the beach.

Whereas the trade winds produce clouds that give rise to the green jungles of the laurel forests, the slopes above the forest are usually bathing in sunlight. Obviously, large weather fronts bring rain (and in extreme cases even snow) every now and then at high elevations, but as Madeira is at the same latitude of northern Morocco, cloudless skies are the norm and rain the exception, especially in summer. Because of the fair weather, you have the exceptional situation that the spring season starts earlier in the high mountains than it does further down in the laurel forests.

View near Pico do Areeiro (route 12).

THE HIGH MOUNTAINS

The peak of the flowering season here is May, some two weeks earlier than on the foggy north slopes.

The sunny balcony of Madeira covers just a small area. From north to south the distance between the Pico do Areeiro and Pico Ruivo is about six kms. East to west this high zone is roughly ten kms across.

'Endemic' is the key word to describe the flora and fauna of the high mountains. In this small area you'll encounter a unique flora and fauna of which a high number of species is limited to just that small range. Here the woodlands have made way to bushy slopes with broom, Shrubby Wallflower (a Macaronesian endemic with bright pink flowers) and the endemic Madeiran Heath, which flowers in summer. In spring, the grassy mountain meadows are a feast of wildflowers, in which the (again endemic) Madeira Early-purple Orchid grows by the thousands. Originally, Madeiran Juniper was a dominant shrub here, but it has become very rare as its timber was in high demand. Famously, the ceiling of the cathedral of Funchal is made of Juniper wood.

The richest haunts of endemic flora are the cliffs. Here the majority of the plants are endemics, either limited to the Atlantic Islands, to Madeira as a whole or even to just the high cliffs of island. If you stand on a ridge with a reasonable all-round view then the habitat for the entire world population of a large number of wildflowers is within your sight!

The same goes for the nesting sites for one of the most extraordinary birds of Madeira – all the world's Zino's Petrels breed on just a few steep cliffs high in the Madeiran mountains. As this bird only comes to land at night, you won't see them here though. For that you need to go out onto the ocean (see page 186). During the day, Plain Swifts, Robins, Blackbirds,

The spectacular Madeiran Early-purple Orchid flowers in large numbers on the high slopes.

LANDSCAPE

THE HIGH MOUNTAINS

Madeira Chaffinches, Berthelot's Pipits, Red-legged Partridges, Buzzards and Kestrels are the common birds. Furthermore, this is the best zone to look for Spectacled Warblers, at least in the breeding season. They are quite common in the thickets of Tree Heath and Broom.

Paúl da Serra

The high zone of Madeira consists of two very different parts, separated by the low-lying Encumeadas Pass. Although climatically, both sections are similar, they have a radically different landscape. Paúl da Serra is a treeless plain, steppe-like in appearance, completely unlike any other part of Madeira.

In the eastern massif the strata are tilted, creating the precipitous slopes, the narrow ridges and the jagged peaks described above. Paúl da Serra is a large, rolling plateau because the soft strata are topped by a hard, horizontal basalt layer.

Apart from areas of grassy vegetation, there are impenetrable, spiny tangles of European Gorse, Common Broom and thickets of Bracken. This is not the natural vegetation. Originally, this Paúl da Serra was most likely covered in a low forest of Tree Heath, Candleberry Myrtle and laurel trees. This forest was cut down completely to create grazing land for cattle. The flat plain is easily crossed on foot or by horse, so it was an ideal hunting ground. The fact that Madeira naturally lacks game was easily fixed: rabbits and Red-legged Partridges were introduced and are still common on these plains. They share their territory with Spectacled Warblers and Berthelot's Pipits, and in summer, with Yellow-legged Gulls. The gull may seem a somewhat surprising bird to find this high up, but apparently, they feed on the locusts which are numerous here in the hot season.

Paúl da Serra has many small depressions where rain accumulates in winter and which dry out in the course of summer. Such temporary pools harbour plant species that are quite familiar to visitors from western Europe: Coral-necklace, Trailing St. John's-wort and Heath Lobelia.

The plateau of Paúl da Serra forms a strangely flat landscape on the otherwise rugged island.

History

History doesn't start for Madeira until the beginning of the 15th Century, when Portugal started to build its overseas empire, discovered the island and colonised it. Although its existence was unknown to the Portuguese at that time, we now know that people had visited Madeira before. There were tales in classical times about islands in the Atlantic that may very well refer to Madeira and Porto Santo. The islands certainly appeared on old portolan charts from 1339, demonstrating that their existence was known, even if their discovery was undocumented. Recently, scientists obtained a new perspective on the pre-Portuguese habitation of Madeira, when they discovered a 1,000 year old bone of a House Mouse. Being a well known human commensal, the mouse must have arrived with humans. An extra surprise came when the DNA of this mouse and that of living Madeiran mice showed a strong affinity with mice from northern Europe, not as one might expect, Iberia. The simplest explanation, which fits neatly with the date, is that mice arrived with an undocumented visit by the Vikings!

For reasons unknown, all these discoverers vacated the island, leaving no written records, so when the Portuguese discovered the islands in the 1418, no-one knew of their existence.

The 15th century was a time of Portuguese expansion. Prince Henry the Navigator organised expeditions to explore the west African coast when strong gales blew two ships off course. The sailors feared shipwreck but fortunately, where the maps just showed the blue of an endless ocean, they found an island. In the nick of time they found shelter in a shallow bay. In gratitude they baptised the island *Porto Santo* – Holy Harbour.

The next year an expedition was sent to claim the island on behalf of the Portuguese crown. To their surprise, the crew discovered a larger island not far from Porto Santo. It was covered in a dense forest and the discoverers called it the *Ilha da Madeira* – Island of wood. On the 1st of July 1419 the first Portuguese disembarked on the gravel beach of what is now the town of Machico – an event that every year is celebrated in a large medieval festival. The Portuguese crown claimed Madeira and Porto Santo and divided them into three captaincies – Porto Santo was ruled by Bartolomeu Perestrelo, the east and much of the north of Madeira was under command of Tristão Vaz Teixeira who was based on Machico. João Gonçalves Zarco governed the remainder (most of the south and the extreme west) from the new town of Funchal. In 1508 Funchal became the official capital of Madeira.

HISTORY

19th century naturalists on Madeira

At the start of the 19th Century much of the natural and geographical world still had to be discovered by the western civilisations. New technologies such as the steamship and the railway made travelling around the world easier and the European wealthy upper classes liked travelling. Naturalists and ornithologists made expeditions to Madeira and some stayed on the island for years. A score of articles on nature, insects and birds of the Madeiran archipelago was published in specialised magazines, especially in Great Britain and in Germany. Such was its fame amongst naturalist that it was one of the destinations that Charles Darwin most wanted to visit on voyage on HMS Beagle in 1832 (in the event it was something denied to him by violent storms and extreme sea sickness).

Nineteenth century ornithologists not only observed birds but also collected them. They mostly did not think about the danger of extinguishing localised species, they were just working on their collections and needed proof of their observations. A well known saying of that time was "what´s hit is history and what´s missed is mystery". We know that Schmitz had stuffed Madeira Wood Pigeons and also obtained its eggs. Hartwig wrote "I finally got the first stuffed Apus pallidus [Pallid Swift] from Madeira on the 10th of October 1891". Often the goal of birding expeditions was to collect specimens, not to observe living birds, which is hardly surprising given the limitations of contemporary field glasses and telescopes. W. R. Ogilvie Grant went in 1890 on a five weeks trip to Madeira, Deserta Grande and Porto Santo to collect birds for the British Museum.

Several German naturalists are important for their research on Madeira birds and wildlife. A famous name is Dr. C. Heineken, who worked as a resident doctor in Funchal from 1820 to 1832. He described the plumages of the Madeiran Chaffinch and attached his name to the Madeira subspecies. The Catholic priest Ernst Johann Schmitz settled on Madeira in the 1870s and lived there about 20 years. He founded what is now the Natural History Museum on Madeira, described the Madeira Wood Pigeon and published about Madeira birds. The teacher W. Hartwig wrote the first extensive article (in German) on the birds of the Madeira islands in 1891, describing 31 breeding birds and 85 vagrants. All this work helped to establish our knowledge of the archipelago's natural history.

A sketch of Madeira, published in 1851, offers a surprisingly detailed account of the geography, places to visit, climate, history and local customs of the island. Moreover, almost half of the book is dedicated to natural history. It includes a plant list (native and cultivated) and a bird list (breeding and visiting). It is almost like a predecessor of this Crossbill Guide!

HISTORY

The arrival
Once the islands were claimed as Portuguese territory, the Crown sent settlers to both islands. Before going ashore, the crew released a pregnant rabbit on Porto Santo. The idea was simple: if it survived and established a population, the conditions would suit people too. Plus, they'd have a healthy and convenient source of protein to hunt.

The first thing the settlers did on Madeira was clearing and burning the forests to create fields for agriculture. It is said that the fires burnt for almost seven years and with such a vigour that people were forced to take refuge in their boats. Just let this sink in for a moment – that paradisiacal island you read about in the brochures and in this book – the first thing people did after its discovery was burning it to the ground! Several species of birds probably went extinct in this time (see also page 33).

Every year in spring, there is a large medieval festival in Machico, celebrating the arrival of the first settlers on the island.

Sugar cane
The first settlers were traders and farmers. Madeira was a perfect stop for traders to Africa and later the Americas. Visiting ships stocked wheat, wine and fresh water on Madeira.

The farmers transformed the blackened soil into fertile land. Wheat and sugar cane did well in the volcanic ground. Wheat was mostly grown on dry Porto Santo, while sugar cane was the cash crop of Madeira. It was called 'white gold' and brought great economic prosperity. Large numbers of African slaves were shipped to Madeira to work in the sugar industry. They built windmills to crush the cane and then refined it after which ships transported the valuable merchandise to Europe. By the end of the 15th century, Madeira was the world´s most important producer of sugar.

The refineries had a huge impact on the natural landscape of the island. In order to produce sugar syrup, the canes were burnt. The remaining as well as the resprouting woodland on Madeira all but completely disappeared in the ovens.

The Cathedral of Funchal is made entirely of different types of local volcanic rocks (bottom).

LANDSCAPE

HISTORY

A replica of Christopher Columbus' ship the Santa Maria is used for dolphin watching out of Funchal (top). Sugar cane (bottom) is still collected and used in the distillery of Porto da Cruz (route 4).

One sugar trader that became particularly famous was Christopher Columbus, the discoverer of America. He married the daughter of Bartolomeu Perestrello, Porto Santo's governor and a plantation owner. Columbus introduced sugar cane to the Caribbean. Later, the Portuguese exported their industrial model to the large sugar fields in their colonies in Brazil and elsewhere where production was cheaper.

On Madeira, the sugar industry began to collapse in the 16th century. The reason was twofold. On the one hand, Madeira had a hard time competing with sugar cane from Brazil. On the other hand, Madeira had exhausted its resources. There simply wasn't enough accessible wood to burn to refine the sugar. In two centuries, Madeira went from a heavily forested paradise to a denuded island on the verge of ecological meltdown.

External aggressions and the British connection

In the first century after its colonisation, Madeira's economy did well, but around 1530, the island's good fortune turned sour. First the sugar industry collapsed and then, not much later, Madeira became a victim of a series of attacks by pirates, the first of which took place in 1497.

In 1566 French privateers sacked Porto Santo. Soon thereafter, they moved to Funchal, where they took the town with little effort. The city was raided and after 15 days, when the attackers withdrew, there was little of value left in town.

HISTORY

Porto Santo suffered more violent pirate attacks. Perhaps the worst took place in august 1617, when a fleet of eight Barbary pirate ships captured a large group of men and women and sold them as slaves in Algiers. The main purpose of these attacks was to capture and enslave Christians.

After several further raids, the Portuguese started to work on the defences of Madeira. The most important fortification lies in the centre of Funchal, close to the harbour (route 1): the São José Fort, built in the eighteenth century.

The development of Madeira took a different direction when in 1581 the Kingdoms of Portugal and Spain were dynastically united by Philip II of Spain. This made Madeira a target of Spain's opponents, mainly the English. When Portugal regained independence from Spain in 1640, English ties with Madeira were strengthened. The heralded a new period of economic prosperity. The basis for the new wealth was the Madeira wine.

Madeira Wine

Just like sugar cane, grapes were an important crop from the very start. Only 25 years after colonising the island, Madeira started to export its first wines, which were soon praised for their quality. A sweet grape from Crete, known as *Malvasia Cândida* (Candid Malmsey) grew best on the island, hence the Madeira wine has its defined, sweet taste.

The French Wine Blight (*Phylloxera*; a small fly) destroyed the Madeira wine stocks in the second half of the 19th century.

Sugar cane plantations were converted into vineyards and the wines became famous for their taste and quality. At first they were sold in the European markets but later the colonies in the Americas became the main buyers. The trade increased steadily and in the 16th century, Madeira´s most important export product became its wine. It was a favourite among royalty and statesmen. The independence of the United States of America in 1776 was toasted with Madeira wine.

Wine of less quality, about one third of the production and named 'low wine', was taken on board of the Portuguese ships. In contrast to water, the quality of the wine, helped by fortification with spirits, only became better, even in a hot climate. It also helped to prevent scurvy, so drinking

HISTORY

A tasting of the famous Madeira wines.

your fair share of wine was considered the healthy thing to do!

Due to the warm relations between Britain and Portugal, there were many British merchants living on the island. They became the most important exporters of Madeira wine. Today, Madeira still ships its wine to all four corners of the world, preserving the fame and prestige as the producer of one of the best wines. Remarkably, despite the passing of centuries, several Madeira producers retain a strong British identity.

The levadas

The south slopes of the island clearly had the more benign climate and topography, so this is where the most important towns and villages were built. The great downside of the south was the scarcity of water. In contrast, on the northern slopes and on the plateau, water is not in short supply.

Shortly after their arrival, the settlers started to build the first *levadas*, contour-hugging mini-canals that carry the water from high mountains and from the north slopes to the south. At first slaves were forced to do the difficult and dangerous task of constructing the canals and the narrow maintenance footpaths alongside them. Some levadas run along perpendicular cliffs and it is difficult to imagine how workmen could labour here! At strategic points the labourers built tunnels to ease and shorten the route to the south side of the mountain. Over time, the levada system was gradually expanded and today 2500 km (!!) of these waterways crisscross the island. It is an impressive monument, a unique feat of hydrological engineering, well known around the world and, although this never was the intention, has turned the extreme rugged island of Madeira into an excellent destination for hikers.

Quintas and flowers – Madeira turns into a paradise

British troops landed on Madeira twice during the Napoleonic wars. This wasn't a hostile invasion, but rather to prevent the island from being taken by a common enemy, the French. That was no coincidence – the link with Britain was already strong. In the 17th century, Portugal signed

HISTORY

treaties with Britain that brought commerce, investments and a growing number of British Upper Class to the island. The first British 'occupation' took place in 1801-1802 and was aimed at controlling the harbour and protecting the citizens of Funchal. Portugal did not resist this 'friendly invasion' of their territory. The second time was in 1807, when Portugal had been invaded by Napoleon. The Royal Navy escorted 13,800 Portuguese refugees to Brazil, including the royal family. Madeira was returned to Portugal in 1814.

In the 18th and 19th century, the local aristocracy and British merchants became wealthy from the wine trade. They built spectacular estates on the hills, especially on the south slopes, near Funchal. The British inhabitants with their tradition of gardening, started to bring large numbers of wildflowers and shrubberies to the island. Ships brought the most spectacular species from the Americas – orchids, agapanthus, Bird of Paradise flower – they all grow well in the fertile soils and the benign climate of Madeira.

This golden age didn't last either, although this time it wasn't geopolitics that destroyed the dream, but something much smaller: lice. The Phylloxera grape lice destroyed the vineyards of the Madeira wines. It arrived on the island in 1852 and its effect on the vineyards was swift and brutal.

Madeira thanks its nickname 'island of flowers' to the many exotic species that were planted here, mainly by the British aristocracy. Although pretty, several of them spread so aggressively that they've become a real threat to the native vegetation.

LANDSCAPE

HISTORY

Tourism

Around the same time the phylloxera lice wreaked havoc in the wine industry, a new economy developed around tourism. In the 19th century, maritime trade with Europe increased and, thanks to steamships, became much faster. Madeira became the place to cure lung diseases. The patients were all upper class British citizens who stayed at luxury hotels. They were the first tourists and heralded an economic field that is now the main source of income for the island.

In the 1950s the first middle class hotels near Funchal opened their doors and provided affordable holidays to an increasing number of visitors. The construction of an airport in 1964 boosted the number of incoming tourists further. Madeira had the questionable reputation of having the shortest runway of any European airport. On the entire island there is only one single spot where the terrain allowed for the construction of a runway, but even that was too short for large modern, commercial aircrafts. In 2012 the runway was extended with pillars into the ocean and now large airbuses can land. Meanwhile, the Funchal harbour became increasingly busy with cruise ships, yachts and cargo vessels. To release the pressure on the harbour, a new cargo port was built in Caniçal and since 2007, all freight ships offload there.

Tourists discovered Madeira as a hiking destination.

What makes Madeira so important in Portuguese history?

The Atlantic islands of Madeira and the Azores were fundamental pillars in building and sustaining the Portuguese empire. During the 15th and 16th centuries, Portuguese explorers used unique cartographical skills and innovative maritime technology to discover the world and establish colonies and fortresses along the coasts. As part of the colonial strategy, Madeira was the link between Portugal and its colonies in Africa and the south American coast and as such indispensable as a staging post and a safe haven for sailors. Funchal was a cosmopolitan place, with sailors from all corners of the Portuguese empire, always busy with people repairing and provisioning the ships. During the 18th and 19th centuries Madeira became an important hub in the commercial shipping industry.

Nature conservation

The first thing the settlers did when they arrived on Madeira, beside torching the place (see page 57), was to introduce alien plants and animals. These changed the environment completely. Before the arrival of people, there were no herbivores of importance on Madeira. Shortly after, the vegetation faced the most destructive of them all: the goat. It was introduced to all islands of the archipelago, including the uninhabited Desertas. Goats are indiscriminate grazers, eating all herbs and reducing scrubs and trees to bonsai level. In addition to goats, sheep and rabbits played a role in denuding the archipelago of vegetation.

The first settlers inadvertently introduced rats and then, partly as a consequence of the first, deliberately brought cats. Both rat and cats are ferocious predators of eggs, birds and small animals.

Even prior to Portuguese settlement, people introduced House Mice (see page 55), notorious for eating birds' eggs. Before the arrival of humans, there were predators (e.g. Buzzards, Kestrels and Sparrowhawks) but not nearly as many or as destructive as cats and rats.

Perhaps the biggest predator of all was Man himself. Centuries of hunting took its toll on some birds that live exclusively on Madeira. Numbers of the Trocaz Pigeon were decimated and the endemic Madeiran subspecies of Wood Pigeon was hunted to extinction. The chicks of shearwaters were considered a delicacy. Annually around 20,000 (!) of them, flightless and helpless, were 'collected' on the Desertas islands.

The biggest blow to the Madeira's native flora was undoubtedly the clearing of forest. This

Invasive species take over the natural vegetation. Especially Eucalyptus and Black Wattle Acacia (inset photo).
These trees make the slopes susceptable to erosion (top) and forest fires.

NATURE CONSERVATION

was done not only for building land and the cultivation of sugar cane and grapes, but also to use the timber itself for fuel or in construction. Huge amounts of native laurel forest disappeared into stoves to refine sugar (see page 57). This went on until the final decades of the 19th century. By that time, there was probably no real laurel forest left. Only isolated trees and small pockets of forest plants survived in the steep canyons. Recent research on the laurel forest suggests that all of the current stands are secondary forest – regrowth after the logging stopped.

The reason the forest was able to regrow is very interesting. The demand for wood was so great that the forest couldn't sustain the sugar refinement industry in the long run. The industry simply collapsed when the resource was depleted, diminishing the demand for wood. At the same time an alternative fuel for heating was developed that made the use of wood in households obsolete.

The development of the modern petroleum industry in the 19th century has had the most profound

Truly old laurel forest is rare on Madeira (top), but fortunately, young forest is regrowing in many places on the north slope.
Unfortunately, Eucalyptus is still planted. Apart from being an ecologically very poor forest, it is very volatile, creating a serious fire hazard (bottom).

NATURE CONSERVATION

impact on our world. Not only did it make much we take for granted in our modern possible, like coal before it, it also relieved the pressure on the use of wood for fuel. On Madeira, this meant the laurel forest could regrow which it continues to do today, making the Madeiran laurisilva the most extensive of its kind in the world. The regrowth of the forest was helped by the recent policy to eradicate all feral goats on the island. In a tremendous effort that cost millions of euros, the island is now free of feral goats, which means another pressure on the natural vegetation is gone.

Porto Santo suffered largely the same problems – rabbits, goats, sheep and the clearance of forest. Here this played out differently because the topography. Porto Santo is not nearly as rugged, steep or high as Madeira. Herbivores could range almost everywhere on the island. The north-east slopes near Pico Branco (route 16) are the exception, hence here is the natural vegetation better preserved. Furthermore, the island is much drier as there is very little land mass high enough to block the trade winds, so clouds form much more sparsely so that rain is less common. The natural vegetation was a dry forest with lots of Dragon Trees, which were soon cut down and the timber used for a variety of things, including making ships. Today, Porto Santo is largely bare, with large areas of arable farming, which in turn is the reason it has a very different birdlife.

Modern conservation problems

Invasive species continue to constitute an important threat. The Eucalytpus or Blue Gum Tree and the Maritime Pine dominate large parts of the island's middle altitudes on the south slope. At lower altitudes of the laurisilva, the vigorous growth of Acacia and Ginger Lily prevent the natural forest from expanding to its previous size.

In the high mountain areas overgrazing has been the main threat to native vegetation. Recently, a total ban on grazing was a drastic but positive measure for the native flora of the high slopes. Introduced rabbits remain a problem though, while cats and the rats present a major threat to the birdlife, including to the very rare and endangered Zino's Petrel. Another issue is the increased risk of forest fires, which is, in combination with the inflammable acacias, pines and Eucalyptus, a constant danger that hangs over Madeira.

Tourism produces its own set of problems. Erosion on busy trails and disturbance of wild animals are the main ones. Madeira has a strict code of conduct for whale and dolphin watching, which, as far as we could assess, is followed by the companies.

NATURE CONSERVATION

There is also an upside to the development of tourism. Most visitors to Madeira are here, at least in part, for the beautiful landscape and wild nature. With tourism being the number one economic activity, this makes nature the island's most important resource – one that, if for nothing else, Madeirans will want to preserve out of self-interest. So one could argue that if you minimise your disturbance to nature and wildlife, your presence is actually favouring the conservation of nature! See page 198 for more information on sustainable tourism and how you can make a difference.

Conservation efforts

Nature conservation movements started later in Portugal than in other western countries. The protection of flora and fauna wasn't an issue until the country entered the European Union in 1986. From that moment the attitude towards conservation on Madeira changed completely. Madeira, Porto Santo, the Desertas, the Selvagens and the Azores became a priority for Portuguese nature conservation. Madeiran natural areas and their flora and fauna were included in the European Habitat and Bird Directives and the Natura 2000 network. A total of 13 sites were protected on all islands of the archipelago, covering about 270,000 hectares (including marine areas). Two thirds of the island of Madeira is protected in some form, which is an unusually high fraction. This is good news of course, but this does not mean these areas are not threatened by the aforementioned issues of invasive species and forest fires.

On Porto Santo there are only few reserves, but all islands and islets of the Desertas and the Selvagens are fully protected as nature reserves, including the ocean surrounding them.

The Desertas Islands and surrounding ocean are protected, for one because of their immense importance to seabirds.

NATURE CONSERVATION

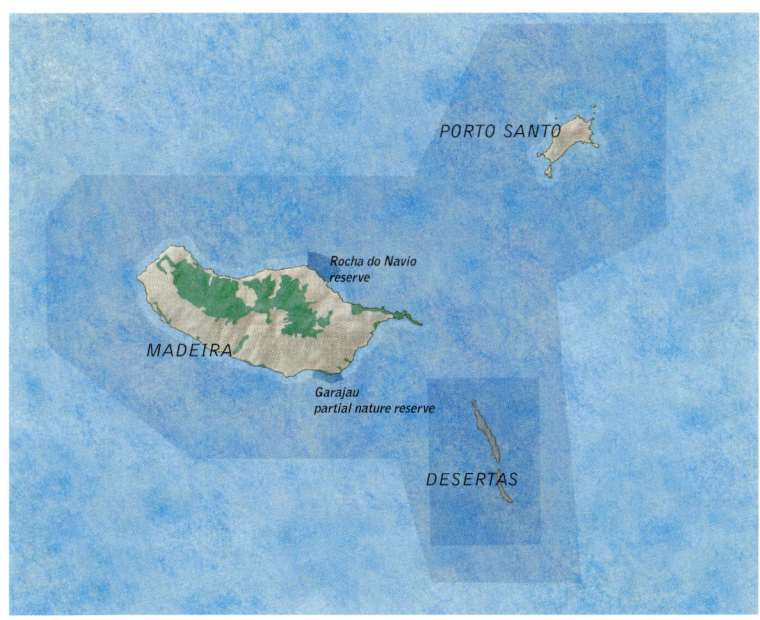

 marine reserve

 special bird reserve

 Natura 2000 reserve

Protected areas in the Madeiran archipelago.

Like Madeira, the Desertas, have a problem with invasive species. The area is so rugged it proved to be impossible to eradicate the introduced goats. Annual hunting campaigns reduce the population as much as possible. In spite of these efforts, it looks like the goat is there to stay.

Two marine natural reserves have been established on the coast of Madeira. Garajau Partial Nature Reserve covers 376 hectares on the south coast, east of Funchal. The Rocha do Navio Nature Reserve is 1,710 hectares and situated on the north coast near Santana. These shallow areas are especially rich and important for breeding fish.

Life projects
The EU LIFE-plus program funds conservation projects of natural environments and endangered species. Lots of species conservation projects on Madeira have been and are still executed by LIFE plus. There have been projects for the conservation of Zino's Petrel, Trocaz Pigeon, Monk Seal, sea Turtles, and cetaceans. The Life project *Recover Natura* focuses on improving the natural habitat for endemic molluscs through the eradication of rodents and invasive plants on Desertas and Ponta de São Lourenço.

FLORA AND FAUNA

The flora and fauna of Madeira is extraordinary. Although the species diversity, with the exception of the flora, is not very high, a great many species that occur here are found nowhere else in the world. They evolved here into unique and often very peculiar and showy forms.
Madeira was never part of any continent. The volcanic eruptions that gave rise to the island, took place far off in the Atlantic Ocean. As a consequence, at its birth Madeira was devoid of life. The organisms that you find today, other than those introduced by man, arrived here by chance and developed in isolation from their relatives (see also page 28), which explains the high number of Madeiran endemics. This happened not only on Madeira, but also on the Canary Islands, the Azores and, much further south, on the Cape Verde Islands. All of these islands are volcanic in origin and were never part of any mainland. Although far apart, they were stepping stones from which plants and birds spread from island to island. Some evolved into species unique to one archipelago, others colonised several archipelagos and remain essentially identical. The Trocaz Pigeon (Madeira) and Bolle's Pigeon (western Canaries) are very closely related for example. In contrast, the Berthelot's Pipit and the Canary occur on most of the Atlantic Islands and are endemic to Macaronesia (the collective name for the volcanic archipelagos of Cape Verde, Canaries, Selvagens, Madeira and Azores). Obviously, there are more endemics among plants and non-flying animals, than there are among highly mobile ones like birds. Most endemic plants (e.g. the marguerites, pericallis, sow-thistles, viper's-buglosses, spurges and houseleeks) are unique to Madeira, but do have close relatives on the Canary Islands which in turn occur only on those islands.
Among the flying animals, Madeira's isolation has given the island an odd 'bipolar' composition of species. This pattern is especially striking among the butterflies all of which fall in the category of either local endemics or widespread and common migratory species that are found nearly everywhere. The first group descends from vagrants that chanced on the island and settled there; the second consists of strong and indefatigable migrants that cross the waters frequently, if not annually.

The unique flora and fauna of Madeira: a Madeiran Wall Lizard on a Small Pride of Madeira. Both species occur exclusively on the island.

INTRODUCTION

Among the more widespread species that occur both on Madeira and on the mainland, the link with the Mediterranean and northern Europe is striking. Madeiran birds like Spectacled Warbler and Rock Sparrow have a distinctly Mediterranean distribution, whereas Blackbird, Robin and Grey Wagtail are widespread north-European species (albeit ones with an outpost in north-west Africa). Elements from the African flora and fauna pale into insignificance by comparison – hardly any birds or butterflies are shared with that continent, which lies actually closer to Madeira than Europe. But there are a few 'Africans', especially among the plants. The curious Disc-leaved Fern* (*Asplenium reniforme*) with its disc-like, leathery leaves is one of them. Several other species have their closest relatives on the African continent, such as the Foxglove Tree (*Isoplexis*).

The final group of flora and fauna are the recent arrivals, all introduced by man, either intentionally or inadvertently. All land mammals belong to this group as do the frogs, the geckos and a lot of plants. They are newcomers that were introduced both from Europe and from Central and Southern America. They were brought to Madeira by the Portuguese from their colonies in South-America or by the British residents of Madeira who had links to colonies all over the world (see page 61). More recently, plants and animals have gained a foothold on Madeira as a result of trade to and from Madeira increasing. Waxbills, Tropical House Geckos, Flowerpot Snakes, Speckled Wood butterflies and Rose-ringed Parakeets are much more recent arrivals. There is a danger that some of these recent newcomers will, like some of their predecessors, develop into invasive 'pests' that threaten the native flora and fauna (see page 65).

All in all, this mix of local and regional endemics, the familiar Mediterranean and European species and the introduced 'foreigners' from America, makes for a very exciting and uniquely Madeiran flora and fauna.

The curious Disc-leaved Fern* (*Asplenium reniforme*) is one of the African elements in the Madeiran flora.

INTRODUCTION

North pelagic
Artctic Skua
(*Stercorarius parasiticus*)

Mediterranean region
Rock Sparrow
(*Petronia petronia*)

European region
Small Copper
(*Lycaena phlaeas*)

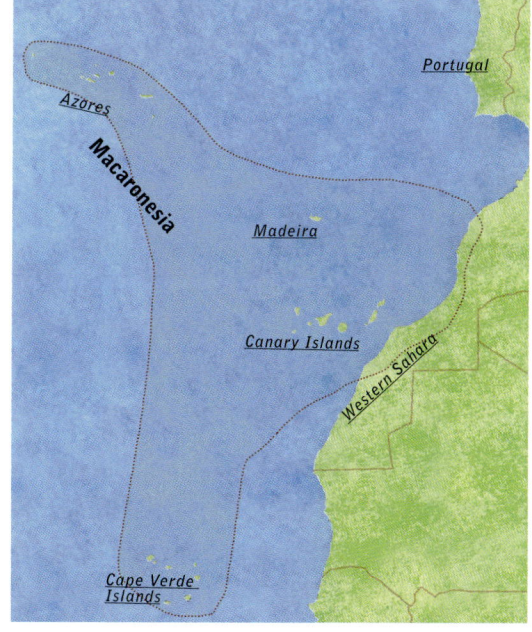

Madeiran endemics
Pride of Madeira
(*Echium candicans*)

Macaronesian endemics
Island Darter
(*Sympetrum nigrifemur*)

South pelagic
Bryde's Whale
(*Balaenoptera brydei*)

FLORA AND FAUNA

Flora

> The best routes for laurel forest plants are routes 6, 8, 11 and 14. Explore the high mountain flora on routes 12 and 13. Rich dryland and cliff flora is found on route 3, 16 and sites D and I on pages 178 and 181.

Plant lovers have a definite advantage over birdwatchers on Madeira. On spectacular walks in the centre and north of the island, there are masses of verdant, flowery, leafy, beautiful species to be found. Some are common and easy to see, others are rare and grow in inaccessible places such as shady ravines or on steep cliffs. Whereas the birdwatchers have just a handful of species to search for, wildflower *aficionados* can spend many fruitful days exploring the Madeiran interior.

Botanists have a disadvantage too. There are very few wildflower guides with which to identify the species and the best, *Flora of Madeira*, is hard to obtain (see page 203).

This is all the more remarkable for a place that is nicknamed 'the island of flowers'. Whether Madeira deserves its famous moniker is a matter of perspective. The spectacular plants you see everywhere in the roadsides, such as the bright blue Agapanthus, the Bird of Paradise flower (*Strelitzia reginae*), Tasmanian Tree Fern (*Dicksonia antarctica*), Jacaranda (*Jacaranda mimosifolia*), African Tulip Tree (*Spathodea campanulata*) and the Pride of Madeira certainly fit the idea of a wildflower paradise. However, most of these exuberant flowers are not native. Amongst the attractive plants we've just listed only the Pride of Madeira, as it name suggests, is a native. The others were brought here by the Portuguese and British to decorate their *quintas*. This is clearly a case where the flower-loving layman and the naturalist/botanist are confused – to the latter, the exotic flowers are hardly the attraction. In fact, they push out the native flora, like the Ginger Lily in the laurel forest, and are thereby an impoverishment rather than an enrichment to the flora. But we won't dwell on that here (see page 65 for a discussion of invasive exotics). Here we'll focus on the native flora. That is a spectacle enough in itself.

The typical feature of Madeira's native flora is not the wildflowers (although some species sport spectacular inflorescences), but the trees, shrubs and ferns. The island's trees stand out because there are so many, both in number (Madeira literally means 'wood') and diversity (given the fact that Madeira is just a small and isolated island). Most of the tall native trees are laurels, which are nearly absent from the nearby mainland

FLORA

and reflect the unique, ancient nature of the island's vegetation (more on that on page 45).

The shrubs are diverse too, but what is so typical here is that many of them are, to western European eyes, just overgrown herbs. Familiar plants like viper's-buglosses, spurges, St. John's-worts, sow-thistles, houseleeks and globularias are large and woody on Madeira, some of them growing as tall as 15 metres. Of the plants that may be regarded as 'conventional' herbs, a relatively large proportion were introduced by man. So the relative diversity of shrubs in comparison to that of herbs was originally even larger than today.

It is thought that on a small island with favourable climate for woodlands and an absence of herbivores, growing tall is the best survival strategy. The original colonising sow-thistles, viper's-buglosses and the other aforementioned herbs evolved here to become shrubs.

Another typical feature of the flora of Madeira are the ferns. Any hike in the laurel forest will yield beautiful stands of them, from the majestic Chain Fern with its bright green 3 metre long leaves to the tiny, see-through Filmy Fern and everything in between. Over 50 species of native ferns grow on the island.

Although Madeira is dubbed 'island of flowers' because of the many introduced species like this Bird of Paradise Flower (right), it is the native flora that forms the greater attraction (left).

FLORA

Ferns are abundant because they naturally thrive in humid places and are well adapted to deep shade – two conditions that are readily available all over Madeira. Being spore plants, ferns are not dependent on insects for pollination, which is an added advantage as Madeira, being the isolated island that it is, has few pollinising insects. This isolation is less of an issue to ferns which produce light spores the wind easily picks up and carries to all corners of the globe. The same goes for mosses, liverworts and lichens, which are also widespread on the island.

Flora of the laurel forests

The first habitat that comes to mind when considering the native flora is the *laurisilva*. This is indeed one of the most spectacular wildflower haunts of the island (although certainly not the only one, as you will see further on). Most of the native plants of the laurel forest are endemic to the Atlantic (*Macaronesian*) Islands, and a large number even to the island of Madeira alone. This richness is not evenly spread throughout the forest though. The hotspots are found in wet places and beside cliffs, where there is a bit more sunlight. This combination of dampness and more open, rocky places is found along many levadas. Levadas are cut out in the mountain which automatically creates a rock wall that accompanies you for the length of your walk. How convenient that some of the best spots in this generally impenetrable forest are found in the few places where access is easy!

The ferns are the first plants you'll notice along the levada. In places there are dense stands of the huge Chain Fern (*Woodwardia radicans*), with its immense leaves. Apart from its size, the Chain Fern is easily recognisable by its leaves that are not as finely divided as the other large ferns on Madeira, but have a simple, feather-like shape. The only other common fern with such a leaf structure is the much smaller Hard Fern (*Blechnum spicant*). Related to the Chain Fern, it also grows widely in temperate Europe and is common in rocky, shady places in the laurel forest.

There are at least a dozen other fern species that are frequent or common on the levada walls. Some may be familiar, such as Maidenhair Fern (*Adiantum capillus-veneris*) and Maidenhair Spleenwort, but you'll need a good flora for a positive identification. The Maidenhair Spleenwort (*Asplenium trichomanes*) already has two doppelgangers (*Asplenium anceps* and *Asplenium monanthes*) which grow in roughly the same spots. Of the more regular-looking ferns there are many different species.

In very wet and shady spots, look out for two small fern species whose

Facing page:
Some laurel forest highlights: Madeiran Blueberry (top), Tree Sow-thistle (centre) and Canary Balm (bottom).

leaves consist of just a single layer of cells and which are therefore almost transparent: the small Filmy Fern (*Hymenophyllum tunbrigense*) and the somewhat larger Killarney Fern (*Vandenboschia speciosa*). Both grow exclusively in very damp places in a dense bed of mosses.

Among the flowering plants, one of the great attractions is the stout Madeira Marsh-orchid*, (*Dactylorhiza foliosa*) which often grows in great quantities along the levadas and in other damp spots. It is a species that only grows on Madeira and as a tall plant with rather few large flowers it's very different from the European marsh-orchids. Another very typical sight is the Canary Buttercup (*Ranunculus cortusifolius*) – again a large species with very big leaves that grows both on Madeira and the Canary Islands and is impossible to confuse with other buttercups. Equally impressive is the large Anemone-leaved Crane's-bill* (*Geranium palmatum*), which is endemic to Madeira and a frequent sight along trails and channels.

Cliffs are the next great wildflower habitat within the laurel forest and, as noted earlier, many cliff plants grow on the rocks above the levadas.

FLORA

Damp cliffs and the bark of old trees share similar species. The Hare's-foot Fern (*Davallia canariensis*) is very common. It is easy to recognise by the thick furry-looking racemes with typical brownish, hair-like scales – hence the name Hare's-foot Fern. It often grows together with Macaronesian Polypody, (*Polypodium macaronesicum*) which is a larger and wider leaved version of the familiar polypody of Europe. Both ferns are common and widespread on all the Atlantic Islands (and also grow in the extreme southwest of the Iberian Peninsula).

The houseleeks, a group of succulent plants, are very typical both of cliffs of the Atlantic Islands. They are hardly found anywhere else. On the Canary Islands there is a confusing diversity of houseleeks, but on Madeira there are just a few (something that also applies to the pericallises, marguerites, sow-thistles and viper's-buglosses that we'll discuss below).

Madeira has two saucer-like house-

Disc Houseleek is a conspicuous cliff plant, even when it is not in flower (top). The Black Parsley is a stout umbellifer (bottom).

leeks of the genus *Aeonium* and two with spreading leaves of the genus *Aichryson*. Both are found on cliffs all over the island, not just in the laurel forest. The Hairy (*Aichryson villosum*) and the Glabrous Aichryson (*A. divaricatum*) are refreshingly easy to tell apart once you realise that 'glabrous' means hairless and that their names refer to their leaves.

The odd Disc Houseleek (*Aeonium glandulosum*) looks like the plant version of a dart board and is often abundant on cliffs in all altitude zones of the island. Somewhat taller is the Viscid Houseleek (*A. glutinosum*), which has a larger stem and leaves that grow up the branches. The *Aeonium* houseleeks

Flora of the laurel forest

Trees and shrubs: Stink Laurel (*Ocotea foetens*)[M,A,CI], Canary Laurel (*Laurus novocanariensis*), Barbusano (*Apollonias barbujana*)[M,CI], Madeira Mahogany (*Persea indica*)[M,CI], Canary Smilax (*Smilax canariensis*)[M,CI], Climbing Butcher's-broom (*Semele androgyna*)[M,CI], Madeira Butcher's-broom (*Ruscus streptophyllus*)[M], Tree Heath (*Erica arborea*), Besom Heath (*Erica platycodon*), Madeiran Blueberry (*Vaccinium padifolium*)[M], Honey Spurge (*Euphorbia mellifera*)[M,CI], Lily-of-the-valley Tree (*Clethra arborea*)[M], Large-leaved St. John's-wort (*Hypericum grandifolium*)[M,CI], Canary St. John's-wort (*Hypericum canariense*)[M,CI], *Sideroxylon mirmulans*[M,CI]

Herbs: Chain Fern (*Woodwardia radicans*), Sweet Violet (*Viola odorata*), Common Dog-violet (*Viola riviniana*), *Oenanthe divaricata*[M,CI], *Peucedanum lowei*[M,CI], *Drusa glandulosa*[M,CI], Black Parsley (*Melanoselinum decipiens*)[M,A], *Teucrium betonicum*[M], Canary Balm (*Cedronella canariensis*)[M,CI], *Bystropogon maderensis*[M], *Bystropogon punctatus*[M], Pride of Madeira (*Echium candicans*)[M], *Normania triphylla*[M], Hairy Aichryson (*Aichryson villosum*)[M], Glabrous Aichryson (*Aichryson glandulosum*)[M], Anemone-leaved Crane's-Bill (*Geranium palmatum*)[M], Giant Herb-Robert (*Geranium maderense*)[M], Massoni's Bindweed (*Convolvulus massonii*)[M,CI], Madeiran Moneywort (*Sibthorpia peregrina*)[M], Wollaston's Musschia (*Musschia wollastonii*)[M], Tree Sow-thistle* (*Sonchus fruticosus*)[M], Madeiran Marguerite (*Argyranthemum pinnatifidum*)[M], Eared Pericallis (*Pericallis aurita*)[M], Broad-leaved Thistle (*Cirsium latifolium*)[M], Mexican Fleabane (*Erigeron karvinskianus*)[in], Sticky Snakeroot (*Ageratina adenophora*)[in], Three-cornered Leek (*Allium triquetum*), Two-leaved Gennaria (*Gennaria diphylla*)

M: Endemic to Madeiran archipelago; M, CI: Endemic to Madeira and Canary Islands; M, A: endemic to Madeira and the Azores; in: invasive species

---

are unique to the Cape Verde, Canary and Madeira archipelagos. This, together with their bizarre appearance, makes them one of Madeira's most special plants, even though they are quite common.

Another peculiar plant with succulent leaves is the Navelwort (*Umbilicus rupestris*), which grows on walls, cliffs and tree trunks. This is one of the few species with a wider distribution range, which includes the entire Mediterranean basin.

The next laurel forest wildflowers will stop you in your tracks because of their size, shape and height: the Black Parsley* (*Melanoselinum decipiens*) is frequent along tracks and one of the few native plants that were grown in the remote villages on the north slope as a vegetable. The Tree

FLORA

Some remarkable plants you are likely to find on Madeira

Since there is a lack of good wildflower guidebooks, we provide here a small selection of easy-to-find and easy-to-recognise plants of the island.

1 - Chain Fern >
Woodwardia radicans
The most conspicuous large fern of Madeira, typically growing in large colonies on wet rocks, along levadas and near waterfalls.
Endemic to the Canary Islands and Madeira.
Routes: 7, 8, 11, 14

< 2 - Hare's-foot Fern *Davallia canariensis*
Strong climber with typical, thick, brown-scaled rhizomes ('roots') that grows in trees and over steep cliffs. Often together with Macaronesian Polypody. Endemic to the Canary Islands, Madeira and a few isolated spots on the extreme south coast of Spain and Portugal.
Routes: 4, 6, 7, 8, 9, 11, 14

3 - Madeira Sea Stock >
Matthiola maderensis
Very conspicuous tall crucifer with grey leaves and deep purple flowers. Common on dry ground, both in the mountains and near the coast.
Flowering time: Feb-Oct
Routes: 2, 3, 4, 5, 9, 12

<4 - Shrubby Wallflower
Erysimum bicolor
This handsome pink crucifer is numerous both in the mountains and on rocky open places in the laurel forest. The name *bicolor* refers to the fact that the flowers at the top are lighter than those lower down. In some plants, this is barely noticeable. As Shrubby Wallflower is the only small pink crucifer, this species is still easy to recognise.
Endemic to Madeira and the Canary Islands.
Flowering time: Nov-Aug
Routes: 7, 11, 12, 13

FLORA

5 - Sinapidenron mustard >
Sinapidendron spp.
The genus *Sinapidendron* is related to the mustards and consists of five species, all of which are exclusive to either Madeira (4 species) or Deserta Grande (1 species). In the photo *S. gymnocalyx*.
Flowering time: March-Aug
Routes: 11, 14, Cabo Girão

< 6 - Pride of Madeira
Echium candicans and *Echium nervosum*
The large, pale-blue spikes of the Pride of Madeira are among the most typical flowers on the island. There are two species. The darker flowers of the 'true' Pride of Madeira can be found on cliffs and other open spots in the laurel forest zone. It is rare in the wild, but often planted in parks and along roadsides. The Small Pride of Madeira (*Echium nervosum*) grows on dry slopes, mostly near the coast, such as on São Lourenço.
Both species are endemic to Madeira.
Flowering time: Apr-Aug (*candicans*) and Jan-Aug (*nervosum*)
Routes: 4, 6, 10, Funchal Ecological Park (*candicans*); 2, 3, 4, 5 (*nervosum*)

7 - Lily-of-the-valley Tree >
Clethra arborea
When flowering, the Lily-of-the-Valley Tree is a spectacular and unmistakable tree of the laurel forest. The spikes of bell-shaped, white flowers spread a wonderful sweet smell. Endemic to Madeira.
Flowering time: Aug-Oct
Routes: 8, 11, 14

< 8 - Madeiran Moneywort
Sibthorpia peregrina
A small, trailing plant with small yellow flowers. Very common on the forest floor of the laurel forest.
Endemic to Madeira.
Flowering time: May-Oct
Routes: 6, 7, 8, 9, 11, 14

FLORA

< 9 - Disc Houseleek *Aeonium gladulosum*
The flat, disc-shaped rosettes of the disc houseleek are a common sight on cliffs, especially on the north slopes and high up in the mountains. The genus *Aeonium* is restricted to the Canaries, Madeira and North-Africa.
Endemic to Madeira
Flowering time: June-Aug
Routes: 4, 5, 7, 12, 13

10 - Viscid Houseleek >
Aeonium glutinosum
The only other native houseleek grows in much the some locations and often together with the previous species. Viscid Houseleek is much taller though, with upright leaves and a large and loose inflorescence.
Endemic to Madeira
Flowering time: May-Oct
Routes: 4, 5, 7, 9, 12, 13

< 11 - Hairy Aichryson *Aichryson villosum*
A succulent plant like the houseleeks, but with much smaller, hairy leaves. Very common on walls, cliffs and also on the trunks of trees in the laurel forest. A second Aichryson, *A. divaricatum*, lacks hairs on the leaves and is equally common.
Endemic to Madeira and the Canary Islands.
Flowering time: March-Nov
Routes: 4, 6, 7, 8, 9, 11, 12, 14

12 - Madeiran Marsh Orchid >
Dactylorhiza foliolosum
A big and large-flowered marsh orchid with many leaves along the stem. Frequent in open wet spots in the laurel forest, especially along levadas.
Endemic to Madeira.
Flowering time: May-July
Routes: 6, 7, 8, 11, 14

CROSSBILL GUIDES • MADEIRA

FLORA

< 13 - Madeiran Early-purple Orchid
Orchis scopulorum
A tall orchid that grows in large numbers in the high mountains of Madeira. Superficially similar to the previous species, but the flowers are different and the leaves are in the form of a basal rosette. Endemic to Madeira.
Flowering time: May-July
Routes: 11, 12

14 - Canary Buttercup >
Ranunculus cortusifolius
Huge and large-flowered buttercup that grows in open spots in the laurel forest and (in a smaller variety) in the high mountains. Endemic to Madeira and the Canary Islands.
Flowering time: March-June
Routes: 6, 7, 8, 11, 13, 14

< 15 - Madeira Marguerite
Argyranthemum pinnatifidum
The marguerites form a group of daisy-like, often bushy plants that are unique to the Atlantic Islands. The Madeira Marguerite is a tall (up to 2 metre) flowery shrub of open spots in the laurel forest. Several other, much rarer species grow on sea cliffs.
Endemic to Madeira.
Flowering time: March-July
Routes: 3, 4, 5, 6, 7, 9, 14

16 - Anemone-leaved Crane's-bill >
Geranium palmatum
The tall crane's-bills you find growing along trails in the laurel forest mostly belong to this species, but there are two other crane's-bills that grow in similar habitat, so for this one you'll need a flora. Endemic to Madeira.
Flowering time: March-Dec
Routes: 6, 7, 8, 11, 14

FLORA

< 17 - Golden Musschia
Musschia aurea
Musschias are among the most spectacular plants of Madeira. The genus consists of only three species, all endemic to the Madeiran archipelago, all bizarre-looking and all rare. Of the three, the Golden Musschia is the easiest to find. Rare and endemic to Madeira.
Flowering time: May - Dec.
Sites: Rocha Alta (page 178); Garajau (page 181)

18 - Madeiran Thrift >
Armeria maderensis
The exuberant pink of the Madeiran Thrift is confined to the highest peaks of island. It is the only species of thrift on Madeira.
Endemic to Madeira.
Flowering time: June-Aug
Route: 12

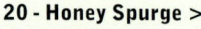

< 19 - Spear-leaved Spurge
Euphorbia piscatoria
On undisturbed slopes on the coast, you'll find the greyish, rounded shrubs of the Spear-leaved Spurge to be quite common.
Endemic to Madeira.
Flowering time: Jan-Aug
Routes: 2, 3, 4, 5, 9

20 - Honey Spurge >
Euphorbia mellifera
This is the only spurge in Europe tall enough to be called a tree and the only one to thrive in the damp laurel forests. It is endemic to the Canary Islands (where it is rare) and Madeira (where it is quite common).
Flowering time: Feb-July
Routes: 8, 11, 14

FLORA

21 - Dragon Tree >
Dracaena draco

The odd Dragon Trees are unique to Madeira, the Canary and Cape Verde Islands. Originally it was numerous in the warm, dry lowland slopes, especially on Porto Santo. Overexploitation has driven the tree close to extinction in the wild. Dragon Trees are widely planted, but have a hard time germinating from seeds. It has been suggested that the seeds best ripen after passing the gut of a now extinct species of bunting.
Endemic to the Atlantic (Macaronesian) Islands.
Routes: Widely planted. E.g. 2, *Nucleo da Dragoeiras* (page 209).

< 22 - Madeiran Blueberry
Vaccinium padifolium

The Madeiran Blueberry is related to the well-known Bilberry, but grows much taller, around 2-4 metres tall. It is a common species in damp open and lightly wooded places above 800 metres. Endemic to Madeira.
Flowering time: May-Dec
Routes: e.g. 6, 7, 8, 10, 11, 14

23 - Eared Pericallis >
Pericallis aurita

The genus *Pericallis* is closely related to the familiar ragworts (*Senecio*), but with purple instead of yellow flowers. The pericallises are unique to the Macaronesian Islands. Of the 14 species, 12 are endemic to the Canary Islands and only one occurs on Madeira. It grows in laurel forest clearings. Endemic to Madeira.
Flowering time: May-July
Routes: e.g. 8, 14

< 24 - Agapanthus
Agapanthus praecox

The bight-blue lily-like flower of the Agapanthus is probably the most conspicuous and common of the introduced flowers found on Madeira. It is found, both planted and feral, along roadsides and in villages all over the island.
Flowering time: May-Aug

FLORA AND FAUNA

FLORA

Extreme rarities

It is three metres tall, with wide leaves and horizontal branches with odd, violet-red flowers and if you haven't been on Madeira you have never seen it before and probably never heard of it either. In fact, even the veteran visitor has likely never seen the Wollaston's Musschia* (*Musschia wollastonii*).

The Wollaston's Musschia is one of those spectacular ultra-rarities of Madeira – it grows on a few steep slopes in the laurel forest, mostly in extremely inaccessible sites. If you chance upon it in the wild, you'll see that it is a very strange plant; one of three members of the genus *Musschia* which sits in an obscure corner of the campanula (bellflower) family. The two other musschias are the Golden Musschia (*Musschia aurea*), known from a thirty odd steep cliffs of Madeira and the tall Desertas Musschia (*Musschia isambertoi*), which has only been discovered in 2006 on even more inaccessible sea cliffs on the Desertas. They are the botanical equivalent of the Galapagos Finches!

Madeira has a number of these extreme rarities and most of them are of a jaw-dropping beauty. The Madeira Foxglove Tree* (*Isoplexis sceptrum*) is a tall bush (up to 2 metres) with exuberant dark orange flowers that grows on just a few cliffs in the laurel forest. The tree is distantly related to our foxgloves, but much closer to two other *Isoplexis* foxglove trees that are endemic to the Canary Islands.

The Giant Herb-Robert (*Geranium maderense*) grows in a few spots in the mountains, if it hasn't gone extinct already. At up to a metre tall this shrub, with its near spherical fan of deep pink flowers, looks like a giant pink pompom. The Madeiran Lady's-tresses (*Goodyera macrophylla*) is an orchid that grows in the wild in just a handful sites in central Madeira, again on cliffs and in canyons in the laurel forest. This habitat is also the haunt of the spectacular Pride of Madeira – a very flowery and bushy version of the viper's-bugloss. It is planted widely, but in the wild, this plant is very rare.

Dry slopes are the natural habitat of the Dragon Tree. Once it was so common on Porto Santo that the first settlers made boats from its wood. Today, only a single tree occurs in the wild, on a cliff near Ribeira Brava on Madeira.

Extreme rarity: the Madeiran Lady's-tresses.

FLORA

All these extreme rarities are virtually impossible to see in the wild. Fortunately, they are frequently planted in botanical gardens, parks, roadsides and levada banks, where they grow for everyone to admire. The Pride of Madeira and the Foxglove Tree are a fairly frequent sight in forest clearings and along levadas in the forest zone, where they grow in their natural environment even if they were planted there. Very good spots to see rarities like the Madeiran Lady's-tresses or the Wollaston's Musschia are in the small botanical gardens of Ribeiro Frio (route 6) and at the Parque Florestal de Queimadas (route 14).

The endemic Madeira Foxglove Tree is a rare plant of semi-shady cliffs in the laurel forest.

Sow-thistle* (*Sonchus fruticosus*) is a tall (up to 4 metres), yellow-flowered sow-thistle which grows (like the Black Parsley) on a large stem, as if their taproot has been halfway pulled out of the ground. The leaves sit at the base of the stem as if it were standing on a pedestal. The white-flowered Madeira Marguerite* (*Argyranthemum pinnatifidum*) is the common Marguerite in gardens and along levadas in the laurel forest zone. In contrast, another relative of the daisies, the Eared Pericallis* (*Pericallis aurita*), has a plump purple heart of florets surrounded by radial pale pink petals. Its leaves are of a typical grey colour. The pericallises form another group of plants unique to the Canary Islands and Madeira.

Summer visitors will enjoy the tall Broad-leaved Thistle* *(Cirsium latifolium)*, again endemic to Madeira.

Deeper in the laurel forest, the plant diversity is clearly lower. One common plant here is the Madeiran Blueberry (*Vaccinium padifolium*), unique to the island and very different from the common Bilberry (which doesn't occur on Madeira). Like so many other plants on the island, the Madeiran Blueberry is tall, growing up to 4 metres in height.

Flora of dry land and the coastline

The dry coastal areas were long seen as simply degraded parts of the islands and therefore not very interesting. Large parts of the coastal lowlands are indeed degraded, threatened by invasive plants, overgrazed by rabbits, swallowed up by the construction of roads and houses or by conversion to farmland. However, the unspoilt parts that remain do have a

FLORA

very special flora. Most of it is found on cliffs, either because the species prefers this habitat, or simply because they have disappeared everywhere else.

On Madeira, the dryland flora is restricted to a few cliffs on the south, west and especially the eastern peninsula of São Lourenço. On Porto Santo, some of the wastelands and the cliffs on the northern part of the island are the top sites for this flora (Pico Branco; route 16). The dry cliffs of the Desertas sport a similar vegetation.

The natural vegetation is dominated by several succulent shrubs and trees. The Spear-leaved Spurge (also called Fish-stunning Spurge; *Euphorbia piscatoria*) with its grey, spherical appearance is quite common. On slightly damper spots, look out for the Willow-leaved Globularia, a bush with pale blue flowers, endemic to Madeira and the Canary Islands. The Madeira Olive Tree* (*Olea maderensis*) in contrast, is only present in a handful of sites that have escaped the urban sprawl. The Dragon Tree is even rarer in the wild, but it is frequently planted.

Various stout plants flower in the dry coastal zone. The peak of the flowering season lies earlier than in the laurel forest, roughly from mid-March to mid-May. It is at this time you'll see the Small Pride of Madeira (*Echium nervosum*), a smaller cousin of the Pride of Madeira (*E. candicans*). The big purple crucifer with grey leaves and the pink flowers is the Madeira Sea Stock* (*Matthiola maderensis*). The white, daisy-like flowers belong to Mandon's Marguerite* (*Argyranthemum pinnatifidum ssp succulentum*).

The Small Pride of Madeira is fairly common on dry grasslands near the coast.

FLORA

Come May, a confusing array of yellow composites pops up. The most eye-catching is a big, branched species with densely furry leaves: Downy Andryala* (*Andryala glandulosa*). A walk on the Peninsula of São Lourenço will reveal many more special species (see box and route 3).

The dryland flora is widespread on the island of Porto Santo. Over much of the island you'll find the small bush *Phagnalon bennettii* with its small yellow flowerheads. Close to the coast, there are masses of Sea Heath (*Frankenia laevis*), Silvery Trefoil* (*Lotus glaucus*) and Hollow-stemmed Asphodels (*Asphodelus fistulosus*).

The highest number of species is undoubtedly found on cliffs and rocky areas. This is where you'll find many endemics. One of them is the Golden Musschia, with pretty yellow flowers but most easily recognisable by the bright green leaves. It shares its habitat with the extremely rare Pinnate Lavander* (*Lavandula pinnata*), the abundant Disc and Viscid Houseleeks, the grey bush *Helichrysum devium*, Madeiran

The Golden Musschia grows only in a few dozen cliffs on Madeira.
It is an odd member of the bellflower family. The entire genus *Musschia*, consisting of only three species, is endemic to the Madeiran Archipelago.

Coastal cliffs and Porto Santo

Helichrysum devium[M], *Helichrysum obconicum*[M], *Helichrysum melaleucum*[M], *Phagnalon bennettii*[M], *Asteriscus aquaticus*[CI, PS], *Carduus squarrosus*[M], Willow-leaved Carline-thistle (*Carlina salicifolia*)[M CI], *Cheirolophus massonianus*[M] *Andryala glandulosa ssp glandulosa*[M, CI], *Crepis divaricata*[M] *Scilla maderensis*[M], Disc Houseleek (*Aeonium glandulosum*)[M], Viscid Houseleek (*Aeonium glutinosum*)[M], Hairy Aichryson (*Aichryson villosum*)[M], Glabrous Aichryson (*Aichryson dumosum*)[M], Madeira Olive Tree (*Olea maderensis*)[M], Pinnate Lavender (*Lavandula pinnata*)[M, CI], Small Pride of Madeira (*Echium nervosum*)[M], Willow-leaved Globularia (*Globularia salicina*)[CI, M], Sea Heath (*Frankenia laevis*) White Sea Heath (*Frankenia pulverenta*), Lowe's Sea Lavender (*Limonium lowei*)[only PS], *Galium productum*[M], Hollow-stemmed Asphodel (*Asphodelus fistulosus*), Pitch trefoil (*Bituminaria bituminosa*), Golden Musschia (*Musschia aurea*)[M], *Wahlenbergia lobelioides*[M, CI, CV], Wild Jasmine (*Jasminus odoratissimum*)[M, CI], *Teucrium heterophyllum*[M, CI], *Lotus glaucus*[M, CI], Shrubby Plantain (*Plantago arborescens*)[M, CI]

M: Endemic to Madeiran archipelago; M, CI: Endemic to Madeira and Canary Islands; M, A: endemic to Madeira and the Azores; in: invasive species.

FLORA

sow-thistle* *(Sonchus ustulatus)*, the white-flowered thistle *Carduus squarrosus*, Shrubby Seakale* (*Crambe fruticosa*), Shrubby Plantain (*Plantago arborescensum*), Mealy Stonecrop* (*Sedum farinosum*) and many others. Some species are restricted to just a few cliffs, such as Garajau, Girão and Ponta do Pargo.

On Porto Santo, the most attractive flora is found on the northern cliffs, where, locally, you may rejoice over the big, knapweed-like *Cheirolophus massonianus*, the Porto Sancto Ironwort* (*Sideritis candicans;* with downy leaves), Disc-leaved Fern* (*Asplenium reniforme*) and the very rare Porto Santo endemic Lowe's Sea-lavander* (*Limonium lowei*).

Highland flora

The highlands are dominated by rocky grasslands, heathlands and thickets of broom and Bracken. The highland flora is radically different from that of the laurel forest and the dry lowlands. The much colder climate distinguishes it from the lowlands, while the extreme sunshine and dry conditions differentiate this habitat from that of the laurel forest. Hence, there is a large number of species that are unique to this area.

This being said, some of the most frequently encountered species are found elsewhere on the island too: the Canary Buttercup (*R. canariensis*;

Madeiran Heath

Highland flora

Tolpis succulenta[M, A], Pinnate Sow-thistle (*Sonchus pinnatus*)[M], *Crepis vesicaria ssp andryaloides*[M], Madeira Sea Stock (*Matthiola maderensis*)[M], *Andryala glandulosa ssp glandulosa*[M], Disc Houseleek (*Aeonium glandulosum*)[M], Viscid Houseleek (*Aeonium glutinosum*)[M], Madeiran Heath (*Erica maderensis*)[M], Madeiran Thrift (*Armeria maderense*)[M], Madeira Saxifrage (*Saxifraga maderensis*)[M], Porto Santo Saxifrage (*S. portosanctana*)[ONLY PS], *Odontites holliana*[M], Shrubby Plantain (*Plantago arborescens*)[M, CI], Madeira Violet (*Viola paradoxa*)[M], Willow-leaved Hare's-foot (*Bupleurum salicifolium*)[M, CI], *Bunium brevifolium*[M], *Satureja varia*[M, CI]

M: Endemic to Madeiran archipelago; PS: endemic to Porto Santo, M CI: Endemic to Madeira and Canary Islands; M, A: endemic to Madeira and the Azores; in: invasive spec here in a much lower growing subspecies), the Downy Andryala (*A. glandulosa*; again a different subspecies), the Shrubby Wallflower (*Erysimum bicolor*) and the Shrubby Plantain (*P. arborescens*). On cliffs, you'll find many Disc and Viscid Houseleeks. All of these are either Madeiran or Macaronesian endemics with beautiful flowers and it is certainly no punishment to spend time among them.

However, the truly exciting species are the different ones. First and foremost, our favourite, the Madeiran Early-purple Orchid (*Orchis scopulorum*), unique to the high mountains of Madeira, where it can turn entire meadows purple. It mixes in nicely with the Madeiran Thrift (*Armeria maderense*), the more subtly coloured Dense-flowered Orchid (*Neotinea maculata*) and, on rocky spots, Madeira Saxifrage (*Saxifraga maderensis*). Cliffs again come up trumps with species, such as Willow-leaved Hare's-ear (*Bupleurum salicifolium*), Madeira Savoury (*Satureja varia*) and various species of *Sinapidendron*-mustards, all of which grow nowhere else but here, on the roof of Madeira.

Mealy Stonecrop, again endemic to Madeira, is quite common in rocky places above the laurel forest zone.

> **Orchids**
>
> Five species of orchids occur on Madeira of which three are endemics: Madeira Marsh-orchid (Dactylorhiza foliosa), Madeira Early-purple Orchid (*Orchis scopulorum*) and Madeiran Lady's-tresses (*Goodyera macrophylla*). Although these three each belong to groups that also occur on the mainland, they are clearly different from and much larger than their mainland cousins. The marsh-orchid (flowering May-July) is widespread and often quite common in the laurel forest. It often grows along levadas. The early-purple orchid (flowering May-June) is abundant around Pico do Areeiro. In sharp contrast, the lady's-tresses, which flowers in late summer, is extremely rare and best seen in the Parque Florestal in Ribeiro Frio.
>
> The other two species are Dense-flowered Orchid (*Neotinea maculata*), which is widespread in the Mediterranean region and the Two-leaved Gennaria (*Gennaria diphylla*), which has its main distribution on the Atlantic Islands and the southwest coast of Portugal. The first grows in large numbers in the upper Tree Heath zone and in the high mountain meadows (flowering April-June) while the latter is locally common in the laurel forest. It flowers very early in the year, from December to March.

MAMMALS

Mammals

> Bats can be seen flying around streetlights and, if you bring a powerful torch, over quiet forest roads at night. A great spot to see Leisler's Bats at close range is around the spotlights for the statue of Christ at Garajau (see page 181). The latter is also a good spot to watch whales and dolphins from land. Other land-based whale-watching spots are found on routes 2, 3 and 15, and sites C, I and M. Your chance of spotting whales and dolphins are clearly higher from a boat. The Porto Santo ferry and a trip to the Desertas are good ways to see whales and dolphins, with the latter offering a real chance of seeing Monk Seal. The best way to see cetaceans, though, is on a special whale-watching trip (see page 187).

Before the Portuguese set foot on Madeira, there were hardly any terrestrial mammals on Madeira. Only bats and a single marine mammal, the Monk Seal, were able to colonise the islands naturally. Crossing the 650 kms from the nearest shore is too daunting a task for even the strongest swimmer, So all the cats, rats, goats and mice followed in the wake of Man.

Bats are represented by three species, of which two have evolved into endemics (one a full species and the other a subspecies). The Madeira Pipistrelle is a Macaronesian endemic species with small populations on Madeira and Porto Santo. It lives in low and middle altitudes, with a preference for areas with pine and mixed forests and shelters in crevices of trees and in buildings. It is the only small sized bat and hunts around streetlights and above roads that cross the forests, such as the one going up to Pico do Areeiro (route 12).

An endemic subspecies of Leisler's Bat (or Lesser Noctule) lives on Madeira (as well on other Macaronesian islands). It roosts in old trees and hunts in forests and over fields. Its population is small and little known.

Short-finned Pilot Whales occur in tight pods and have a typical, easily recognisable dorsal fin.

CROSSBILL GUIDES • MADEIRA

MAMMALS

The Grey Long-eared Bat occurs on Madeira and has also been found on the Desertas. It lives both in the forest and in agricultural areas, where it roosts in houses.

House Mouse, Black and Brown Rats were all introduced to Madeira accidentally. They have done tremendous harm to seabird populations on the islands (none of them being accustomed to predators) by eating their chicks and eggs. On Bugio, the southernmost island of the Desertas, poison is used to eradicate them. Introduced cats too are a problem. Domestic Goats and Rabbits (deliberately released by the earliest settlers) are also doing harm to the native flora and fauna of the islands.

Marine mammals

Spotting a big whale or a pod of smaller whales or dolphins always gives a thrill. Even if you fail to identify to the precise species, just seeing these elegant yet mighty beasts breaking the surface is breath-taking.

The Madeiran waters are on the migration routes of many cetaceans (the collective name for whales and dolphins) and most species are only seen during a part of the year. May to October is the best period to spot sea mammals as their numbers are greater and the sea is calmer.

At least 21 species of cetaceans have been recorded in the Madeiran waters. This enormous diversity is thanks to the blessed combination of food-rich waters and the position of Madeira in a small zone where northern and southern species meet.

The Striped Dolphin is frequently seen during dolphin trips.

Seven species are typical of warm temperate waters and two are home to colder, northern seas. Bryde's Whale and Atlantic Spotted Dolphin serve as examples of southern species while Minke Whale is an example of a northern species. Twelve have a cosmopolitan distribution.

Six species are common and often seen on whale-watching trips. One of them is the Sperm Whale, with its typical long, grey body and massive head, is present all year round. It migrates from tropical waters to the polar zones and family groups are seen around Madeira. It is the largest toothed whale and thus the largest toothed predator in the world. The males measure up to 18 metres in length and weigh 57 tonnes!

MAMMALS

Sperm Whales visit the Madeiran waters in summer (top). The Rough-toothed Dolphin is seen only occasionally (bottom).

The Bryde´s Whale is a typical baleen whale of warm waters. It has a long, grey body with a pale underside and a small dorsal fin placed at the end of its back. It is seen from April to December and measures up to 14 metres.

The much smaller Short-finned Pilot Whale has a rounded, bulbous forehead and a dorsal fin set forward on the body. It is a slow swimmer that often lies motionless on the surface. The Common Dolphin with its attractively patterned skin is a fast swimmer that approaches boats and ferries. It is seen in winter, from December to May. The uniformly grey Bottle-nose Dolphin and the Atlantic Spotted Dolphin with its three-toned pattern are both seen all year, though mainly from March to October. Fin Whale and Sei Whale, are regularly recorded and other less common species are Minke Whale, Killer Whale, False Killer Whale, Cuvier´s Beaked Whale, Risso´s Dolphin, Striped Dolphin and Rough-toothed Dolphin.

The Mediteranean Monk Seal

The Mediterranean Monk Seal is one of the most endangered species on the planet, with a world population thought to be less than 700. They breed on small, uninhabited islands in the Mediterranean and eastern Atlantic.

The human role in the decline of the Monk Seal has been decisive. Hunting Monk Seals by the Portuguese along the African west coast has been documented since the 15th century. The skin and the extracted oil was sold. Prolonged hunting caused a long decline and human persecution, disturbance and bycatch of the fishing industry still take their toll. A new threat has emerged with ecotourism. People who want to see them in the last locations where they breed approach and disturb colonies. Today, the distribution of the Monk Seal is highly fragmented. Outside the eastern Mediterranean coast of Greece and Turkey only two colonies survive – one in Mauretania and the other on the Desertas Islands.

In Madeira the Monk Seal was called *Lobo Marinho* (Sea Wolf), a reference to their barking and howling voice. The first navigators found a colony on the south coast of Madeira and this place was called *Câmara de Lobos* (Bed of Wolves). The seals were numerous and used beaches and caves to breed, unaware of the threat from humans. Following their decline, they disappeared from Madeira but survived on the Desertas. They were more secure on these uninhabited islands but population fell to 50 in 1978 and then to only 6-8 in 1988. The islands were legally protected in 1990 and in twenty years the population recovered to 25-30 individuals.

Spotting the Monk Seal in the Madeira Archipelago remains difficult. There are few animals, which are shy and hide in inaccessible places. When in the water, only their head and a part of their back can be seen. That said they sometimes appear elsewhere (including Funchal) so it's always worth keeping an eye out for them.

Whale hunting and the Whale conservation

Whale hunting started on Madeira surprisingly late, in about 1941. At first it was in primitive wooden vessels with sails, hand thrown harpoons attached to the boat with hemp rope. Lookout posts were established to locate the whales. The first such post was in Porto Moniz but others were set up on the east coast. On the sighting of a spout from a whale´s blowhole, a signal from the lookout post alerted the whalers in the harbour. They then sailed out on the hunt.

Later, motor boats equipped with harpoon cannons were used and tug boats helped to tow whale carcasses back to port. In the island´s factory, the blubber and meat went into a pressure cooker which extracted the primary product, oil. Remaining solids were dried and ground up with bones to make 'whale meal', used as animal feed. Bones and teeth that were too hard to grind were used to create art, jewellery, and instruments.

Most of the whales hunted were Sperm whales. Almost six thousand of these animals were killed. They were abundant in Madeira waters and easy to retrieve after killing as their carcasses floated.

The whaling industry continued to 1981 and stopped when the demand for whale meat fell. Soon after, whale watching tours started on Madeira that helped to set up whale conservation projects and educate tourists as well as inhabitants of the island. The Whale Museum (**www.museudabaleia.org**) at Caniçal tells the whaling history and organises conservation and education projects.

BIRDS

Birds

> Best trips for finding Trocaz Pigeon, Madeira Goldcrest and other laurel forest birds are routes 1, 6, 11, 14 and site K on page 183). Open land birds such as Red-legged Partridge, Hoopoe and Berthelot's Pipit are best searched for on routes 2, 3, 10 and 15. For seabirds, try route 2, 4 and 15, and sites C and L on pages 177 and 183. Better still, book an excursion on the ocean (see page 186).

Since the beginning of the 19th Century, when naturalists started to travel the world in search of new discoveries, the Atlantic islands have been in the spotlight. One of the first to describe the Madeiran fauna was Dr. Karl Heineken, a German who lived on the island for several years (and no relation of the family that gave their name to the famous beer brand). Heineken described several birds that live exclusively on Madeira such as the Trocaz Pigeon, the Madeira Firecrest and the now extinct local race of the Wood Pigeon. The local subspecies of Blackcap still bears Heineken's name.

Today, the archipelago draws its fair share of European birdwatchers who mostly come for the endemic species and the huge numbers of seabirds. With the consequent better coverage of the islands, some migratory species (particularly waders and some seabirds) have proved to be less scarce than previously thought – an added bonus for visiting birders.

The total number of bird species on the archipelago is low, though. Only

Madeira is a spectacular place for seabirds. Elsewhere hard-to-spot species like this Bulwers Petrel (left) and Madeiran Storm-petrel (right) can be seen here when you go out on a seabird excursion (see page 190).

BIRDS

35 land birds breed annually, plus an additional 11 different species of seabirds, which is a proportionally high number. If you spend a week on Madeira, you may expect to see about 40 different species, 50 if you visit Porto Santo too, and more still if you seriously search for seabirds. The Madeiran archipelago lies too far out in the ocean to be on one of the main migration routes. However, it has hundreds of kilometres of open ocean around it, so any stray bird that comes across Madeira or Porto Santo is likely to drop down to rest and feed, sometimes staying for months on end. Naturally, this happens during spring and autumn migration. These vagrants never appear in big numbers, but there are enough to seriously boost the variety of birds on the island.

Pretty much any migrating species on the western flyway between Europe and Africa may wind up on Madeira. In 2011 the checklist of the birds of the archipelagos of Madeira and the Selvagens included 344 species and subspecies and the list is growing every year. On it are quite a few American vagrants, since Madeira sits isolated in the Atlantic and is one of the earliest landfalls open to birds arriving from the west.

Some species, like Grey Heron, Cattle and Little Egrets, House Martin and Swallow, Turnstone and Whimbrel are found fairly regularly as non-breeding visitors.

> **Madeira´s birdlife in a nutshell**
>
> **Madeira endemics (full species):** Zino´s Petrel, Desertas Petrel (sometimes regarded as a subspecies of Fea's Petrel), Madeira Firecrest, Trocaz Pigeon
>
> **Madeira endemics (distinct subspecies):** Linnet, Sparrowhawk, Barn Owl, Grey Wagtail, Madeira Chaffinch
>
> **Atlantic Island endemics:** Macaronesian Shearwater, Plain Swift, Berthelot`s Pipit, Canary
>
> **Atlantic Island endemics (distinct subspecies):** Buzzard, Kestrel, Yellow-legged Gull, Blackcap, Quail
>
> **European land birds:** Coot, Moorhen, Mallard, Kentish Plover, Hoopoe, Red-legged Partridge, Woodcock, Pallid Swift, Robin, Spectacled Warbler, Blackbird, Spanish Sparrow, Rock Sparrow, Goldfinch, Greenfinch, Turtle Dove, Rock Dove, Collared Dove
>
> **Frequent non-breeding visitors from Europe:** Grey Heron, Cattle Egret, Little Egret, Turnstone, Whimbrel, Dunlin, Sanderling, House Martin, Swallow
>
> **Seabirds:** Cory´s Shearwater, Manx Shearwater, Bulwer´s Petrel, Roseate Tern, Common Tern, White-faced Storm-petrel, Madeiran Storm-petrel
> Non-breeding seabirds include Great Shearwater, Sooty Shearwater, Wilson´s Storm-petrel, Leach's Storm-petrel, European Storm-petrel, Northern Gannet, Great Skua

Due to its western and isolated position, Madeira receives a lot of American vagrants, such as this Spotted Sandpiper.

FLORA AND FAUNA

BIRDS

Birds of parks, gardens and agricultural areas

Quite a number of the Madeiran land birds have adapted to living in human-made environments. In large gardens and parks, you should have little difficulty finding Canaries, Robins, Blackbirds and Blackcaps, while Plain Swifts wheel overhead from spring (roughly late March) well into autumn. If there is a bit of water, you are likely to add Grey Wagtail to that list too. In Machico and Lugar de Baixo, there is a population of Waxbills. Collared Doves are a little more widespread. They have recently colonised the island and are rapidly expanding.

The greatest variety of urban birds is undoubtedly in villages and towns where streams run down to the sea, such as in Machico or São Vicente. Here you may see Madeira's few water birds, such as Moorhen and Mallard (both of which breed), Grey Heron, Little Egret (both frequent visitors) and various waders (many of which are vagrants). There are only a few areas of open water on the islands, the most notable ones being on Porto Santo (El Tanque and the Golf Course (see page 171) and Lugar Baixo on Madeira (see page 176). These are favourite haunts for vagrant water birds like herons, ducks, rails and Spoonbills.

In agricultural areas, you may look for some of the less common species, like Greenfinch, Goldfinch and Linnet, which occur along with the abundant Canaries. Red-legged Partridge and Quail occur here as well, the latter being one of the very few migrant land birds that fly back and forth to Madeira every year.

Blackcap (top) and Canary (right) can be seen in the parks of Funchal.

CROSSBILL GUIDES • MADEIRA

Madeira Archipelago subspecies

Buzzard (*Buteo buteo harterti*) is similar to a dark morph Common Buzzard *B. b. buteo*. Some ornithologists contest the status of *harterti* as a subspecies.
Eurasian Sparrowhawk (Macaronesia subspecies *granti*) is smaller and darker, with thicker barring below.
Common Kestrel (Madeira/Western Canaries subspecies *canariensis*) is smaller and darker, and the male's head is of a darker grey.
Quail (Macaronesia subspecies *confisa*) is smaller, darker and is partially resident. Some ornithologists contest the status of *confisa* as a subspecies.
Yellow-legged Gull (Macaronesia subspecies *atlantis*) is generally smaller and darker.
Rock Dove (subspecies *atlantis*) has many black spots on the upperparts, black on mantle and upper wing. Some ornithologists contest the status of *atlantis* as a subspecies.
Barn Owl (Madeira subspecies *schmitzi*) is rather small and has a heavy tarsus and toes.
Berthelot's Pipit (Madeira subspecies *maderensis*) has a longer bill and middle toe.
Grey Wagtail (Madeira subspecies *schmitzi*) is fairly small and has a long bill.
Blackbird (Madeira/Western Canaries subspecies *cabrerae*) is deeper black (male) or darker brown (female).
Blackcap (Madeira / Western Canaries subspecies *heineken*) is smaller and often darker. Its upperparts are olive-brown and underparts darker and greyer. The rare hooded form (2% of the population), unique to Macaronesia, is largely found here on Madeira.
Spectacled Warbler (Macaronesia subspecies *orbitalis*) is inseparable from the mainland form. Some ornithologists contest the status of *orbitalis* as a subspecies.
Chaffinch (Madeira subspecies *maderensis*) has a pink breast, green back and blue head, a louder and more melodious song – all in all a very different bird from the European chaffinches.
Linnet (Madeira subspecies *guentheri*) has rather short wings and slender bill.

Open fields form a good place to look for Madeira's raptors, Buzzard and Kestrel and at night for the island's only species of owl, the Barn Owl (which may also be found in large city parks). Where agricultural land borders the forest, you may be lucky and find a Sparrowhawk, which is the least common of the raptors on Madeira. Fields bordering the laurel forests are in autumn a good spot to see Trocaz Pigeons, which come down to feed on the spilt seeds.

BIRDS

Birds of dry land – São Lourenço and Porto Santo

One of the most diverse habitats for birds are the dry grasslands, abandoned fields and native scrublands, which you mostly find on the eastern Peninsula of São Lourenço and on the island of Porto Santo. In addition to the ubiquitous Canary, these are the places for seeing the Berthelot's Pipit, endemic to Madeira, the Canaries and Azores. It is a typical pipit with long legs, brown above and streaked below and, vagrants aside, there are no similar birds on the islands, so it should be easy to recognise. The dry lands are also the place to look for Rock Dove, Rock Sparrow, Linnet and Hoopoe, the latter two being much more common on Porto Santo than on Madeira. Porto Santo is also the island to go if you want to see Spanish Sparrows. They used to occur in eastern Madeira as well but seem to be extinct there. Also exclusive to Porto Santo is the Kentish Plover, a few pairs of which breed on quiet sections of the coastal plain.

Berthelot's Pipit is a typical bird of dry, open areas areas such as the coast, the highlands, Porto Santo and the Desertas.

Birds of the laurel forest

The laurel forest is an obvious destination for birdwatchers as it is here that you can find the most emblematic birds of the island. The big prize is of course the Trocaz Pigeon. This large pigeon hides extremely well in the forest and is most often seen when it flies from one place to another above the canopy.

Whereas the Trocaz Pigeon is not easy to see well in this habitat, the opposite applies to the Madeira Chaffinch, an endemic subspecies. Females are virtually identical to European birds but the male looks quite different with its darker cap, greyer back and flanks and pale face. It is more akin to the Chaffinches of North Africa and the Canary Islands.

The third great attraction that is not hard to find either is the Madeira Firecrest which resembles its European namesake albeit with a far shorter white supercilium. It prefers stands of Tree and Besom Heath, where it is common and, though restless, easy to watch.

Apart from these three attractions, the laurel forest is remarkably poor in birds. Robins, Blackbirds, Grey Wagtails and Blackcaps are numerous

BIRDS

The pretty Madeiran Chaffinch can be extraordinarily tame, such as here at Ribeiro Frio (route 6).

and besides these, there are really just two other laurel forest birds: the Sparrowhawk and the Woodcock. Both live hidden lives deep within the forest and are not easily seen. The woodcock is best found on clear spring evenings, when it flies its courtship flights over the forest.

Birds of the high mountains

The rocky and scrubby world above the trade wind clouds are, like the laurel forest, a habitat with very few but special birds. Most spectacular is the Zino's Petrel, a sea bird whose entire world population breeds in the mountains of Madeira (see page 102). It only comes to land at night, so the Zino's Petrel is not a bird you'll actually see while walking in the mountains – you may see it during the day on the ocean though (see page 186) or hear it on specially arranged trips to the mountains at night.

Fortunately, the other mountain birds show themselves much better. Apart from Robin, Blackbird and Madeira Chaffinch, which are

Spectacled Warbler

FLORA AND FAUNA

BIRDS

Downfall and recovery of the Trocaz Pigeon

In 1829 the German ornithologist Karl Heineken described a new kind of pigeon. He found this bird to be different from the Wood Pigeon, a race of which which then also bred on the island, but was much rarer and was last shot in 1904. Heineken noted that the pigeons did not interbreed. He suggested giving this new species the name 'trocaz', which was simply the Madeiran name for pigeon. At the time of its official discovery, the Trocaz Pigeon (sometimes called the Long-toed Pigeon), was not rare on Madeira, but often just as elusive as it can be now. Heineken wrote that "*It is found in the most wooded and unfrequented parts of the island, and is so shy and difficult to get at, that I can learn but little of its habits*". Although still not always easy to see, for reasons noted below, they are less hard to find than thirty years ago and probably also easier than in Heineken's time.

Trocaz Pigeons feed on laurel berries, especially the Madeira Laurel and Stink Laurel, and in spring and summer, when the berries are scarce, on leaves of a variety of species. The pigeons, deprived of much of their original forest habitat, found new food supplies in the crop fields and started to feed on cabbage, cherry flowers and vine shoots. Farmers were obviously not amused and started to hunt the pigeons. Introduced Black Rats also added more pressure by predating on the eggs and young. As a result, the Trocaz Pigeon disappeared on Porto Santo Island and suffered greatly on Madeira.

Hunting continued until 1986, the year Portugal entered the European Union. By that time only about 2,700 birds survived and on only 15% of the island where the laurel forest remained. Conservation projects were launched aimed at stopping shooting and increasing the available natural habitat. Awareness campaigns were established to change the negative attitude towards the Trocaz Pigeon. The bird itself was thoroughly studied to know more about its ecology, especially its diet and feeding behaviour. All in all, this was very successful. Today, the distribution area has more than doubled and the population has increased to an estimated 10,000-14,000 birds. However, illegal hunting still occurs, especially where birds feed on agricultural fields.

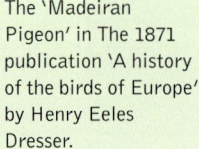

The 'Madeiran Pigeon' in The 1871 publication 'A history of the birds of Europe' by Henry Eeles Dresser.

BIRDS

all numerous, the birds to look out for are the Berthelot's Pipit and the Spectacled Warbler. The latter bird is quite common in gorse, heath and broom bushes of the high mountains. In winter, it descends to scrubland near the coast. Also very attractive in the mountains are the big flocks of Plain Swifts. You may see them all over the island, but in the mountains you can see large numbers of them speeding along the cliffs at eye level. Mountain passes are the best to see this spectacle at close range.

Buzzards, Kestrels and Red-legged Partridges are other frequent birds of the high mountains.

Coastal and seabirds

The highest bird diversity is seen on the coast and at sea. Common Terns and Yellow-legged Gulls are most common, breeding all along the coast. More local, the rare Roseate Tern breeds in the same colonies as the Common Terns. It can be seen frequently at Funchal and São Vicente (routes 1 and 4). Furthermore, a score of wader species is present on the islands, mostly in places where rivers pour out into the sea, or where tidal pools remain between the pebbles. Although any type of shorebird can turn up (including American vagrants) only Turnstones, Sanderlings, Dunlins and Whimbrels are tolerably frequent (esp. in winter) whilst Grey Plovers, although scarce, may have been previously overlooked. Little Egret and Grey Heron are also frequently present.

The coastal cliffs of Madeira and the surrounding islands play host to enormous colonies of Bulwer's Petrels (about 7,000 breeding pairs), Cory's Shearwater (about 3,000 pairs), Madeiran Storm-petrel (about 1,000 pairs). Manx Shearwaters (about 500 pairs) and Macaronesian (or Barolo) Shearwater (about 400 pairs) breed on higher slopes. You won't see these birds from land, but if you are on Madeira in spring, you may hear their unearthly calls after the sun has set and the shearwaters come in to land. If you have never heard a Cory's Shearwater, then google its bizarre call and imagine hearing tens or hundreds

Cory's Shearwaters breed in massive numbers on inaccesble cliffs and on uninhabited islands. The adults come to shore only at night, making the most awesome bird 'songs' you've ever heard.

BIRDS

Re-discovery of the Zino´s Petrel

Madeira's most enigmatic bird is undoubtedly the Zino's Petrel. This rare pelagic bird breeds high up on steep cliffs of the Pico do Areeiro and nearby but nowhere else in the world! During much of the year, it roams widely over the oceans but come May, all the birds gather in the ocean around Madeira. Only at night, they fly into the mountains to visit their burrows. This makes the Zino's Petrel one of the most difficult birds in the world to see – only on a trip around the seas close to Madeira during the breeding season, you have a chance, but even then, sightings are far from guaranteed as there are so few birds on a very large ocean!

The story behind the Zino's Petrel is a fascinating one. For a long time it was thought to be extinct. There were only old tales about the presence of a 'Soft-plumaged Petrel' on Madeira (a species otherwise found exclusively in the southern hemisphere). No-one had seen this petrel for a long time though. Or at least, no-one who knew what he was looking at. And there were many myths and old wife tales about Madeira anyway. One famous one was that if you went out into the mountains at night, you could hear the forlorn cries of the lost souls of deceased mountain dwellers. This was a classic shepherd's tale from the people of the village of Curral das Freiras.

In 1969, the ornithologist Francis Zino made the connection between the two stories. Could the eerie sounds the shepherds talk about be the calls of the petrel that was considered to be extinct? He organised a nightly expedition to find out what these sounds really were and he indeed discovered that it came from the lost petrel! There were just a few birds though, and the rediscovery was kept quiet for years to protect them.

Together with the shepherds a conservation program was set up that included locating, capturing and weighing the remaining birds. It turned out that they belonged to a different species from the Soft-plumaged Petrel (it had been

Dusk in the high mountains. The souls of the dead (aka Zino's Petrels) are about to start their concert...

assumed that birds seen in the seas around the island belonged to this bird of the southern oceans). In honour of its discoverer, it was named the Zino´s Petrel. The breeding area is now strictly protected, as the world's entire breeding population does not exceed 80 pairs. The birds are still highly threatened by stray cats and rats. Soil erosion and the permanent threat of forest fires are another danger to its existence. During the big fires of 2010 only 1 of the 38 monitored chicks survived! Fortunately, the Zino´s Petrel is long lived but as pairs lay only one egg a year, the recovery of the population takes a long time.

The Zino's Petrel has two close relatives, the Desertas and Fea's Petrel. As its name suggests, the Desertas Petrel breeds exclusively on the Desertas (on the southern island, Bugio) and is thus also endemic to the archipelago. The rugged terrain makes it hard to put a number to its population, but it is thought that there are currently around 300 birds, making it about four times as numerous as the Zino's Petrel, which is still very rare. It is still sometimes regarded as a race of the third species, Fea's Petrel, which breeds on the Cape Verde Islands (as seabirds wander widely this species may visit Madeiran waters but, being so similar to Desertas Petrel, their identification at sea remains a mystery).

Zino's, Desertas and Fea's Petrels are very hard to tell apart. Nevertheless, they are considered to have evolved separately since the early Pleistocene, some 900,000 years ago. One piece of evidence for this is found by comparing parasitic lice of the birds' nests from each population. These lice only transfer from one animal to the other on the nest, so that they have a different lice fauna suggests a complete separation of the populations of the Zino's, Desertas and Fea's Petrels.

One of the rarer seabirds of Madeira – the Macaronesian Shearwater (also called Little or Barolo Shearwater).

BIRDS

of these birds in chorus. You can sometimes hear them from the terrace of houses in coastal villages, but an evening trip to Garajau (site I on page 181) is the best!

There are several good vantage points for seeing seabirds (e.g. site C and L on pages 177 and 183). Here you may see hundreds of birds fly low over the ocean. Cory's Shearwaters are most numerous and easily visible from land. Sometimes, Manx Shearwater is common as well. In winter, you may see Great Skua or Gannet.

The other seabirds are less easy to spot from land, but on a boat trip, you are likely to see Bulwer's Petrel and maybe even a Zino's or Desertas Petrel, or a Great Shearwater on passage. In winter, various gull species (e.g. Kittiwake), skuas and Gannet may turn up.

The small storm-petrels are notoriously hard to spot and are most easily found on an organised seabirding trip (see page 190). Theoretically, you could see five different species: Leach's, European, Wilson's, Madeiran and White-faced Storm-petrel. Leach's and European are visitors from the north (although a few European breed), while Wilson's is a bird from the southern hemisphere that visits the Madeiran waters in summer. Madeiran Storm-petrel is the most common storm-petrel in these waters as there are large colonies of this bird, mainly on the Desertas. Finally, there is the handsome White-faced Storm-petrel, with its long legs, yellow webbed feet and its odd tendency to bounce over the water like a ping-pong ball. This bird breeds in large numbers on the Selvagens (60,000 pairs) and small numbers venture as far north to the waters around Madeira.

Stray shorebirds frequent Madeira's pebble shores and can stay here for months. The turnstone is one of the more frequently found species here.

Identification key for Madeiran shearwaters, petrels and storm-petrels

Cory´s Shearwater Large with a wingspan of about 110 cm, upperparts grey-brown and underparts largely white, a pale yellow bill and a flight that is characterised by long glides over the water on bowed wings with occasional wingbeats. Around Madeira it is the most abundant of this group.
Feb - Oct; abundant

Manx Shearwater Medium sized with black upperparts descending below the eye on the head and white underparts. Flight that is characterised by long glides followed by series of rapid wingbeats.
Feb-July; Sept; common

Macaronesian (Barolo) Shearwater Very similar to Manx but smaller and with a white face, shorter, rounded wings often with a greyish panel on the upper wing. Flight faster with quicker wingbeats and shorter glides.
Year-round; scarce

Bulwer's Petrel Small, exceptionally long wings and tail. It is all dark with brownish band across the upper wings. In flight the wings seem to be pressed forward and slightly bowed and a bat-like flight with rapid, erratic movements, with quick changes in direction.
Mid-April - Sept; common

Desertas Petrel Size between Manx and Cory's Shearwater, with grey upperparts, greyish shoulder patches and darker flight feathers, pale below with dark markings on underwing contrasting with white belly. Flight characterized by glides alternated with rapid wingbeats and zigzag movements. In strong winds it flies in very pronounced arches, rising many metres above the sea.
Mid-May - November; scarce

Zino´s Petrel Very similar to Desertas Petrel – indistinguishable at sea without excellent views and preferably good photos. It has a smaller body and bill. Flight as Desertas Petrel. April - Sept; very scarce

Madeiran Storm-petrel Small, blackish-brown plumage, a somewhat rectangular white rump, pale wing-bar across the upper-wing. Like other storm-petrels it flies close to the surface with fast fluttering wing beats interrupted by short glides. It can be confused with other storm-petrels, like European Storm-petrel (which is a white patch on the underwing), Leach's and Wilson's Storm-petrel.
Year round; frequent

White-faced Storm-petrel Small, but the biggest storm-petrel and the only one with whitish underparts, extensively grey above and a dark 'mask', long legs. It has a characteristic bouncing flight. It seems to 'jump' up and down the water surface.
April - Aug; scarce

Reptiles and amphibians

> Madeira Wall Lizards are very common and especially easy to find in the lowlands near viewpoints and parks (e.g. routes 1, 2, 3, 4, 5, 15 and 16). Look for both geckos on walls of villages and towns close to the coast on Madeira's south coast. We found both species at Garajau (site I on page 181). For sea turtles, go on one of the boat trips on the ocean (see page 186).

The theory that the isolation of an island determines the diversity of species is clearly reflected in the number of reptile and amphibian species on Madeira. There is only one native species in the archipelago: the Madeira Wall Lizard. The Selvagens Islands host another, the Selvagens Island Gecko. These are is the only reptiles that lived here before people arrived. Five other species of reptile and two amphibians have been introduced, in part by accident.

The endemic Madeira Wall Lizard with a maximum head-tail length of 20 cm has a highly variable colour pattern. It is abundant in all sunny environments of Madeira, Porto Santo and Desertas, from sea level to the highest mountain peaks, including urban areas. Highest densities are in areas with lots of sunshine. An interesting feature of Madeira Wall Lizards in their readiness to climb of the stems of wildflowers. Have a look at wildflower beds and you could well find one of the smaller specimens pottering about on the flower heads. The animals go for the nectar and it is very likely that they play a role in the pollination of the flowers.

Apart from the native lizard, there are repeated records of the introduction of the much larger Tenerife Lizard in the Botanical Garden of Funchal. It is unclear whether it still occurs here.

The only native gecko in the area is found on the Selvagens archipelago: the Selvagens Islands Gecko (sometimes considered a subspecies of the Boettger's Wall Gecko of the Canary Islands).

REPTILES AND AMPHIBIANS

On Madeira, two gecko species occur, both of which have been introduced to Madeira and survive in villages and towns in the warm areas close to the coast. The Moorish Gecko arrived on Madeira in the 1990s and on Porto Santo in 2008. It was first detected in Funchal and populations are growing. Moorish Gecko has been found between Garajau and Camara dos Lobos on the south coast. Tropical House Gecko, with its characteristic dark V bands, was first found in Funchal in 2002. It is an African species (although widely introduced in the Americas), whose distribution and population size on Madeira is insufficiently known. We found it, together with Moorish Gecko, in Garajau.

The Flower Pot Snake is a small and thin snake (6 – 17 cm) with rudimentary eyes that could be mistaken for an earthworm. It was first discovered in Funchal in 2013 and a population possibly exists on Madeira. It has been introduced to many islands around the world and it is believed that it can have offspring from an unfertilized egg. Finally, the Red-eared Slider, the popular pet terrapin, has locally been introduced to ponds in Funchal.

Most likely there is only one species of amphibian on the island: the Spanish Water Frog. It is introduced on Madeira and Porto Santo and on both islands it is widespread and noisy. The Stripeless Tree Frog was introduced by the first navigators to Madeira but it is not certain if any of them survive.

The Loggerhead Sea Turtle is frequently seen on sea trips (top) Madeira Wall Lizards are abundant in all open habitats (bottom).

Sea Turtles

The sea turtles are most attractive and vulnerable animals of the sea. They lay their eggs on undisturbed beaches and are live in the ocean for the rest of their lives. There is a good chance of seeing one on a boat trip around Madeira. They may be curious and swim towards the boat and show well. Sightings from the coast are much more difficult.

Five species have been recorded around Madeira, wandering from (sub)tropical waters into the temperate zone. The Loggerhead Sea Turtle is the most common, while Green Sea Turtle and Leatherback Sea Turtle regularly occur. Hawksbill Sea Turtle and Kemp's Ridley Sea Turtle have occasionally been seen.

INSECTS AND OTHER INVERTEBRATES

Insects and other invertebrates

> Great haunts for butterflies are found on routes 1, 2 and 3 (for Monarchs, Canary Red Admiral, the blues and Clouded Yellows) and on routes 10, 12 and 13 (for Canary Red Admiral, Madeiran Grayling and other upland species). The Madeiran Speckled Wood and Madeiran Brimstone are best searched for in Ribeiro Frio (route 6) and Chão da Ribeira (site K on page 183).
> For dragonflies, try the rivers (e.g. routes 2, 4, 6, site K and M on pages 183-185). The freshwater pond of Lugar de Baixo (site A on page 176) is also worth visiting. Good spots for watching invertebrate sea life are found on routes 2, 4, 5 and 15.

Two speckled woods occur on the island. The Madeira Speckled Wood (top) is overall darker than the Common Speckled Wood (bottom).

Butterflies

The Madeira Archipelago's butterfly list doesn't exceed the 17 species, and one of the species on the list, the Madeira Large White, recently went extinct. So Madeira has a low diversity of butterflies, but one that contains a few special species. Three are endemic (Madeiran Speckled Wood, Madeira Brimstone and Madeiran Grayling) and one is a Macaronesian endemic, the Canary Red Admiral (which is sometimes called Indian Red Admiral as it was once thought to be a subspecies of that butterfly).

It is clear that this low number of butterflies can be blamed on Madeira's isolation in the Atlantic. Even strong migrants such as Bath White and Plain Tiger didn't make it over here. Or at least, if they did, they weren't able to survive.

A striking common feature of oceanic island ecosystems is the absence of insects that are well represented on the nearest mainland. Only a few species succeed in establishing themselves and there is evidence that these occupy such a wide range of habitats, that new arrivals have a hard time founding a population.
The widespread Madeiran species include Small White, Small Copper,

CROSSBILL GUIDES • MADEIRA

INSECTS AND OTHER INVERTEBRATES

Long-tailed Blue, Red Admiral, Clouded Yellow, Canary Red Admiral and Painted Lady. Lang´s Short-tailed Blue and Queen of Spain Fritillary are more localised and therefore more difficult to find. The Monarch has many populations in the coastal zone, especially in parks and gardens of villages. A few strongly migratory butterflies reach Madeira occasionally, such as the African Migrant (*Catopsilia florella*) and the False Plain Tiger (*Hypolimnas misippus*).

All species of the archipelago occur on the main island of Madeira. Porto Santo is a lot less diverse, while on the Desertas, no more than a handful occur.

Endemic butterflies

Of the four endemic butterflies of Madeira, the Madeiran Brimstone (or Madeiran Cleopatra) is the rarest. It is classified as endangered on the IUCN red list. Small populations live on Madeira in laurel forest between 500 and 1,500 m. It is frequently seen in Ribeiro Frio (route 7) and other open places in the laurel forest, as well as on flowery spots just above the tree line.

The Madeiran Speckled Wood can be found on Madeira all year round. It is widespread in laurel forests and mixed woodlands between 350 and 1,100 m but less common than the Speckled Wood, which occurs all over the island. The population of the Madeiran Speckled Wood is decreasing and is apparently being replaced by the Common Speckled Wood which arrived in 1976. In contrast to the rapid flight and restless behaviour of the Madeiran

The Canary Red Admiral (top) has more extensive red patches on the wing than the familiar Red Admiral (bottom).

INSECTS AND OTHER INVERTEBRATES

Lang's Short-tailed Blue (here a rather worn specimen) can be found in Funchal's city parks (top). Madeira Grayling is quite common at higher altitudes, but only flies in the summer months (bottom).

Speckled Wood, the Common Speckled Wood prefers to perch on open sunny patches in woodlands to guard their territory.

The Madeiran Grayling is a high mountain butterfly which is very numerous in its montane habitat. It lives above 1,000 m in heathlands, grasslands and open patches in the Tree Heath zone. Look for them on bare soil or in the shade when the sun is strong. There is only one generation which flies between half July and half September.

The Madeiran Large White is now considered extinct. Once it inhabited the laurisilva in the northern valleys and flew between March and October. The causes of its extinction are not entirely certain, but competition with the introduced Small White, combined with habitat loss are the most likely reasons for its disappearance.

The Canary Red Admiral occurs on all of the islands of the archipelago. Like the Common Red Admiral, it inhabits in parks and gardens, but can also be seen in flowery parts of the high mountains and open patches in the laurel forest. At the coast, it can be seen in every month of the year.

The Madeiran subspecies of the Small Copper lives on both Madeira and Porto Santo. It is widespread but not very common and occupies a broad range of habitats, from farmlands to laurel forests.

Moths

Approximately 315 species of micro and macro moth have been recorded on Madeira, of which more than 50 are exclusively found here. In addition to those specialties, there are also some familiar species. The following you may recognise from Britain and Europe.

When walking through levada tunnels, use your torch to scan the tunnel walls and you'll probably find the Herald (*Scoliopterix libatix*). It is also worth to look for specimens pressed against on bright walls near street lights, including Angle Shades (*Phlogophora meticulosa*), Golden Twin-spot (*Chrysodeixis chalcites*) and Cotton Bollworm (*Helicoverpa armigera*) are frequently found. The *Ascotis fortunata* is a pale-coloured member of the geometer family (*geometridae*) that inhabits laurel forests and can

---

Insecta Maderensia, discoveries by the 19th Century naturalist Wollaston

The collection of specimens of flora and fauna increased enormously in the 18th and particularly in the 19th centuries. On Madeira, it was Thomas Vernon Wollaston (1822-1878) who first described the local insect diversity in his *Insecta Maderensia* (1854). Charles Darwin called it "an admirable work", which is not an exaggeration for this 700 page overview that contains 13 great colour plates.

Wollaston stayed on Madeira for the benefit of his health. He passed two winters at Funchal and started collecting beetles for amusement and to 'relieve the monotony of a winter's exile in a distant land'. Working on his collection his interest and knowledge grew, he systematically searched all minor islands and rocks and added a summer visit to the islands.

Wollaston sent his beetles to various European universities for identification. In total he collected 270 species new to science, many of them endemic to Madeira. For the author, most striking and incredible was the total absence of families and genera that were well-known and common in other places. Without realising it, he stumbled upon a key element of island ecology and evolution, namely the crucial role colonisation plays in the evolution of life on islands. He even described a classic island adaptions: the lack of wings in many species. Wollaston considered 86 species of beetles to be introduced by people, many of which were winged. Wollaston's collections from Madeira as well as those he took from the Canaries, Cape Verde Islands and St. Helena are now in the Oxford University Natural History Museum.

INSECTS AND OTHER INVERTEBRATES

be found almost throughout the year. The striking Crimson Speckled (*Utetheisa pulchella*) is a migratory moth that prefers flowery grasslands. Hawk-moths stand out even to the layman, because of their size, colours and typical shape. They become active at dusk and if you search carefully you may find one. The beautiful Madeiran Spurge Hawk-moth (*Hyles tithymali gecki*) is a Madeiran subspecies, which occurs in the drier parts of the island where the Spear-leaved Spurge grows. The well-known Hummingbird Hawk-moth is common on Madeira from the coast to the high mountains and can be seen feeding on flowers of, amongst others, the Pride of Madeira.

Dragonflies

Madeira is not a stronghold for dragonflies. Only six species occur on the island, most of which have only small and localised populations. When looking for dragonflies you have to find fresh water – small pools, water reservoirs and levadas are the places to be.

The Island Darter is the only dragonfly on Madeira with a small distribution range – it is endemic to Madeira and the Canary Islands. It is fairly common and widespread and can be found far from the waters where it lays its eggs. Make sure not to mistake

There are few dragonfly species on Madeira, but the island does have some attractive species, such as the Vagrant Emperor (top) and the Island Darter (right).

INSECTS AND OTHER INVERTEBRATES

the Island Darter for its look-alike, the Red-Veined Darter. Both can be seen on twigs, rocks and other open spots where they perch to oversee their territory. The Red-veined Darter is most common, but either darter species can show up anywhere.

Near reservoirs Blue Emperor and Lesser Emperor patrol over the water (in small numbers). A third species, the Vagrant Emperor, is strongly migratory and is usually seen hunting over low vegetation in coastal areas. On Madeira this species is relatively frequently seen, which suggests (given the island's isolated geographical position) that it has some small permanent populations on the island.

The final 'odonate' is the Small Bluetail. It is the only damselfly on the island. This species is rare as a result of the lack of underwater vegetation. It is frequently seen on the channel in Machico, where fresh water flows through suitable habitat for this species.

Other invertebrates

Recently, a report was published on all the animal species found on Madeira up until 2014. The list contains over 3,000 insect species and 315 different spiders. This reflects quite a large diversity, particularly since some species we currently know from Madeira are not noted on this list. Of 109 species of Madeiran beetles, nine were introduced and 58 are endemic to the island. They include several endangered, specialised animals like ground beetle *Eurygnathus latreillei*, many ground beetles of the genus *Trechus* and the leaf beetle *Chrysolina fragariae*.

Six out of the twenty recorded bee species on Madeira and Porto Santo are endemic. Surprisingly this group holds only one parasitic bee, in contrast to the mainland of Europe where a quarter of the total number are parasitic. Parasites cannot survive as their hosts are not present.

The report lists 26 species of grasshoppers and crickets. Among them is the conspicuous Handsome Cross Grasshopper (*Oedaleus decorus*). This striking species inhabits dry grasslands and rocky slopes. They rely, as most ground-dwelling grasshoppers, on open patches as they need a warm microclimate.

The huge Desertas Tarantula is endemic to a single valley on the Deserta Grande Island.

INSECTS AND OTHER INVERTEBRATES

The endemic bee *Amegilla maderae* forms loose colonies on the ground. It is frequently seen visiting the island's flowers.

On dry and shrubby grasslands you might encounter the somewhat sluggish Southern Wartbiter (*Decticus albifrons*). On Madeira this carnivorous grasshopper is already active in March, unlike in the Mediterranean, where adults are usually found from July.

The inconspicuous *Aiolopus thalassinus* is a threatened grasshopper of which the majority of individuals on Madeira is melanistic (dark). You may find them on the grassy slopes in coastal areas.

Cattle grazing threatens the Madeiran Steppe Bush-cricket (*Montana barretii*) and the Madeira Pincer Grasshopper (*Calliptamus madeira*). Thanks to the irradiation of feral goats (see page 63), their populations seem to recovering again.

A truly spectacular spider is the endemic Desertas Tarantula (*Hogna ingens*), which only lives in the inaccessible central valley of Deserta Grande. This giant spider with zebra-stripe legs is considered Europe's largest spider species (although this title is claimed for several other species as well). Unfortunately, this eight-legged beast is threatened by the introduced Bulbous Canary-grass that takes over the open habitat.

Sea shells, crabs and other marine life

The rocks on the shoreline host an entirely different wildlife. It is the realm of crabs, molluscs, seaweeds and all sorts of mostly dead marine organisms that get washed ashore. Like the insect life, it is hard to get a thorough picture of all that occurs here, so we restrict ourselves to the most visible and typical species that you are likely to find when exploring this rough and unique habitat.

One of the first animals you'll notice in the calmer parts of the coastline are the crabs, which rest mostly just above the water line. One common crab is the Sally Lightfoot Crab, which has a carapace of about 3 cm, a dark body and legs with flaming red or bright yellow rings. With age it acquires more and more red lines. It is a herbivore which anchors itself to the rocks by putting its long legs and claws in cracks and holes to resist the crashing waves and violent riptides.

INSECTS AND OTHER INVERTEBRATES

Attached to the rocks on the tideline are the limpets – sea snails with a conical shell that cling firmly to the hard substrate. They graze on the moss-like seaweeds that grow on this borderland of sea and land. The China Limpet (or Rough Limpet, *Patella ulyssiponensis*) has a flat shell, fine radiating ridges and is white inside. *Patella candei*, an endemic species of the Atlantic Islands, is almost the same size and is also rather flat but its shell is thicker and the inside colour is brown on the edge and bluish going to white in the centre. *Patella piperata*, also an Atlantic Island endemic, shows dark spots on its shell and a cream band in the inside, bounded by a reddish colour. Other sea snails with a smaller size (10 – 20 mm) and a conical shell can be found. *Gibbula candei* is again a Macaronesian endemic. The Dogwhelk or Atlantic Dogwinkle is a widespread Atlantic predatory sea snail on mussels and barnacles, which has a more pointed shell. The Top Shell (*Monodonta edulis*) is a grazer with a dark green shell that is eaten by local people.

Barnacles spend their whole adult life firmly attached to a substrate, usually on rocks but it can also be the skin of a whale. When the barnacle is covered by water it opens and holds out its modified legs to catch and eat plankton. The barnacle on Madeira is a warm water species, *Pollicipes stellata*. It lives on more exposed rocks.

Sea life: the Portuguese Man-o-War (top) and the Sally Lightfoot Crab (left).

FLORA AND FAUNA

PRACTICAL PART

In this section we describe 16 routes, 14 sites and 6 guided excursions by which you can discover the Madeiran archipelago. The sites and 14 of the routes are located on Madeira itself, while two routes (number 15 and 16) explore the much smaller island of Porto Santo. This much drier island has a rather different flora and fauna.

Furthermore, the ferry trip to the island enables you to see some of the spectacular seabirds, whales and dolphins for which Madeira is famous.

The splendid marine life and the seabirds are also the reason that we put emphasis on the guided tours. It is very fortunate that there are several companies on the island that provide specialised seabird and whale-watching trips. Booking a tour with one these companies is also the only way to see a bit of the spectacular, uninhabited Desertas and Selvagens Islands.

Madeira itself is a highly varied island. We've described several of the finest laurel forest walks with the highest diversity of plants, birds and butterflies (routes 6, 7, 8, 9, 11 and 14). Walks in the highlands (routes 10, 12 and 13) and in the lowlands (1, 3) add to the variation. With the exception of route 12, none of these walks are particular difficult, but their length varies making some easy and other fairly demanding (see introduction of each of the routes).

In addition to walks, we've also included several car trips with stops and short walks on the way (routes 2, 4, 5 and 10). These have the advantage of covering more ground and are thereby more diverse. They form the perfect introduction to the nature and wildlife of Madeira.

The numbers in the white squares refer to the routes that are described on page 118 and further. The letters are a reference to the sites described on page 176 and further, while the purple letters pertain to the guided excursions described on page 186 and onwards.

The beautiful and easy-to-walk levada trails bring you to the wildest and remotest parts of the island (Levada do Furado; route 7).

Route 1: The Funchal area

FULL DAY

Get to know colonial Madeira, including its wildlife.
Shady, subtropical parks where stately Monarch butterflies drift by.

Habitats city parks, sea shore
Selected species Canary, Blackcap, Grey Wagtail, Plain Swift, Common Tern, Roseate Tern (rare), Madeira Wall Lizard, Moorish Gecko, Monarch, Speckled Wood, Lang's Short-tailed Blue, Long-tailed Blue, Canary Red Admiral, Lesser Emperor, Island Darter

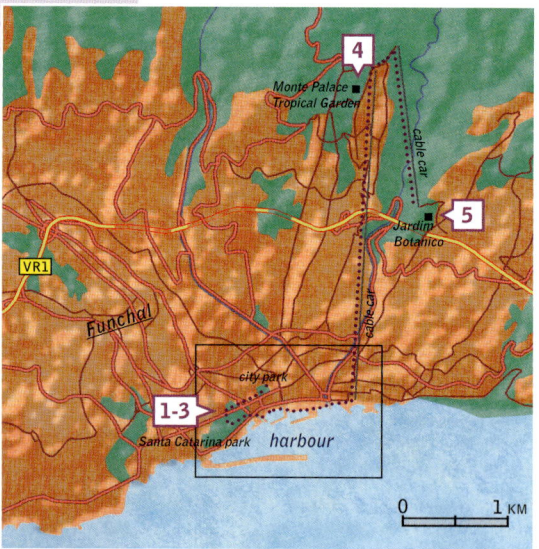

Funchal spreads out over an area of roughly 8 by 4 km – a leafy residential area with houses, hotels, estates and parks, built on the mountain slopes around the old city. It is a busy yet pretty place. There are many parks and gardens, where the more common Madeiran species can be found. You can see your first (endemic) birds, plants, butterflies and reptiles right here in the heart of the old town. Canaries are in every garden, often close to the hotels, while Plain Swifts can be seen flying over town at any point. The flowery gardens attract Monarchs and other butterflies. Moorish Gecko and Barn Owl should enliven your evening strolls.

This route describes a walk through the historic centre and the harbour, where you can book your excursions for whalewatching, birdwatching or trip to the Desertas (see page 188). Then you visit some of the gardens in the upper reaches of the city, which can easily be reached by bus or cable car.

Starting point City Park (Jardim Municipal do Funchal)

ROUTE 1: THE FUNCHAL AREA

1 The Jardim Municipal do Funchal, (8,300 m²) is in the heart of downtown Funchal and surrounded by historical buildings. Very near is the *Cathedral Sé do Funchal*, built in the late 15th century and one of the oldest buildings on the island. Different kinds of lava taken from Cabo Girão were used for the walls. and for the ceilings, wood from the endemic (and now very rare) Madeira Juniper.

Central Funchal exudes an atmosphere of modern cosmopolitanism mixed with a colonial past.

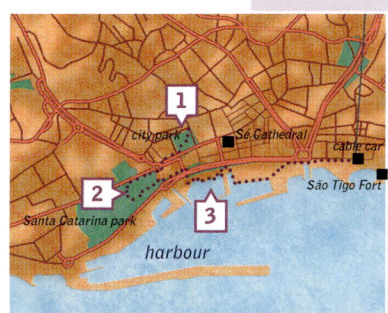

The Jardim Municipal do Funchal is a great spot to watch butterflies. Among the flashy Monarchs and Canary Red Admirals, there are also the tiny Lang's Short-tailed and Long-tailed Blues (the latter on photo below).

The city garden is an enchanting place with flowers and old trees, most of which are originally from South America. Birds that can be found are Canary, Goldfinch, Robin, Blackcap and Blackbird, while the butterflies include Monarch, Canary Red Admiral, Clouded Yellow, both Lang´s Short-tailed and Long-tailed Blue and Speckled Wood. There are also dozens of Madeira Wall Lizard around.

Leave the park in its southwestern exit and follow the *Avenida Arriaga*. Cross by the roundabout to reach Santa Catarina Park.

2 At 36,000 m², Santa Catarina Park is a good deal larger than the Jardim Municipal. It has many trails and open spaces and offers

PRACTICAL PART

ROUTE 1: THE FUNCHAL AREA

good views over Funchal Bay and the harbour. There are again many exotic plants from the Americas and the birds, butterflies and reptiles are similar to those in the Jardim Municipal.

Go down to the harbour and walk along the quay. This is where the kiosks are where you can book your birdwatching excursions and whalewatching trips, and your visit to the Desertas Islands.

3 Although you can't access the main pier, you can see it from the harbour wall. Scan the pier for terns. Common Tern is regular and Roseate Tern may also be seen, particularly after the nesting season. Between the rocks in the harbour, there are many Sally Lightfoot Crabs and it is a good place to see some of the common fish species. From the harbour wall, waders such as Whimbrel, Dunlin, Sanderling, Turnstone and Common Sandpiper can be seen and Little Egret sometimes also shows up. Black-headed Gull and Lesser Black-backed Gull come here outside the breeding season. The Grey Wagtail, which is a regular bird in Funchal, searches for food along the water line. Hundreds Madeira Wall Lizard live on rocks and walls of the promenade.

Common Terns (top) and, much rarer, Roseate Terns (bottom) can be seen in the harbour of Funchal.

As you proceed to the end of the quay, you have a choice. Turning left you enter the old town where the historic churches, the town hall and (book) shops offer more cultural diversions. Alternatively, you can take a bus or the cable car further up town to visit one or more of the following gardens.

Just beyond the cable car entrance lies the old fort of São Tigo, built in the 17th and 18th century to protect the young city against attack (now housing a museum of contemporary art).

4 The Monte Palace Tropical Garden (70,000 m²) holds more then 100,000 species of plants (including native and Macaronesian ones) from all over the world.

CROSSBILL GUIDES • MADEIRA

ROUTE 1: THE FUNCHAL AREA

The garden also has 700 minerals on display. Canaries, Blackcaps, Blackbirds and Plain Swifts can be seen here. Among insects that can be encountered are Common Speckled Wood, Canary Red Admiral, the endemic dragonfly Island Darter and Blue Emperor.

The Tropical Garden is open from 09.30 h. to 18.00 h. It is serviced by bus n° 21, 22, 23 and 48 and the cable car. Entrance € 12.50 (2018 prices).

5 In the beautiful Botanical Garden (Jardim Botânico da Madeira; 35,000 m²) you can find 2,000 plants originating from all continents and 200 Macaronesian endemics. The small Natural History Museum (see 19th century naturalists on Madeira, page 111) here is interesting, as it displays stuffed birds and other animals from Madeira (some specimens are in poor condition). Similar birds and butterflies can be seen as in the Jardim Tropical. Among the masses of Madeira Wall Lizards, introduced Tenerife Lizards are reputed to be around. Pay attention to the small Blues. This is the best place on the island to see Lang's Short-tailed Blue which is smaller than the Long-tailed Blue, a common species seen all over the island.

The Jardim Botânico is 3 km from the city centre and is serviced by bus n° 29, 30 and 31. Entrance € 8.– (2018 prices), open from 09.00 h. to 18.00 h.

Funchal has beautiful botanical gardens such as the Jardim Tropical Monte Palace (left) with exotic plants like the Bird of Paradise flower (top).

PRACTICAL PART

ROUTE 2: MACHICO TO PONTA DE SÃO LOURENÇO

Route 2: Machico to Ponta de São Lourenço

4-6 HOURS

Easy birdwatching and spectacular scenery on the east coast.

Habitats city park, river, sea shore, dry cliffs and grasslands, ocean
Selected species Whimbrel, Turnstone, Greenshank, Grey Wagtail, Common Waxbill, Little Egret, Iberian Water Frog, Monarch, Clouded Yellow, Island Darter, Small Pride of Madeira*, Madeira Sea Stock*

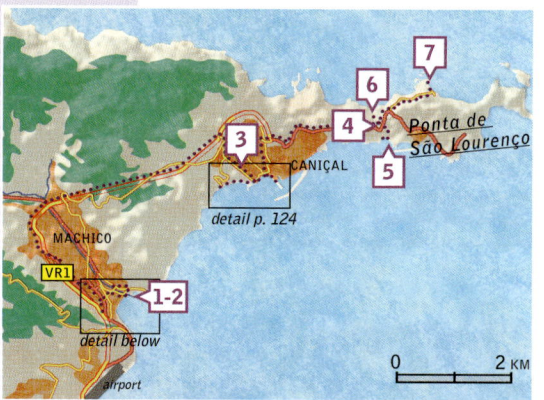

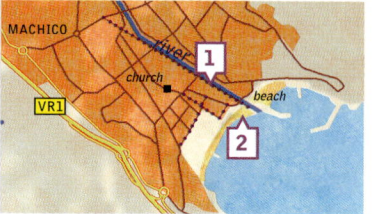

This route explores the dry south-eastern coast of Madeira, around the laid-back coastal villages of Machico and Caniçal. Both are pleasant places with a seaside promenade (and excellent fish restaurants), where you can see gulls, terns and shorebirds. This area is the best for several hard-to-find-birds, such as Waxbill and Moorhen. But there is more – Monarchs in the village parks, Madeira Wall Lizards on the pavement, a chance of spotting whales, a fabulous geology and superb views.

This is a relaxed route that combines short walks through the villages with several viewpoints. You can also treat it as a prelude to the walk over the spectacular Peninsula of Ponta de São Lourenço (route 3), making it a full day visit.

Starting point Machico

Getting there From the Motorway, take exit *Machico Sul* and find a parking place in the centre. Find your way to the pretty church and walk the circuit shown on the inset map.

CROSSBILL GUIDES • MADEIRA

ROUTE 2: MACHICO TO PONTA DE SÃO LOURENÇO

The river of Machico attracts many birds.

1. The riverbed is full of reeds and herbs and is usually wet even in the dry season. From the elevated walkway along the bank you have a good view over the river. Little Egret, Grey Heron, Grey Wagtail, Moorhen and different waders are often present along the stream. Listen if you can hear the weak nasal call of the tiny Waxbill, which is often discovered by its voice before it is seen. Small groups search for seeds in the dense vegetation. In summer and autumn, this is also a good place for dragonflies, such as Small Bluetail, Blue Emperor and the endemic Island Darter. The village gardens and trees are good for Canary and Goldfinch, plus a range of butterflies: Monarch, Speckled Wood, Clouded Yellow, Painted Lady and Hummingbird Hawk-moth.

2. At the river mouth there is a small beach (with sand imported from the Sahara) on the left and volcanic pebbles brought in by the ocean currents on the right. The beach is shielded by a pier that you can walk down. All these sites can be attractive for migrant Redshank, Greenshank, Whimbrel, Turnstone, Sanderling, Dunlin, Green Sandpiper and other waders. It is also a favourite place for Yellow-legged Gull and Common Tern.

Return to the VR1 motorway and follow signs to Caniçal. After the tunnel, turn right to Caniçal and follow the signs to the whaling museum, which is right on the beach front. Park there (see map).

PRACTICAL PART

ROUTE 2: MACHICO TO PONTA DE SÃO LOURENÇO

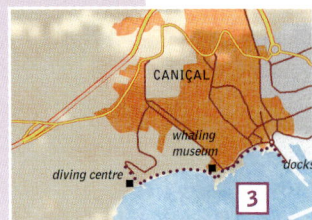

3 Madeira's main freight harbour is situated at Caniçal. The village is not much visited by tourists and has kept a laid-back charm. Potter about the pebble beaches and walk up the short pier (the long one is closed to the public). Just as in Machico this is a good place for shorebirds, gulls and terns. It is even better for more pelagic seabirds and mammals. With telescope, you may spot Cory's Shearwaters, whales and dolphins. During two visits in May 2018 we saw a group of Sei Whales, some unidentified dolphins and a Monk Seal in the harbour! An excellent spot for seawatching is right beside the whale museum.

The first Collared Doves on Madeira bred in Caniçal and are now plentiful. For Spanish Sparrow you need to look harder. Caniçal is the last place where this formerly widespread bird is seen – perhaps it has disappeared here too (it is still common on the island of Porto Santo; route 15).

There are a few kiosks in the harbour that exhibit whale bones and sell products made of bone. Do not worry, the bones are very old as whaling has been forbidden for a long time.

Whilst here, walk the track along to the shore to the west and turn right into the valley (behind the diving club). There are lots of Willow-leaved Globularias here and a large population of Monarchs. Snorkelling enthusiasts will find easy access to the sheltered bay just in front of the diving centre. Finally, the Whale Museum *(Museu do Baleia)* is worth visiting as well (see page 208).

The only natural beach of Madeira, consisting of dark, volcanic sand (point 6 of this route).

ROUTE 2: MACHICO TO PONTA DE SÃO LOURENÇO

Thousands of petrified roots stick out of the ground, reminders of the extensive forests that once grew in the area (see page 26).

Go back to the main road and follow the signs *Pta. S. Lourenço*. Once you pass the commercial port of Madeira you get into a barren landscape with little more than a few isolated buildings and palm trees.

4 After 1.5 km there is a large parking area with a viewpoint. Make a stop here to admire the coastline. This is another lookout point for pelagic birds, dolphins and whales that prefer the calmer sea on the south side of Madeira. You need clear viewing conditions and a good telescope though, as they are usually not near the coast (unless driven by strong onshore winds).

5 Walk towards the end of the parking area. On your left there is a track onto the grassy headlands, with several small cliffs and rocky parts. Look around the latter and you'll find a geological curiosity: thousands of petrified roots lie scattered around on rocky spots or stick out of the cliffs (see also page 26).

6 From the viewpoint there is a path of about 300 m that leads to the only natural beach of Madeira. It consists of black (volcanic) sand. Walk the path to the beach (signed *Prainha*). It is a scenic spot, excellent for snorkelling. On your walk down, note the many (planted) Dragon Trees and look for butterflies (mainly Long-tailed Blue, Clouded Yellow and Small Copper) and Madeira Wall Lizards.

PRACTICAL PART

ROUTE 2: MACHICO TO PONTA DE SÃO LOURENÇO

The Downy Andryala is a frequent plant on coastal cliffs (top).
A Dunlin on Machico's pebble beach (bottom).

Proceed and at the roundabout (300 m) take the second exit.

7 The landscape becomes increasingly attractive. Stop after another 800m at the car park. This is a most photogenic place. You see Caniçal on the south coast where you came from, the steep rocks on the north side of the island and the coastline of the Ponta de São Lourenço Peninsula with Porto Santo and its islets on the horizon. Beneath are reddish sea cliffs, black rocks and an ever-moving ocean. If it is not too windy, walk to the viewpoint *Miradouro Ponta do Rosto* on your left. You will probably find some very tame Berthelot´s Pipits near a food truck or at the picnic tables. Look for Hoopoe and Red-legged Partridge as well.

This is a popular place and the vegetation is pretty trampled. If you venture a bit further afield, you can find Madeira Sea Stock* (*Matthiola maderensis*), *Helichrysum devium* (a plant that is endemic to São Lourenço!), Mandon's Marguerite* (*Argyranthemum pinnatifidum ssp succulentum*) and Downy Andryala* (*Andryala glandulosa*).

Return the same way, or proceed to the car park of Ponta de São Lourenço for the peninsula walk (see next route).

Route 3: Ponta de São Lourenço

4-5 HOURS
MODERATE

Trail along spectacular seaside cliffs.
Unique flora and some special birds.

Habitats sea shore, dry cliffs and grasslands, ocean
Selected species Quail, Hoopoe, Berthelot´s Pipit, Rock Sparrow, Canary, Manx Shearwater, Grey Heron, Pallid Swift, Small Pride of Madeira, Madeira Trefoil, Sea Campion, Mandon's Marguerite*, *Helichrysum devium*, Desfontaines Bean-caper*, Ascherson's Plantain*, Downy Andryala*, many other endemic plants

!
Exposed route, be careful in strong gales!

This popular walk explores the narrow peninsula *Ponta de São Lourenço* that juts out into the Atlantic on the eastern end of Madeira. The landscape is spectacular and, with its scant vegetation, radically different from any other part of the island. It resembles the landscape of Porto Santo

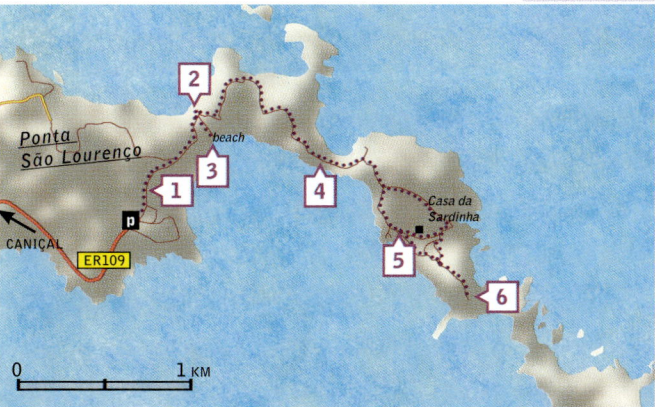

and of the Desertas islands, which you can see on a clear day to respectively the north and south. The landscape is dry and barren from June to October, but turns green with the autumn rains and dries up again at the end of spring.

The peninsula has a fascinating flora and fauna. Of the about 160 vascular of plants that occur, 31 are endemic. Furthermore, there is an extraordinary high number of endemic snails (24!). Birders will enjoy views of Rock Sparrow and Hoopoe which are much easier to see here than elsewhere on Madeira, while the cliffs hold important seabird colonies.

PRACTICAL PART

ROUTE 3: PONTA DE SÃO LOURENÇO

This route follows a spectacular, linear trail which is generally easy to walk, but there are some steep sections and the ascent to the summit can be slippery. Start your walk early, preferably at sunrise, as it becomes very busy later in the day.

Starting point Car Park at the end of the ER109 road, east of Caniçal. The trail starts directly from the roundabout.

Views of the start (top) and end point of this route (bottom).

1 The first section of the trail is rather grassy – a result of grazing by rabbits, which have reduced the native vegetation on the easily accessible western part. The fantastic flora of the peninsula is confined to the more remote and rocky parts, and will present itself further along the route. You may pick-up your first birds of the route though – Kestrel, Berthelot´s Pipit, Rock Sparrow, Canary, Goldfinch, Hoopoe, Red-legged Partridge, Rock Dove, Pallid and Plain Swifts and in spring singing Quails can all be found along the trail. There are hundreds of Madeira Wall Lizards (no exaggeration), especially on this first section of the path.

2 After 15 minutes you arrive at a crossing, near a windbeaten viewpoint with a vista of the northern cliffs and sea stacks. Erosion

caused by strong winds from the north shaped the steep cliffs on the north of Madeira while on the south the coast they raise more gently from the sea.

The first attractive wildflowers appear. From here onwards, look for the stout, pink-flowered Madeira Sea Stock*, Mandon's Marguerite* (*Argyranthemum p. ssp succulentum*), *Helichrysum devium*, Downy Andryala* (*Andryala glandulosa*), Sea Campion, Small Pride of Madeira* (*Echium nervosum*), Madeiran Sow-thistle* (*Sonchus ustulatus*), Iceplant, Pitch Trefoil, Caterpillar Plant, Spear-leaved Spurge, Desfontaines Beancaper* (*Zygophyllum fontanesii*) and Ascherson's Plantain* (*Plantago aschersonii*), to name but a few.

At the crossing turn right on the path that leads down to a small beach.

3 this stretch of coastline is visited by wading birds like Whimbrel and Turnstone. Grey Heron and Little Egret are often present, attracted to the fish rearing pens in the ocean. The pens are enclosed with nets, but the birds seek out the centre, where the nets bend down just deep enough to reach the fish.

Return to the main path and continue.

4 The path climbs to a narrow ridge with steep drops on both sides of the path and reaches a plateau. On this section, you'll see some spectacular dykes – fissures in the cliff filled with a different kind of lava (see page 23).

Young Rock Sparrows out after a rain shower.

5 On the plateau, follow the circular trail that leads to the house surrounded by palm trees, *Casa da Sardinha*. This is the station of the guards of the Natural Park. There is a small tank of fresh water near the house, that, together with the palm trees, attract Canaries, Rock Sparrows and other songbirds. This is a good spot to photograph them.

6 Continue to the final lookout point on the cliff, from which you overlook the inaccessible islets of Ponta de São Lourenço. Further out, you can see the Desertas to the south and Porto Santo in the north. A spectacular sight.

Route 4: The northeast coast

6 HOURS-FULL DAY

Leisurely route through a traditional Madeiran landscape and along spectacular cliffs.
Broad selection of flora and fauna, with a mixed tern colony as highlight.

Habitats sea cliffs, sea shore, native scrubland, farmland, river mouth, ocean
Selected species Roseate Tern, Common Tern, Manx Shearwater, Canary, Madeira Sea Stock, Brookweed, Viscid Houseleek, Disc Houseleek

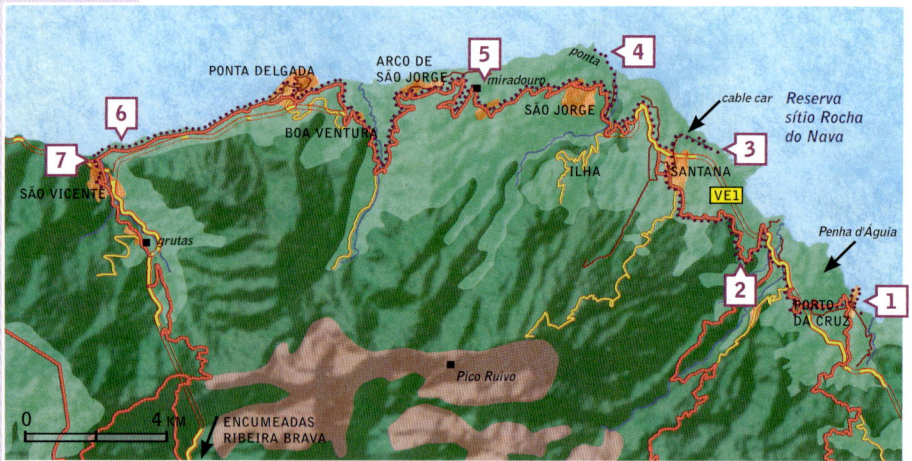

The northeastern coast of Madeira is verdant and green, and its villages are traditional and quiet. On a clear day, this part of Madeira offers a wonderful backdrop for exploration of the coast.
This is a simple route, of interest for all types of naturalists. It combines wonderful scenery, pretty villages (with good cafés and restaurants) and short walks along the coast, with birdwatching, some attractive flora and butterflies. In other words – a route with something for all!
The itinerary follows as much as possible the old winding road that connects the villages near the sea.

ROUTE 4: THE NORTHEAST COAST

Starting Point Porto da Cruz. Park near the coast, where the sugar cane refinery is situated.

1 Porto da Cruz lies right next to a huge, flat-topped mountain known as the Penha d'Águia, or eagle's cliff. Eagles don't breed here, and it is doubtful they ever did, but even without them, the mountain is impressive. The village has two black pebble beaches, separated by a small peninsula, with a promenade along the coastline. Walk along this road. It is one of the better spots on the island to observe the marine fauna of the intertidal zone. Scan the sheltered edges of the rocks for limpets. There are three species here, *Patella ulyssiponensis* and the Macaronesian endemics *Patella candei* and *Patella piperata*. Sally Lightfoot Crabs are often seen on the rocks.

Porto da Cruz is a centre for rum production on the island but distilleries are now reduced from fifty a couple of generations ago to less than a handful. Madeiran rum is traditionally made directly from cane syrup (rather than, as elsewhere, from molasses) and then matured in old Madeira wine casks. The sugar cane processing factory is the last of its kind on Madeira. It uses steam engines to extract syrup from the cane, which is used in the traditional *bolo de mel* (honey cake) that you can buy all over the island.

The beautiful northeastern coast of the island.

Leave Porto da Cruz on the old road ER108 direction Faial /Santana.

2 You are crossing Madeira wine country. The grapes are grown in small plots between the small farmhouses that dot the slopes. Note the small plots of sugar cane too, which is grown in the surrounding of Porto da Cruz and is used in the production of Rum. As you proceed, you cross fine-looking forests. Sadly, on closer inspection, they are all Eucalyptus forest with Black Wattle Acacia (*A. mearnsii*) undergrowth – the two most vigorous and destructive invasive species on the island (see pages 63-65).

PRACTICAL PART

ROUTE 4: THE NORTHEAST COAST

Once in Santana (notice the original thatch-roofed Madeiran houses, for which Santana is famous), follow the signs *teleférico*. Park there. You can choose to walk down (45 minutes along a steep trail) and return via cable car (€ 3.–), or simply take a return fare (€ 5.–).

3 On Madeira, most cable cars don't bring you up into the mountains, but glide down sea cliffs to the *fajãs* – small, fertile plains at the base of sea cliffs (see page 25).
This particular fajã is a wonderful, laid-back, unspoilt spot with small vineyards, narrow trails and some original coastal scrublands, with massive cliffs in the background with an all too scenic waterfall that drops down to the coastal plain. On the trails, there are masses of Madeira Wall Lizards and on the rocky, boulder strewn beach (take care as you negotiate it) there are many limpets along the shoreline.
The sea around the fajã is part of the Marine Natural Reserve *Reserva Sítio da Rocha do Navio*. The place takes its name ('Ship Rock') from a shipwreck of a Dutch XIX century schooner. There is a small visitors' centre in the fajã near the cable car station dedicated to the biosphere reserve.
The footpath down to the fajã (should you decide to walk) has an attractive cliff flora, with houseleeks and Willow-leaved Carline Thistle.

A big Madeiran Wall Lizard is sunning on the wall of the Miradouro das Cabanas (point 5).

Return to Santana and follow the old road to São Jorge. Just before the village, right after crossing the river, turn right on the signs *Piscina* and *Ruinas*. Park at the end of the road, where the river flows into the ocean.

4 From the car park, walk the easy, if vertiginous, trail to *Ponta de São Jorge*. This trail is quite spectacular as it hugs the cliffs, partially along boardwalks tacked onto them, to the old harbour. Several small streams pour down from the cliffs. This is a good spot to enjoy the cliff flora of Madeira. The Disc Houseleek *(Aeonium glutinosum)*, Willow-leaved Globularia, Madeira Sea Stock*, Madeiran Sow-thistle* *(Sonchus ustulatus)*, *Sedum nudum* and *Tolpis succulenta* are common. On the streams there is a lot of Brookweed and locally the Japanese Holly Fern *(Cyrtomium falcatum)*. After 20 minutes (1.5 km) you reach the old pier where in times long past the small boats found some protection against the violent waves.

ROUTE 4: THE NORTHEAST COAST

Return to the main road and proceed the main road direction São Vicente.

5 After about 11 km, just behind a holiday village, there is a viewpoint at a sharp bend in the road (you can't miss it). At almost 500m the views from here, *Miradouro das Cabanas*, are spectacular. It is not surprising that once this was one of the whale observation points (see page 93). With some luck you may see Trocaz Pigeons flying by on the slopes above you and dozens of Plain Swifts rush over the viewpoint (mostly at the start and end of the day). Madeira Wall Lizards are common on the stone walls.

Continue through Arco São Jorge and Boa Ventura villages to Ponta Delgada. There, don't take the direct VE 2 motorway to São Vicente, but enter Ponta Delgada instead. At the junction, turn left and follow the old coastal route to São Vicente. There is another viewpoint on the right and a little further, a diving school and several restaurants. Park here.

6 Just off the coast, there are some small islets. On the largest, flat-topped one there is a tern colony. There are plenty of Common Terns but the real highlight is the presence of several pairs of the rare Roseate Tern. Use your binoculars or, better yet, a telescope to pick them out by their paler plumage (they almost 'light up' as it were, among the Commons), faster wingbeats and their angled dive feeding technique.

7 Continue to São Vicente and park near the bridge. On the pebble beach there are often terns resting – a good spot to see the Common and Roseate Terns at closer range.

Continue into the pretty village of São Vicente to end this trip.

The mixed tern colony (Common and Roseate) on an offshore islet near São Vicente.

PRACTICAL PART

Route 5: Madeira's wild west coast

FULL DAY
EASY

End of the world seascapes.
Spectacular cliffs and *fajãs*.

Habitats dry scrubland, cliffs, sea shore, pastures, fajã
Selected species Quail, Berthelot´s Pipit, Rock Sparrow, Madeira Wall Lizard, Spear-leaved Spurge, Disc Houseleek, Madeiran Squill, Small Pride of Madeira

Madeira's western shores are dominated by some of the highest cliffs of the island. It's a humbling feeling, standing on the edge of a 400 metre high cliff and overlooking the seemingly endless ocean that stretches all the way beyond the horizon to America.

This route explores several beautiful sites on Madeira's wild west coast, including its special cliff flora and fauna. You'll drive through a few rather sleepy villages and explore the headlands, the precipitous rock faces and some of the *fajãs*: small, relatively fertile plains on the base of the cliffs, only reachable by spectacular trails or by cable car.

Starting point The docks (porto) of Paúl do Mar.

1 The traditional fishermen's village of Paúl do Mar is built on a fajã. Until the late 1960s, before road tunnels were constructed, the village could only be accessed from the ocean by boat.

In the docks on the eastern end of the village is a conspicuous statue of a naked man. From here the *Verada da Doca* trail leads up to the village of Prazeres, high up in the mountains. It is worth walking part of the trail (fairly strenuous), which runs along steep cliffs and enters

ROUTE 5: MADEIRA'S WILD WEST COAST

a narrow valley some 100 metres above sea level. Walk into the valley and marvel at the spectacular cliff flora, which is almost completely natural. The odd blobs of Disc Houseleeks are common, Small Pride of Madeira* frequents the slopes, there are many Spear-leaved Spurges, Madeira Sea Stock*, Willow-leaved Globularia, the cabbage *Crambe fruticosa* and the Madeira endemic, white-flowered thistle *Carduus squarrosus*, amongst many other, mostly endemic flowers.

Near the river there is Grey Wagtail, while Kestrel and Plain Swift breed on the cliffs.

Leave Paúl do Mar in the direction of Fajã do Ovelha.

2 The road snakes up to the mountain village of Fajã do Ovelha. It crosses one of the few larger coastal valleys on Madeira that retains large areas of the original, warmth-loving 'thermophilous' scrubland (see page 40). Parking is difficult, but there are a few viewpoints that are worth a stop and where you can see a similar flora as at point 1. You also have great views over the fajã of Paúl do Mar.

Cross Fajã do Ovelha and turn left on the T-junction, direction Ponta do Pargo and Porto Moniz.

3 Now follows a sobering stretch of the route. These fairly flat headlands, once terraced for agriculture, have been planted with Eucalyptus and pines, while broom and gorse grow in the abandoned plots. For several kilometres, it is a challenge to find a single plant that is native to the island. Consequently, the fauna is poor here as well. Best to leave this part behind you quickly.

The wild valleys such as this one near Paúl do Mar (top) are safe havens for the threatened warmth-loving coastal flora. One of the species you can encounter here is the endemic thistle Carduus squarrosus *(bottom).*

PRACTICAL PART

ROUTE 5: MADEIRA'S WILD WEST COAST

When you arrive in Ponta do Pargo, follow the signs *Farol* and later, *Miradoura* and *Casa de Châ*.

4 From the Miradoura (368m. above the sea) you have spectacular views over the empty ocean. You are now almost at the most westerly point of the island (the most westerly is the bluff of land just beneath the lighthouse – the next stop of this route). This whole area breathes a quiet, somewhat forlorn atmosphere.
With binoculars, scan the cliffs – *Crambe fruticosa*, Madeira Sea Stock*, Small Pride of Madeira*, both houseleeks and the grey bushes of the Madeiran endemic *Helichrysum maleleucum* grow just beneath the viewpoint. Further down lies a *fajã* that is now abandoned and overgrown with the grey bushes of the Spear-leaved Spurge.

Walk the 1 km trail to the lighthouse and back

5 The Ponta do Pargo headland is open terrain with a particular birdlife. Look and listen for Quail, Red-legged Partridge, Hoopoe, Berthelot´s Pipit, Rock Sparrow, Spectacled Warbler, Linnet, Goldfinch, Canary, Buzzard, Kestrel and Plain Swift. Most of them are scarce though. Being the first landfall birds encounter on the ocean, rarities sometimes turn up. American vagrants, have been found more often at this spot than elsewhere on Madeira. Stray Wheatears and Chiffchaffs can be found in high numbers during migration.

Return to Ponta do Pargo village, turn left on the main ER 101 and at the right turn, go left to Ponta das Fayas. In front of the small restaurant *O Farolim* (50 metres ahead on your left), follow the road right to the viewpoint Miradouro Garganta Funda. Park at the small car park on the end of the track.

6 You walk towards a viewpoint on the edge of the cliff, overlooking a beautiful waterfall. Here you have another chance on seeing the birds noted at Ponta do Pargo. Amongst the butterflies, look for Painted Lady, Clouded Yellow and Long-tailed Blue.

The endemic *Helichrysum maleleucum* grows on coastal cliffs.

ROUTE 5: MADEIRA'S WILD WEST COAST

Return and drive back to the main ER 101 road. Turn left (direction Porto Moniz) and drive to the village of Achadas da Cruz, 11 km north of Ponta de Pargo. Here, follow the signs *teleférico*.

7 The *Fajã dos Quebrada Nova* is arguably the most spectacular site on this route. So far, you've seen headlands, cliffs and the developed fajã of Paúl do Mar – now you descend the 470 metres from a cliff down to the isolated fajã which is still used by locals to grow crops.

The trip down (either on foot or by a very steep cable car) is spectacular; the peace and quiet on the traditional fajã is wonderful and the steep cliffs above it border on the intimidating. It is an ideal place to contemplate the landscape. There are only a few birds and masses of Madeira Wall Lizards, but it is the end-of-world atmosphere that is most exciting. The flora is rich, with lots of Spear-leaved Spurges, Small Pride of Madeiras and other plants that you've seen at the previous points. In the autumn, the cliffs are one of the few sites for the rare and spectacular endemic Madeiran Squill. Equally rare and spectacular is the spring-flowering Giant Herb-Robert* (*Geranium maderense*), which flowers on the cliffs just beneath the upper cable car booth.

The cable car operates between 08-00 – 12.00 and 13.00 – 18.00; € 3.– return ticket (2018).

Fajã dos Quebrada Nova is a wildflower paradise. On the photo Spear-leaved Spurge and *Helichrysum maleleucum*.

PRACTICAL PART

Route 6: Ribeiro Frio

2-3 HOURS
EASY

Perfect first introduction to the laurel forest.
Splendid scenery and birdwatching on the 'balcony of Madeira'.
Small botanical garden with some of the rarest plants of the laurel forest.

Habitats laurel forest
Selected species Trocaz Pigeon, Madeira Chaffinch, Madeira Firecrest, Madeira Marsh-orchid, Madeira Foxglove Tree, Wollaston's Musschia, Madeiran Lady's-tresses, Madeiran Speckled Wood, Madeira Brimstone

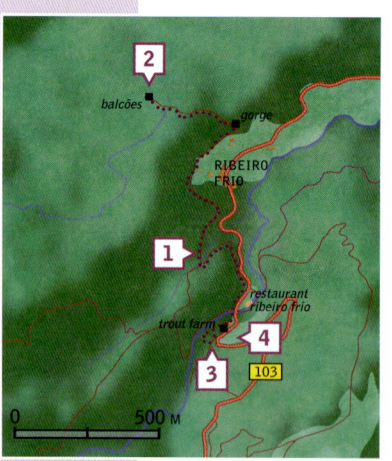

For most scenic spots in the laurel forest you need to walk quite a way. The *Balcões* at Ribeiro Frio is the major exception to this. Hence this route is perfect for a first acquaintance with this the most famous of Madeira's habitats and its flora and fauna. The spectacular balcony is the place to see (and photograph!) some the area's star birds, like Trocaz Pigeon and Madeira Firecrest, plus a fine range of butterflies and wildflowers. Even though it is just a short trip, take your time to discover the wealth of plants and to get good views of the birds.

Ribeiro Frio (which means cold stream) is a small village at 860 m with some restaurants and tourist shops from which several well-known levada walks start.

Make sure you start early, as it is a popular place. Around nine o'clock the first coaches disgorge their passengers and Ribeiro Frio quickly becomes crowded.

Starting point Ribeiro Frio. Park near the restaurant of the same name (just south of the village).

1 First head out to the *Balcões*. Cross the road and walk down a little before following the levada path that branches off to the left, signposted *Balcões*. Along this trail you'll see the laurel forest trees that grow here:

ROUTE 6: RIBEIRO FRIO

the Canary Laurel (here easily recognisable by the large, antler-like fungi *Laurobasidium lauri* which grows on the trunks), Madeira Mahogany, Madeira Blueberry and Noble Bush-madder* (*Phyllis nobla*), a shiny-green bush related to the bedstraws. It is not all laurel forest though. Along the trail there are a great number of introduced trees too: Pedunculate Oak, Sweet Chestnut, Tree Fern and London Plane Tree (*Platanus x hispanica*). On the forest floor, look for Anemone-leaved Crane's-bill, Madeiran Moneywort, Hairy and Glabrous Aichrysons and a wide range of native ferns, including the Macaronesian Polypody and Hare's-foot Fern, which grow on tree branches.

This stretch is excellent for seeing Blackcap, Blackbird, Robin and some confiding Madeira Firecrests (although they're often heard before they're seen). Among the butterflies you can find several attractive species like Madeiran Speckled Wood, Madeira Brimstone and Canary Red Admiral.

After 1 km you are half way and there is a turn to the left where you enter the forest and pass a small gorge, dug out in the cliff. On the other side, the laurel forest is pristine and original. Another 400 metres and you arrive at the *Balcões*.

On the Balcões you see two types of birdwatchers – on the left (hands out) those who long for a close encounter with the tame Chaffinches (bottom) and on the right the people scanning for a glimpse of the elusive Trocaz Pigeon (next page).

2 It is worth staying here a while to enjoy the superb views and study the surroundings. The slopes around you are clad in original laurel forest. Beneath is the valley of Fajã da Nogueira with a network of streams and an electric power plant on its end (see site J on page 182). On clear days you may see the island's third highest peak, Pico do Areeiro (1,817 m), the central mountain chain and the spectacular chunk of rock known as the *Penha d'Águia*.

Madeira Chaffinches are very tame and easy to photograph. The prize bird here is the endemic Trocaz Pigeon, which flies over the tree tops and with luck you can

PRACTICAL PART

ROUTE 6: RIBEIRO FRIO

see some perched on a branch. Take your time – eventually you'll be able to see them. On the cliffs grows the Madeiran endemic *Helichrysum melaleucum* with its typical grey leaves.

Return to the restaurant along the same path.

3 Pay a visit to the trout farm across the road from the restaurant. The garden around the basins (known as the *Parque Florestal de Ribeiro Frio*) holds a fine collection of very rare, native wildflowers of the laurel forest. Besides a large population of Madeira Marsh-orchids and tall specimens of Black Parsley* (*Melanoselinum decipiens*), there are Pride of Madeiras (the rare, tall species native to the laurel forests), Madeira Marguerites, Anemone-leaved Crane's-bills* and Canary Buttercups. In (late) summer this is also the place to see the rare Madeira Foxglove Tree* and the extremely rare Wollaston's Musschia and the even rarer Madeira Lady's-tresses (*Goodyera macrophylla*; known from just a handful of completely inaccessible sites in the wild).

The Balcões is one of the better places on the island to see the rare Trocaz Pigeon.

4 It is worth continuing just a little uphill where there are lots of wildflowers along the stream. This point is also part of the Levado do Furado walk (next route).

The trail to the viewpoint leads through a mature laurel forest.

Route 7: Levada do Furado

**4-5 HOURS
EASY-MODERATE**

A beautiful laurel forest walk with a rich flora.

Habitats laurel forest, levada
Selected species Trocaz Pigeon, Madeira Firecrest, Madeira Chaffinch, Madeira Marsh-orchid, Chain Fern, Filmy Fern, Anemone-leaved Crane's-bill*, Hairy Aichryson, Madeiran Speckled Wood

The Levada do Furado trail is perhaps the most famous of all the levada walks. It runs from Ribeiro Frio all the way to Portela. Alternatively, you can make it a circular walk, by crossing over a small plateau to the main road. It is this latter route we describe here.

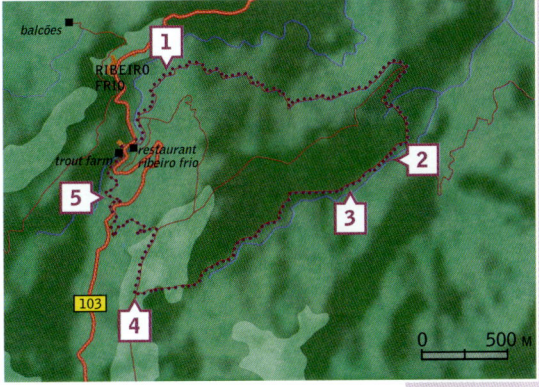

This is above all a very scenic walk, with moss and lichen-covered branches, fairy-tail tree heath scrub and, here and there, spectacular views.

Starting point Restaurant Ribeiro Frio in Ribeiro Frio.
Next to the restaurant, follow the PR 10 walk to Portela.

1 The trail along the levada starts as a wide path but gradually becomes narrower as you proceed. It leads along steep drops with views into the valley, alternating with more gentle slopes, where the forest is most dense. Along levada and on wet cliffs, you'll see masses of ferns (including the tall Chain Fern), both Aichrysons, lots of mosses, liverworts, Shrubby Wallflower and other plants. Wherever you have views, pause for a moment for a chance encounter with a Trocaz Pigeon as it breaks cover and flies along the slope. The endemic Madeiran Speckled Wood butterflies can be seen flying over the canopy.

PRACTICAL PART

ROUTE 7: LEVADA DO FURADO

The damp, north-facing slopes (top) are the habitat of the small Filmy Fern, which received its name for its very thin 'filmy' leaves of only, one cell layer thick.

2 After 3.2 kms, you arrive at a bridge over a picturesque stream, which makes a good spot to take a break. Tame Madeira Chaffinches come to collect their share of your picnic. Look for Chain Ferns and Madeira Marsh-orchids along the river just upstream, and masses of Filmy Ferns on the trunks of the trees – a plant that is special because its leaves contain only one layer of cells, making them nearly transparent.

Just before the bridge, follow the levada trail that runs upstream.

3 The next gentle but long climb follows a fast flowing levada that brings you into a new vegetation zone, dominated by the fine-leaved

CROSSBILL GUIDES • MADEIRA

and elegant Tree Heaths. This is prime habitat for Madeira Firecrest, and it shouldn't be hard to see a few of these handsome birds. We also flushed a Woodcock when we were here.

4 Near the summit, you reach an open area with pastures, Bracken and Purple Foxglove. It is an area grazed by sheep, without too much of interest, although Buzzard, Kestrel and Plain Swift may show themselves.

At the high point, just after a patch of young Tree Heath, you see a farm house to your right. Walk towards it (there is no clear path, but it is easy and open terrain), and pick up the track that passes by the buildings. After 200 metres, a path branches off to the left (marked with a pile of stones, roughly where the fencing ends of a field on your right).
Follow the steep, broad path down to the road (careful, it may be slippery). Once on the road, turn right and after 150 metres, just before the lay-by, take the path to the left again, which brings you back to the trout farm.

5 This last section leads you again through mature laurel forest with more attractive species, including many Madeira Marsh-orchids, Giant Sow-thistle, both Aichrysons, Maidenhair and Filmy Fern.

The endemic Madeira Firecrest is neither shy nor rare along the Levada do Furado. Getting good views of this tiny, restless bird isn't easy though.

PRACTICAL PART

Route 8: Rabaçal

3-4 HOURS
EASY-MODERATE

Enchanting tree heath forest and majestic waterfalls. Rich flora.

Habitats tree heath forest, laurel forest
Selected species Madeira Firecrest, Madeira Chaffinch, Sparrowhawk, Madeira Foxglove Tree*, Eared Pericallis*, Anemone-leaved Crane's-bill*, Madeiran Speckled Wood, Madeira Brimstone

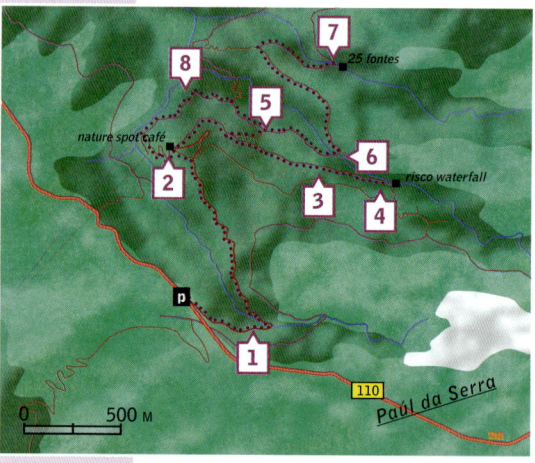

Rabaçal or the 'fairytale forest' is one of the most visited hiking areas in the whole of Madeira and that popularity is well deserved. In contrast to the other levada walks, this one does not enter the laurel vegetation belt proper, but, at an elevation of 1,100 metres, crosses the upper reaches of the forest where the laurels give way to a wonderful Tree and Besom Heath woodland. Thick heath trunks sprout and twist in serpentine bends and curves. There are many springs and waterfalls, adding to the almost otherworldly luxuriant ambiance. The flora along the trail is spectacular, particularly in the summer months.

There are various well-maintained trails in the area and all of them are clearly signposted. We describe here the one to the famous Risco waterfalls and a loop through the forest. This route is undemanding and can be done by anyone in reasonable condition.

A word of advice – start early, preferably at sunrise, as later in the day, the hundreds of visitors that rush off to the Risco Waterfall and 25 Fontes (the other hiker's goal of Rabaçal) break the spell of the enchanted 'fairytale forest'.

ROUTE 8: RABAÇAL

Starting point Car park on the ER110 road on the edge of the Paúl da Serra plateau, 3.5 km west of the crossing with the ER109.

Walk down the tarmac road to the Rabaçal Nature Spot Café. (On return, you could take the minibus service; € 3.– in 2018, or € 5.– to go both ways).

1 This walk illustrates how, as you drop down from an open plateau, you initially find low dense heathland which gradually becomes taller and more impressive as you descend. Naturally, the lower slopes, being more firmly under the influence of the north slope fogs, are covered in forest that is taller and more impressive. The low heathland in the first stretch of the trail is not the original vegetation, which was a forest that burnt down in 2016 by an enormous forest fire that started in the south moved up and just over the mountain. It nearly destroyed Rabaçal too, but was just halted in time by the joint efforts of Madeiran and Portuguese firemen.

The botanically interested should check the roadside near the bend through the river valley. Dense-flowered Orchid grows here.

Take the steps down to the Rabaçal forest house (through the first section of original tall heathland).

2 The historic foresters' house, built in 1835 has been converted to a beautifully situated café / restaurant. From the terrace you overlook the fine forests of Rabaçal. Tame Madeiran Chaffinches will gladly join you on your sandwich break. The open,

The Risco Waterfall

PRACTICAL PART

ROUTE 8: RABAÇAL

sunny environment around the house and the many flowers make this area a good spot to look for the butterflies of the laurel forest – above all Madeiran Speckled Wood and Madeira Brimstone.

Various trails head towards Risco. Follow the one that starts next to house by the water fountain.

3 The broad and level path to the Risco waterfall is a great spot to look for wildflowers. There are plenty of Canary Buttercups, Anemone-leaved Crane's-bill, Glabrous Aichryson and Madeira Pericallis. Noble Bush-madder* (*Phyllis nobla*), Madeiran Blueberry, Lily-of-the-Valley Tree (*Clethra arborea*) and *Bystropogon maderensis*. Along the levada there are some Madeira Marsh-orchids – all of these plants are unique to either the Madeiran laurel forests or the Atlantic islands.

The thick, horizontal branches of the Besom Heath are most impressive. Listen carefully for the high pitched calls of the Madeira Firecrests, which are plentiful here and can be observed at close range.

Anemone-leaved Crane's-bill in the valley of 25 Fontes.

4 The Risco waterfall drops down from the plateau of Paúl da Serra, forming a spectacular view. Look along the trail here for the rare Madeira Foxglove Tree* (*Isoplexis sceptrum;* see page 84-85).

Return and follow, after 700 m, the trail down in the direction of the 25 Fontes.

5 This trail ends on another levada path, where you're faced with a choice – turning left (not signposted) will complete the loop, turning right leads you to the 25 Fontes.

6 Turning right brings you further down to the river valley that is fed by the Risco

ROUTE 8: RABAÇAL

waterfall. You have great views over the laurel forests deeper down in the valley. Madeira Saxifrage grows near the path at this point.

7 The 25 Fontes (25 sources) is a beauty spot where many small waterfalls, ranging in size from a trickle to a small stream, fall down a cliff in a *caldeira*, a crater-like valley with high, steep cliffs. The walk over to 25 Fontes leads through thick, dark and species-poor Tree Heath vegetation along a narrow and difficult to navigate path. As you need to go back and forth (and so will the 100-odd other hikers), this is a logistical bottleneck, so you may consider skipping the 25 Fontes...

8 Turning left beneath the steps at point 5, you follow the broad levada trail through a spectacular mix of tall heath and laurel trees. Similar flora and wildlife occurs here as on the trail to Risco.

After 1 km take the steps to the left (not signposted) which brings you back to the Rabaçal house. Should you miss this turn – just a few metres further on is the long tunnel to Canhal, which is a clear sign for you to retrace your steps.

The trail starts on plateau which lies usually above the clouds. You then descend through some fine Tree Heath stands to the laurel forest.

PRACTICAL PART

Route 9: Ribeira da Janela and Fanal

3-4 HOURS
EASY

Spectacular old laurel trees draped in mosses.
A taste of the old Madeira.

Habitats Laurel forest, grassland, sea cliffs
Selected species Canary, Plain Swift, Goldfinch, Common Tern, Roseate Tern, Grey Wagtail, Madeiran Chaffinch, Woodcock, Madeiran Speckled Wood, Madeiran Cleopatra, Hare's-foot Fern, Glabrous Aichryson, Deer's-tongue Fern*, Lily-of-the-Valley-tree

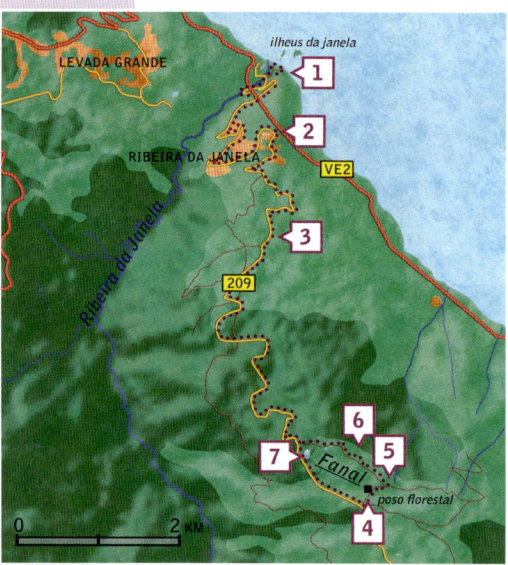

Fanal is an exceptional site – massive laurel trees, clad in epiphytic plants and mosses, grow in an open woodland. The site was used to collect timber and fodder for animals, but many trees of over a hundred years old remain (mostly Stink Laurels; *Ocotea foetens*). Some trees are said to pre-date the Portuguese settlement.

The main objective on this route is Fanal, which can be explored by a short and easy walk. However, the drive to Fanal from Ribeira de Janela has a number of attractive sites, so we've included those in the route as well. A visit to Fanal is also easily combined with a visit to Paúl da Serra (see next route).

Starting point Highway VE2, junction to Ribeira da Janela village. Head down to the coast.

1 Where the Janela, Madeira's largest river, flows into the ocean, there are a number of sites of interest. First is the freshwater pool at the

ROUTE 9: RIBEIRA DA JANELA AND FANAL

base of the water purification installation. In the river and the pool you can see birds such as Mallard, Grey Wagtail and sometimes waders. This little spot is known to attract vagrant birds, especially of American origin. However, in recent years Muscovy Ducks have been bred here which has seriously polluted and disturbed the water, making this site a lot less attractive than it once was.

On the other side of the road you see a cliff with beautiful columnar basalt. The typical, almost mathematical structure of the columns are the result of the shrinking and cooling of the lava. In the cliff is a small catholic shrine. Walk down to the beach and look at the impressive sea stacks. Scan the Common Terns carefully for Roseate Terns, which are regularly seen among them. To the right, the cliffs have a fine, natural coastal cliff vegetation with many original Madeiran species, such as Spear-leaved Spurge, Madeira Sea Stock*, Disc Houseleek, Pinnate Sow-thistle and the grey bushes of *Helichrysum maleleucum*.

Noisy flocks of Plain Swifts often fly low and fast over the Ribeira da Janela viewpoint.

Return and turn left, following the signs Ribeiro da Janela, Fanal and Paúl da Serra.

The road winds up the cliffs and into the village of Ribeiro da Janela. There is a viewpoint on your left and some 50 metres further, another viewpoint – the *Miradouro da Eira da Achada*.

2 Both viewpoints look down on the spectacular northern coastline, the beach and the ocean. In the village birds such as Canary, Goldfinch, Robin, Blackbird and Barn Owl breed and groups of Plain Swifts pass the viewpoint at eye level.

Continue. Outside the village the road narrows and the Ribeira da Janela river is on the right hand side. The slopes are covered with dense laurel forest.

PRACTICAL PART

ROUTE 9: RIBEIRA DA JANELA AND FANAL

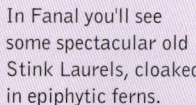

In Fanal you'll see some spectacular old Stink Laurels, cloaked in epiphytic ferns.

3 The road passes through a large area of low laurel forest, dominated by heathers. This entire area, originally laurel forest that was cleared for grazing, is now abandoned. A young form of laurel forest is taking over and, given time, will develop to a mature forest. Over the slopes you can see groups of Plain Swifts flying fast and low over the vegetation. This is also the haunt of the secretive Woodcock, which is seen flying along the road every now and then.

Some 8 km after the viewpoints, turn left at the sign *Poso Florestal do Fanal* and park.

4 Here all three laurel Tree species of Madeira stand together and the island's oldest laurel trees (Stink Laurels; *Ocotea foetens*) grow. Part of the forest has been cleared to create meadows for cattle and you can find several drinking pools, creating a landscape that is very different

from that of the rest of the laurel forest. The ancient trees have a sacred beauty. The trunks and branches are heavily draped in epiphytes – plants that grow on other plants.
Several hiking trails cross and we advise to walk around for some time to see more of the surroundings.

Follow the path in direction of Paúl da Serra and walk the steps to a viewpoint.

5 From the viewpoint you look into the beautiful valley of Chão da Ribeira (site K on page 183). On clear days, look out for Trocaz Pigeons flying over the laurel-clad slopes.

6 Follow the rather unclear path along the ridge to left of the viewpoint. As the landscape here is open and fairly level, walking is straightforward; if you stick to the ridge, you can't go wrong. Along this route, the trees are spectacular – old, gnarled, with huge trunks and draping branches. In foggy weather, it feels like a forest out of Tolkien's Middle Earth.

Grey Wagtails are common on the river.

Further ahead, the path becomes clearer. It leads past a drinking pool for cattle and then proceeds on to the road. Turn left at the road and take the first path on the left.

7 After a few metres the scrub gives way to reveal an open area, either bare with some stones at the centre in summer or covered with water in winter. At first site, this spot is rather unremarkable, but it is special nonetheless, as it is one of just two crater lakes on Madeira.

Return to the road, turn left and take the first footpath left once more. It leads to a picnic area at the side of the road. Take the trail left here and the bear right to return to the car park.

Route 10: Paúl da Serra plateau

3 HOURS
EASY

Unique open plateau.
Special geology, birdlife and, in summer, butterflies.

Habitats shrubby plain
Selected species Buzzard, Berthelot's Pipit, Spectacled Warbler, Red-legged Partridge, Madeira Firecrest, Plain Swift, Madeiran Grayling, Madeiran Speckled Wood, Queen of Spain Fritillary, Trailing St John's-wort

Paúl da Serra is unlike any other place on Madeira. This high plateau that forms the top of the western massif, is the flattest part of the island. It covers roughly 24 km2 at an altitude of between 1,300 and 1,500 m.
The odd geological structure is a result of very resistant horizontal basalt layers that protect the underlying soft strata. The plateau is the most important source of freshwater on Madeira. From here, levadas take the water to all parts of the island.
The Paúl da Serra plateau is covered with gorse and broom brush and masses of Bracken that colonised the plain after the herds of sheep and goats disappeared (which had roamed here since colonisation). As water doesn't easily penetrate the hard top layer, there are many seasonal ponds and marshy spots, which appear as open grasslands in summer. These are great places to find butterflies.
Paúl da Serra is the kind of place you want to have seen, because it is such an unlikely relatively flat area in an otherwise steeply sloping island. In late spring and summer there are a number of birds and butterflies that make the area attractive for naturalists as well.
A visit is easily combined with a walk in Rabaçal (route 8) or Fanal (route 9).

Starting point Bica da Cana.

ROUTE 10: PAÚL DA SERRA PLATEAU

Getting there the deserted house of Bica da Cana lies on the E.R. 110 that runs up from the Encumeadas pass to Paúl da Serra. The house is hidden in the woods; the small car park is in the left bend after the first straight stretch on the plateau.
On foot, follow the cobbled road to the Bica da Cana house.

1 The track bends to the left and climbs up the ridge towards a viewpoint. Thickets of gorse and broom (both brought to Madeira by the British) line the trail. Other plants that grow here also occur in western Europe: Trailing St John's-wort between the cobbles, Changing Forget-me-not and Crane's-bill.
Look here and for the remainder of the trip for butterflies. Even if the rest of the island is underneath a sheet of clouds, Paúl da Serra is often sunny. In summer, there can be many Madeiran Graylings. Other frequent butterflies include Red Admiral, Canary Red Admiral, Clouded Yellow, Small Copper, Madeiran Speckled Wood and Queen of Spain Fritillary.

2 The viewpoint offers magnificent views of the jagged eastern massif, where you can make out the Ruivo, Torres and Areeiro peaks. What a pronounced contrast it makes with the gently undulating Paúl massif you are on now! On the eastern massif, the hard basalt layers, which on Paúl da Serra function as a protective roof are tilted, allowing the softer bedrock to erode.
Noisy flocks of Plain Swifts often fly low around the viewpoint. This is a good place to observe them at close range.

View from Bica da Cana over the Encumeadas pass (in the mist) to the eastern massif of Pico Ruivo and Pico do Areeiro.

PRACTICAL PART

ROUTE 10: PAÚL DA SERRA PLATEAU

Madeira Grayling (top) and Red-legged Partridge (bottom) – two frequent species on the plateau of Paúl da Serra.

Follow the small trail around and down the peak. Where it reaches a broader trail, turn right to return to Bica da Cana.

3 Look for Madeira Firecrests in the mature pine forest in front of the house.

For a further exploration of Paúl da Serra, you can either walk the trail that goes down into the valley (point 4 below), or drive along the ER 110 road and make stops along the way; point 5). Similar species can be seen in either points.

4 The trail heads down a slope where various small streams have their source, although in summer they are all dry. Look and listen for Blackcap, Robin, Berthelot's Pipit and Blackbird in the shrubbery. The three star bird here is Spectacled Warbler, which is quite at home in this bushy environment during the breeding season. Buzzard hunts over the area in search of Rabbits, which are plentiful here.

Walk on for as far as you like and return by the way you came.

5 While driving on along the road, seek out the spots with open areas flanked by bushes. Park and explore these sites on foot. The birds mentioned in the previous point should be present. Madeiran Grayling, Queen of Spain Fritillary and Small Copper and Clouded Yellow are common butterflies in summer. Among the plants, Coral-necklace is plentiful in the lowest parts.

Route 11: The valley of the Lily-of-the-Valley Tree

3-4 HOURS
MODERATE

Simple, short walk through the laurel forest.
One of the richest routes for forest flowers.

Habitats laurel forest
Selected species Madeiran Goldcrest, Trocaz Pigeon, Madeira Brimstone, Lily-of-the-Valley Tree, Madeiran Early-purple Orchid, Madeira Marsh-orchid, Wollaston's Musschia, Anemone-leaved Crane's-bill, Chain Fern, Honey Spurge

! Wet tunnels: Bring torch and wear waterproof footwear

Folha is the Portuguese name for *Clethra* or the Lily-of-the-Valley Tree, an endemic tree of Madeira's laurel forests which flowers spectacularly in August and September and is especially common in this *Folha* valley. The entrance to the valley is like a portal to the lost world. You start on the south slope, pass through a long tunnel and on the other side, you immerse yourself in the spectacular emerald scenery of one of the most intact laurel forests on Madeira. In comparison to the other routes, the *Folha* valley is steeper and more open, giving better views of the forested slopes. However, this route lacks the dramatic waterfalls that form the highlight of the other laurel forest walks. Perhaps that is the reason why this route is less popular with tourists than the others. The two long and rather hard to penetrate tunnels are another reason. In any case this otherwise easy walk is one of the best botanical routes.

ROUTE 11: THE VALLEY OF THE LILY-OF-THE-VALLEY TREE

Lily-of-the-Valley Tree in flower.

Madeira Marsh Orchids grow in large numbers along the levada.

Starting point Encumeadas pass

1 The Encumeadas pass is the nexus of Madeira. From the viewpoint you can, when the weather allows, see the ocean both to the north and south of the island. At the same time, the mountains rise in the east to the jagged peaks of Areeiro and Ruivo and in the west to the high plateau of Paúl da Serra. From the viewpoint, take the small trail down to the snack bar on the ER 228 just underneath the pass (south side), where a sign *Folhadal* leads you along the levada in the right direction (see map).

2 The route follows a broad path along a levada that brings water to the town of Ribeira Brava on the south coast. Along the path you'll see a mixture of laurel forest species and planted vegetation. You should be able to pick out the first Tree Sow-thistles* (*Sonchus fruticosus*) and Honey Spurges. In May and June, you'll see many Madeiran Early-purple Orchids* (*Orchis scopulorum*) in flower – an endemic species that is much more common in the high mountains. In the pines and tree heath, look for Madeira Firecrests.

3 Get out your torch and walk the 600 m tunnel on your right through which both the broad levada and the narrow trail pass. Because the tunnel is low and narrow, it is not an easy walk, especially for tall people or for those carrying large backpacks. Note that it is a long tunnel and that it is very difficult to pass oncoming hikers, so look carefully to make sure no-one is coming towards you. Be careful not to bump your head either.
This is one of the tunnels through which water is transported from the rainy, uninhabited north slopes to the drier residential areas on the south slope.

4 As you cross from the south to the north slope, you enter a spectacular jungle of laurel forest with

CROSSBILL GUIDES • MADEIRA

ROUTE 11: THE VALLEY OF THE LILY-OF-THE-VALLEY TREE

numerous Honey Spurge trees, Tree Sow-thistles*, Anemone-leaved Crane's-bill* (*Geranium palmatum*) and large drifts of Madeira Marsh-orchids*. Note that the latter look similar to the orchids on the south side, but are a different species with many leaves all along the stem. Between the laurels there are quite a few Lily-of-the-Valley trees, an endemic tree that flowers in profusion in late summer. The flowers are attractive and fragrant but the plant is toxic to humans. Birdwise, this is a typical forest patch: Robin, Blackcap, Blackbird, Madeira Chaffinch and Madeira Firecrest are common. Wherever you have clear views over the valley, keep an eye out for Trocaz Pigeon. This elusive bird lives a hidden life in the canopy, but you may see it flying by as it moves from tree to tree.

Pass through the next tunnel (which is even longer, but higher, so easier to walk through).

5 On the other side, the landscape is broadly similar. Directly after the tunnel, there is a short trail to the left to a waterfall. If you continue along the levada you arrive at a second waterfall some 400 metres ahead. This is one of the few accessible sites where the rare Wollaston's Musschia grows (see page 84-85). It flowers in August and September.

With stop five you have covered roughly half of the walk to Lombo do Moro. You can continue to enjoy more of the laurel forest. The return is by the way you came.

A spectacular endemic flower that grows only in a handful of sites is the Wollaston's Musschia. In detail one of its flowers, visited by another endemic species, the Madeiran Speckled Wood.

PRACTICAL PART

Route 12: Pico do Areeiro to Pico Ruivo

!
Tunnels:
bring a torch

Don't try this route in stormy weather

FULL DAY STRENUOUS

Spectacular and popular high altitude walk. Super views and ditto flora.

Habitats high mountain area
Selected species Plain Swift, Spectacled Warbler, Buzzard, Madeiran Grayling, Canary Red Admiral, Disc Houseleek, Madeiran Early-purple Orchid*, Madeiran Thrift*, Shrubby Wallflower*, Canary Buttercup, *Odontitis holliana*, Madeira Violet*, Madeira Saxifrage

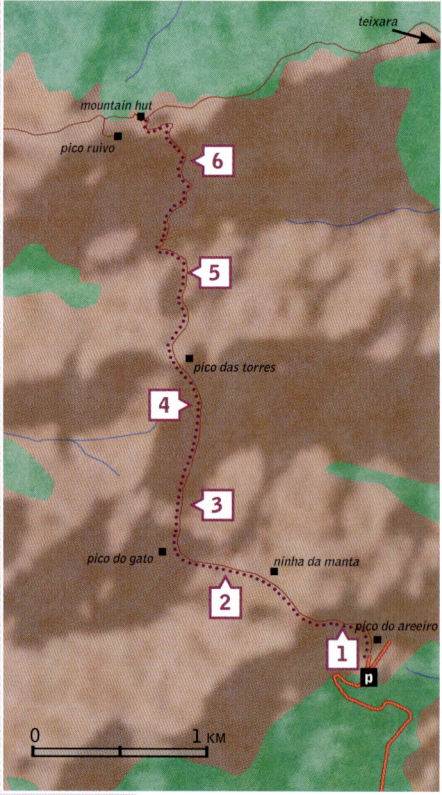

The high mountain traverse from the Pico do Areeiro to Pico Ruivo is one of Madeira's most spectacular walks. The walk follows an unreal, steep itinerary, starting from the car park at Pico do Areeiro (the third highest peak of Madeira) underneath the Pico the Torres (the second highest peak) and over to Pico Ruivo, the highest mountain of the island. The views are beyond amazing, especially when the clouds start to form (as they frequently do) and you find yourself looking down upon a downy blanket.

The route is botanically fabulous. Most of the wildflowers here occur exclusively at altitude on Madeira – a unique flora in other words.

So whilst there are enough reasons to embark on this journey, there are a few challenges too. First, it is an exhausting trip, only recommended for the fit and experienced visitor. The slopes are extremely steep with the abyss unblinkingly staring at you just a metre or so from your feet, so this route is definitely not for you if you are afraid of heights. However, the trail is

ROUTE 12: PICO DO AREEIRO TO PICO RUIVO

The trail to Pico Ruivo is utterly spectacular.

in good state and there are ropes and handholds everywhere so, as long as it's taken seriously and carefully, it shouldn't be too perilous. The weather is changeable and usually quite different from lower down – it can be both windier and much colder up in the mountain, but also, as you are usually above the clouds, much sunnier and hotter. So come prepared for all weather conditions.

Finally, this is a very popular walk. Large groups of people come on organised hikes. They mostly arrive between 9:00 and 10:00 and can be quite noisy, so for the best experience start walking at sunrise. This route is really worth getting up for in the early hours. For much the same reason, walk this route in the direction given here. This is the most popular direction in which to start this route so if you intend to return by the way you came then starting very early will minimise the number of people you'll have to pass on the narrow and steep trail. Hence an attractive alternative is to continue on to Achada da Teixeira having arranged to be picked up there. This extension is the same trail of route 13 of this book, but in reverse direction.

Starting point Pico do Areeiro (for a site description of the Pico, see page 180). Follow the trail that starts next to the peak, just above the restaurant.

ROUTE 12: PICO DO AREEIRO TO PICO RUIVO

1 The first part of the trail over to the viewpoint of *Ninho da Manta* is in-your-face stunning. The trail runs across the jagged peaks and steep ridges, with vertical drops on both sides (thankfully the fencing protects you and gives you grip). You'll cross areas of brittle tuff-stone as well as hard 'dykes' of basalt. These dykes, once the filler of cracks, stand out as the softer tuff-stone in between eroded away, which explains the extreme topography of the area.

The softer eroded rock provides the last refuge for Zino's Petrel which are protected from introduced ground predators by steep inaccessible slopes. The slopes of the Pico Arreeiro and Pico del Torre (just ahead) are the only places where this extremely rare seabird breeds. You won't see them though – they are only here at night (see page 102 and 191).

From the first metre of this route, the flora is spectacular. Along the first kilometre, there are masses of Madeiran Early-purple Orchids on the slopes and equal amounts of the pink Shrubby Wallflower* (*Erysimum bicolor*), which is endemic to the Atlantic Islands. On the rocks, another member of the cabbage family, this time with yellow flowers: *Sinapidendron frutescens*. Not only is this species restricted to Madeira – the entire genus is endemic to the island. Other common endemics are Madeira Saxifrage, Madeiran Thrift, the vetch *Anthyllis lemanniana*, the yellow Madeira Violet* (*Viola paradoxa*) and the eyebright *Odontites holliana*.

2 After the viewpoint of *Ninha da Manta*, you start a steep descent to the low ridge that connects Pico Arreeiro with Pico das Torres. There are many more (rock) flowers here and also the very interesting Red Beard Lichen – a rare and conspicuous, bright-orange lichen. This is perhaps the only place in the world where it can be seen at eye-level. This section ends on the grassy ridge where you have little bit of space to manoeuvre. It is a good point for a break and to look for butterflies. Madeiran Grayling, Canary Red Admiral, Red Admiral and plenty of Small Coppers can be seen here.

Some plants along trail: Red Bear Lichen (top), Madeiran Saxifrage (centre) and Madeira Early-purple Orchid (bottom).

CROSSBILL GUIDES • MADEIRA

ROUTE 12: PICO DO AREEIRO TO PICO RUIVO

3 The next section passes between the Pico do Gato and Pico das Torres. It is fairly level but very narrow, as the trail is squeezed against the vertical cliffs. You'll pass through several tunnels. Note here the big blotches of Disc Houseleek* (*Aeonium glandulosum*). There are many more Madeiran Early-purple Orchids as well as Dense-flowered Orchid and many more wildflowers. In the broom and heather slopes, look and listen for Spectacled Warbler among the much more common Robins and Blackbirds.

4 Next comes an intensely steep and exhausting climb up to the ridge.

5 After a short descent you pass onto the east slope of the Pico das Torres – again a massive cliff, but this time a drier one. Notice the ravages of the 2012 forest fire. Splendid old Tree Heaths were burnt, but young ones are now growing up. More attractive wildflowers are on the rock faces. Madeira Figwort* (*Scrophularia hirta*), Willow-leaved Hare's-ear* (*Bupleurum salicifolium*), Mealy Stonecrop, Navelwort, Madeiran Sickle Fern (*Polystichum falcinellum*), Canary Buttercup, the houseleek *Aichryson divaricatum*, Pride of Madeira, Shrubby Wallflower*, *Sinapidendron frutescens*, *Crambe fruticosa*, Madeira Hawkweed* (*Tolpis macrorhiza*), Willow-leaved Carline-thistle (*Carlina salicifolia*) and the Porto Sancto Mountain-tea* (*Sideritis candicans*) can all be found here.

6 A long but not too steep ascent brings you to the abandoned mountain hut at the foot of the Pico Ruivo, end point of this route. Either return by the same route or follow route 13.

View along the trail.

PRACTICAL PART

Route 13: Pico Ruivo

3-4 HOURS
EASY-MODERATE

A gentle climb to Madeira's highest mountain.
Spectacular views on the 'island in a sea of clouds'.
The flora and fauna contain some attractive species.

Habitats low heathland, rocks
Selected species Madeira Chaffinch, Berthelots Pipit, Spectacled Warbler, Plain Swift, Madeiran Grayling, Madeira Brimstone, Dense-flowered Orchid, Canary Buttercup, Shrubby Plantain*, Shrubby Wallflower*

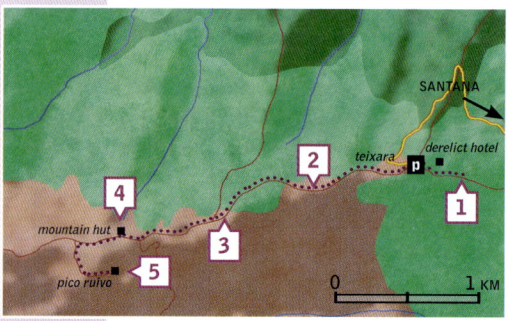

The climb up from Achada da Teixeira to Madeira's highest peak, Pico Ruivo, is a fairly simple affair. The slope is gentle and the trail is well maintained and easy. In the prevailing weather conditions, if you start early, you will soon be well above the clouds (which tend to rise in the afternoon) offering you spectacular views of the forested slopes bathed in mist beneath you, while you walk under a crisp blue sky.
In spring and summer the shrub-dominated landscape makes this is one of the best places to see the sought-after Spectacled Warbler.

Starting point Car park of Teixara.

Getting there From VR in Santana, follow the signs *Parque Temático* and follow the signs *Pico Ruivo*. This will bring you all the way up to the car park. En route you pass through a small area of laurel forest where you may stumble upon Trocaz Pigeons.

1. Before starting your walk up to Ruivo, walk some 100 metres in the opposite direction, past the derelict hotel. Just beyond is a curious rock formation, known as the standing man (for obvious reasons). It is a

ROUTE 13: PICO RUIVO

remnant of a dyke (see page 23). You can also find the endemic cabbage *Sinapidendron frutescens* here.

2 Follow the trail to Pico Ruivo. Next to the trail there are many wildflowers which are endemic to either Madeira or the Atlantic Islands: Madeira Hawkweed* (*Tolpis macrorhiza*), Downy Andryala* (*A. glandulosa*), Shrubby Wallflower* (*Erysimum bicolor*), Shrubby Plantain* (*Plantago arborescens*), Madeira Thyme* (*Thymus micans*) and Canary Buttercup. Look carefully and you'll find Dense-flowered Orchid too. There are thousands of them on these slopes, but due to their modest appearance, you need to develop an eye for them. In spring, listen carefully for Spectacled Warbler, which breeds quite abundantly in the open heath scrub. Other birds of interest are Plain Swift, Berthelot's Pipit, Kestrel and Buzzard.

The walk towards Pico Ruivo leads over slopes that are often above the clouds (bottom).
In spring and summer, this is the habitat of the Spectacled Warbler (top).

3 The trail crosses the north slope of the mountain before returning to the crest. Looking south, you see the white skeletons of old tree heaths– reminders of the devastating fire that destroyed these slopes in 2012 and was halted just before they could cross over

PRACTICAL PART

ROUTE 13: PICO RUIVO

to the north slope where it would have wreaked havoc on the pristine laurel forest of Calderão Verde, which is beneath you on your right (and is the goal of route 14).

At the junction, follow the signs to Pico Ruivo.

4 A few metres further on you arrive at the mountain refuge, which is closed but its terrace remains a tempting spot to stop for a sandwich, which you'll share with many tame Chaffinches. At the time of our visit (2018), many had a curious and nasty papillomavirus infection that deformed their toes and seriously troubled the birds.

5 Continue to the peak of Ruivo. A short climb further (with the pretty Madeira Violet* *(Viola paradoxa)* in the side of the trail) you're on the top of the island. Weather permitting, you'll see the plain of Paúl da Serra to the west (with the wind turbines) and the Pico do Areeiro (with the dome) to the south. Notice too the many dykes (hard basalt layers) that lace the softer tuffstone.

Return the way you came.

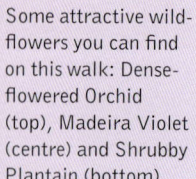

Some attractive wildflowers you can find on this walk: Dense-flowered Orchid (top), Madeira Violet (centre) and Shrubby Plantain (bottom).

CROSSBILL GUIDES • MADEIRA

Route 14: Queimadas and Caldeirão Verde

6 HOURS - FULL DAY; 13 KM
EASY-MODERATE

One of the finest laurel forest trails of the island.

Habitats laurel forest
Selected species Madeira Chaffinch, Madeira Firecrest, Trocaz Pigeon, Madeiran Cleopatra, Madeiran Sow-thistle*, Disc-leaved Fern*, Madeira Marsh Orchid, Two-leaved Gennaria, Chain Fern, Honey Spurge

!
Wet tunnels:
Bring torch and wear waterproof footwear

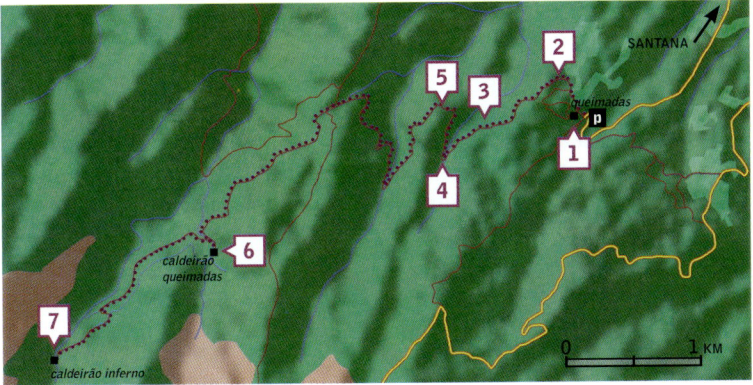

This fascinating, easy but long walk follows the *Levada do Caldeirão Verde* over almost its entire length. The route has a double objective: the *Caldeirão do Queimadas* and for those who want to for those who want to walk the whole route, the *Caldeirão do Inferno*. For the latter you'll have to do a short, sharp climb.

Caldeirão is Portuguese for a steep dead-end valley that originated from (in the case of Madeira) a landslide. Both caldeirãos on this route are spectacular spots with massive walls clad in ferns and mosses, with water trickling down from all sides. The walk over to them is beautiful, with pretty much all the native wildflowers, birds and butterflies the Madeiran laurel forest has to offer.

Note that this impressive walk has become popular in last years. We advise you to beat the crowd and start early.

PRACTICAL PART

ROUTE 14: QUEIMADAS AND CALDEIRÃO VERDE

Starting point Queimadas

Getting there From the Via Rápida, follow first the signs *Parque Temática* and subsequently *Queimadas*. On your way up, notice the Eucalyptus woods with Acacia undergrowth – two extremely damaging invasive species. You'll notice the contrast with the natural forest on your walk.

1 Queimadas is a wonderfully restored, traditional thatch-roofed house. Right around it, you'll see the first spectacular laurel forest plants: the tall bushes of Madeira Marguerite (*Argyranthemum pinnatifidum*) and Tree Sow-thistle* (*Sonchus fruticosus*), both endemic species of the Madeiran laurel forest. As this is an open spot in the laurel forest zone, it is an excellent place to look for the laurel forest butterflies Madeira Brimstone and Madeiran Speckled Wood.

2 The first half kilometre of the trail is a little unexpected – some spectacular trees grow here along the trail, but most of them are not laurel forest species at all. There are impressive specimens of Japanese Red-cedars (*Cryptomeria japonica*), European Beech (*Fagus sylvatica*), Pedunculate Oak and Sycamore.

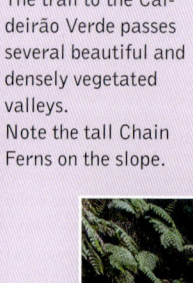

The trail to the Caldeirão Verde passes several beautiful and densely vegetated valleys.
Note the tall Chain Ferns on the slope.

3 Gradually, the non-native species disappear and you enter the true laurel forest. Tame Madeiran Chaffinches walk on the trail in front of you, Madeira Firecrests appear in stands of Besom Heath and wherever you have views over the slopes, keep an eye out for Trocaz Pigeons flying by.

Plantwise, almost all laurel forest plants appear along the trail. On the rock above the levada you'll find mats of ferns (many Hard Fern, but all in all there are easily a dozen or more species),

ROUTE 14: QUEIMADAS AND CALDEIRÃO VERDE

Hairy Aichryson, Disc Houseleek, Madeira Marsh-orchid, Willow-leaved Carline Thistle, the white crucifer *Crambe fruticosa*, Madeiran Moneywort (*Sibthorpia*) and mats of Selaginella, mosses, liverworts and lichens.

4 You reach a bridge over a small river. It is an enchanting wet and shady jungle here. There are many huge Chain Ferns, Honey Spurges (the only spurge in Europe that grows to the height of a small tree), the stout Canary Buttercup and the Black Parsley* (*Melanoselinum decipiens*).

5 The forest becomes more and more spectacular. Orchid aficionados who are here in early spring should look out for the small, green-flowered Two-leaved Gennaria. For this section, you'll need to get out your torch, because you'll pass through a few tunnels.

6 About 5.5 km beyond the bridge you arrive at the Caldeirão Verde with its spectacular long waterfall. If you thought the laurel forest was cool, moist and shady, then you haven't yet experienced the *Caldeirão*. There is hardly any direct sunlight here and the air is permanently damp. The result is a densely green vegetation, with lots of Chain Ferns and mosses. Some very rare plants grow here, like the Madeiran Elder.

7 The last section is much tougher, as you climb over a 100 metres and walk through some low and very wet tunnels and cross spectacular narrow gorges. It is amazing how the levadas were engineered here in this extreme terrain. Eventually you arrive at the Caldeirão do Inferno where there trail ends. Here you'll find wild Pride of Madeiras growing and Wollaston's Musschia is reputed to occur – one of the rarest plants of the laurel forest.

Return the way you came.

A waterfall plunges down on the levada.

PRACTICAL PART

Route 15: Porto Santo daytrip

FULL DAY

In every respect different to Madeira.
Dry habitats, with a special birdlife.
Ocean crossing with lots of seabirds and cetaceans.

Habitats ocean, beach, dry scrub vegetation
Selected species Common Dolphin, Bottlenose Dolphin, Cory´s Shearwater, Manx Shearwater, Bulwer´s Petrel, Desertas/Zino´s Petrel, Great Skua, Kentish Plover, Hoopoe, Red-legged Partridge, Berthelot´s Pipit, Rock Sparrow, Spanish Sparrow, Monarch

Porto Santo is Madeira's pleasure island. It is where Madeirans themselves spend the weekend as it is much sunnier and has a natural, 4 km long sandy beach – two perks that Madeira lacks.

For naturalists a visit to Porto Santo is time and money well spent. The trip over on the large and steady vessel (important for those prone to sea-sickness) offers excellent opportunities for watching seabirds and dolphins. The island itself, being much drier and having a more open vegetation, has a different birdlife too. The flora contains some interesting species but for those, you'd best climb the Pico Branco (next route).

ROUTE 15: PORTO SANTO DAYTRIP

Once on Porto Santo, it is best to combine a visit to dry areas with places of fresh water in order to find the most birds in the roughly 9 hours you have available on a day trip. Or better yet, spend a night here and explore at your leisure.

There is no obvious route to follow on the island and your access to the sites largely depends on how you decide to get around (see boxed text), so we've simply described the best sites here and leave it up to you which ones you wish to visit.

The daily boat service to Porto Santo starts in Funchal at 8.00 am and departure from Porto Santo is (mostly) at 7.00 pm. Book your ticket in advance on **www.portosantoline.pt** (€ 59.44 return, 2019) or at the office near the harbour of Funchal.

The ferry crossing

On the ship, find yourself a place on the rear deck from where you have the best views. Lower decks on the sides on the front are usually better for close views and photography. Look for a place out of the wind and with the light behind you.

The ship follows the coastline of southern Madeira, offering great

Sunrise over the São Lourenço Peninsula, seen from the ferry.

Getting around on Porto Santo

Porto Santo is small, but still too large to cover on foot. If you are here only for a day, you'll need to make sure you're on time for the ferry back to Madeira. Hence it is important to work out the logistics. Here are your options:

Taking your hire car on the ferry: the easiest but most costly option. Set aside an extra € 100.- for bringing your car. Note that drivers need to be at the ferry earlier to embark.

Hiring a car: from the boat, a short bus ride takes you to the taxi rank and bus stop in Vila Baleira. This is the main logistic hub for the entire island. Here you can hire a small car to take you around the island. Easy and less costly.

Taking the taxi: head to the same taxi stand and have yourself dropped off at any spot you wish. Make sure you get the driver's phone number and check if you and the driver have a language in common so you can arrange a pickup. Mobile Phone reception on the island should not be a problem.

Taking the bus: a bus runs along the boulevard on the south side of the island, which takes you to some of the sites, but not to the more beautiful ones to the northeast. A bus time table is available at the taxi rank.

PRACTICAL PART

ROUTE 15: PORTO SANTO DAYTRIP

views of the cliffs. You'll pass Garajau with the statue of Christ (dolphins are frequent in this area), the airport with the landing strip that juts out into the ocean and finally the Peninsula of São Lourenço.

Around São Lourenço and on to Porto Santo you are in excellent waters for pelagic birds. The most abundant species will be Cory´s Shearwater, one of the larger shearwaters with a wing span of more than a metre. Some will come close to the ship and expect to see a few hundred during the crossing between March and October. Bulwer´s Petrels are also often seen – all dark, with an erratic, bat-like flight (May-Sept). Manx Shearwater is much scarcer, while storm-petrels and Macaronesian shearwater are exceptional. On most crossings between June and September one or two Desertas/Zino's Petrels (indistinguishable at sea without previous experience or good photographs) may be seen, spotted from a distance thanks to their habit of repeatedly arcing high above the sea.

Northern Gannet and Great Skua occur in winter. Search either side of the ship for groups of Common, Bottlenose, Spotted or Atlantic Striped Dolphin. Near Porto Santo, you'll start seeing terns, mostly Common and, in winter, Sandwich Tern.

The dry grassy slopes of Porto Santo form a sharp contrast with the damp, vegetated slopes of Madeira. This photo was taken in the northeast, near the Pico Branco trail (route 16).

Sites on Porto Santo

1 – Vila do Baleira
The village of Vila do Baleira is Porto Santo's capital. Here you can swim and sunbathe on the beach or visit the village to look for Canary, Spanish Sparrow (the only sparrow in the present), Monarch butterfly, Long-tailed Blue, Blue Emperor and Madeira Wall Lizard. Much of this you'll see when you walk from the taxi stand along the river bed into the village. Iberian Water Frogs occur in large numbers in the river.

2 – El Tanque reservoir
Just above Vila do Baleira lies the reservoir El Tanque – a small freshwater site that attracts birds, especially on migration. Spoonbill, Whimbrel, Little Ringed Plover and many other water birds have been seen here.

Rare or absent from Madeira but common on Porto Santo – the Spanish Sparrow.

3 – Ring road
Around the central mountains of the island lies a ring road that brings you into the deserted interior of Porto Santo. The rather barren landscape has its own appeal. There are a few original windmills on the south side worth seeing, as well as some small reservoirs on the northeast, all of which attract birds. Plain Swift, Kestrel, Buzzard, Hoopoe, Berthelot's Pipit and Spanish Sparrow (breeding in the palm trees) are the common birds here.
Along the way you pass the starting point of the Pico Branco walk (see next route).

4 – The beach
In the low season, the deserted beach has its share of birdlife too. Sandwich Tern, Common Tern, Sanderling, Kentish Plover and other waders and seabirds may be present. A few pairs of Kentish Plover even breed on Porto Santo, in the scant vegetation just above the beach.

5 – Golf course
The golf course hardly qualifies as a site of natural beauty if it weren't for the fact that it attracts birds like a magnet. The fertile, irrigated greens and small freshwater ponds are frequented by species that are not normally part of Madeira's birdlife. Little Egret, Cattle Egret, Grey Heron, Glossy

ROUTE 15: PORTO SANTO DAYTRIP

Ibis, Coot and Moorhen concentrate in the lakes and any kind of wader could be present. Resident Hoopoe and migrants such as Wheatear feed on the fields.
Views on the Golf Course are best from the car park or, better yet, the restaurant's terrace. Ask at the reception – we never had problems entering the premises.
Looking in the other direction, you have good views of the low *Pico de Ana Ferreira*, which has a beautiful crown of columnar basalt.

The man-made freshwater pools on the golf course are a magnet for birds. Especially during migration, this site can offer great birdwatching.

6 – River

Roughly in front of the golf course, a small stream which runs down to the ocean, usually flows with water. The ribbon of vegetation along the stream is attractive to birds and birdwatchers alike. Look for Berthelot's Pipit, Spanish Sparrow, Rock Sparrow, Buzzard, Kestrel, Red-legged Partridge, Collared Dove, Plain Swift, Canary, Linnet and Goldfinch.

7 – Ponta de Calheta

The western point of the island overlooks the uninhabited *Ilhéu de Baixo*, also known as the *Ilhéu da Cal* or chalk island. The mixture of lava and limestone from fossilised reefs is special. Large dykes criss-cross the island (see page 23) and the rocks on the shoreside have an interesting geology of basalt and sandstone.
This is also a beautiful spot for a swim or to watch the sun set.

Dolphins like this Bottlenose are frequently seen from the ferry.

Route 16: The Pico Branco

3-4 HOURS
MODERATE

Porto Santo's richest site for flora.
A quiet and scenic walk.

Habitats dry grassy slopes, cliffs, Cypress forest
Selected species Berthelot's Pipit, Rock Sparrow, Linnet, Plain Swift, Madeira Wall Lizard, *Cheirolophus massonianus*, Porto Sancto Mountain-Tea, Madeira Savoury*, Sea Heath, Disc-leaved Fern

Most of the natural vegetation of Porto Santo has deteriorated, with one wonderful exception – the steep slopes of the White Peak or *Pico Branco*. And what a fine area this is! A short and fairly easy walk (with a final short and steep ascent), brings you in a stunning landscape with a rich flora, some attractive birds and more Madeira Wall Lizards than you can count. Along the way, you pass several attractive points on the circular road around the centre of the island (see previous route).

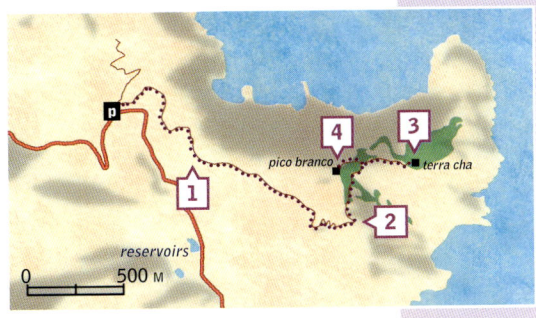

Starting point Pico Branco car park.

Getting there From Vila do Baleira, follow the signs *Serra de For* and follow the circular route. After passing the second reservoir (on your left) the start of the trail appears on your right.

1 The first section of the trail runs through open country with wide views over this abandoned part of the island. Note the terraces on the opposite slope – signs of former cultivation. Porto Santo was discovered before Madeira, and due to its gentler topography, it was easier to cultivate. This is why so little of the original vegetation remains – except for a few steep seaside slopes, as you'll see further on.

ROUTE 16: THE PICO BRANCO

The extreme rarity Cheirolophus massonianus (top) and thick blankets of beard lichens (bottom) are just a few of the botanical attractions on this route.

Along the trail, there are already some fine wildflowers, such as Small Pride of Madeira* (*Echium nervosum*), Downy Andryala* *(Andryala glandulosa)*, lots of Sea Heath (rare on Madeira, common on Porto Santo), the grey bushes of Madeira Wormwood* (*Artemisia argentea*), Shrubby Plantain (*Plantago arborescens*), the tiny bellflower relative *Wahlenbergia lobelioides*, and Madeira Savoury* (*Micromeria thymoides*). Plain Swifts wheel overhead. Listen too for the nasal call of Rock Sparrows, which share the slopes with Linnet, Canary and Goldfinch.

2 The last section ascends steeply before crossing over to the other side. There the steep slopes are radically different, as they are clad in a Monterey Cypress forest with a large number of extremely rare native plants. About a quarter of the plants here are endemic, either being restricted to the Atlantic Islands, the Madeira archipelago and some even to Porto Santo itself, these slopes being the most important site of their occurrence.

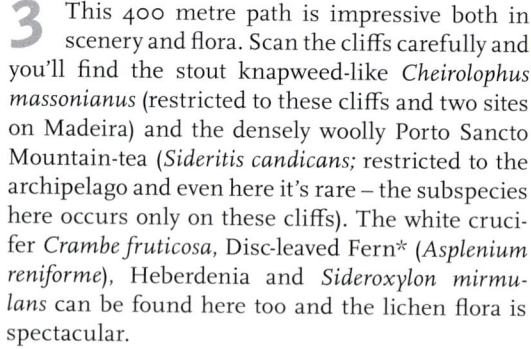

The track splits in two with one path leading to the lookout point of Terra Cha and the other to the Pico Branco itself. We describe the Terra Cha branch first.

3 This 400 metre path is impressive both in scenery and flora. Scan the cliffs carefully and you'll find the stout knapweed-like *Cheirolophus massonianus* (restricted to these cliffs and two sites on Madeira) and the densely woolly Porto Sancto Mountain-tea (*Sideritis candicans*; restricted to the archipelago and even here it's rare – the subspecies here occurs only on these cliffs). The white crucifer *Crambe fruticosa*, Disc-leaved Fern* (*Asplenium reniforme*), Heberdenia and *Sideroxylon mirmulans* can be found here too and the lichen flora is spectacular.

4 Return and climb the 200 metres to the Pico Branco, from which you have stunning views all around.

ROUTE 16: THE PICO BRANCO

Views of the coast and the Monterey Cypress forest from the Pico Branco.

PRACTICAL PART

ADDITIONAL SITES

Additional sites

Location of the sites described on the following pages.

Although small, Lugar de Baixo (bottom) is Madeira's largest marsh and attracts all sorts of vagrant birds, such as this Little Crake (top).

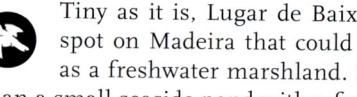

A – Lugar de Baixo

Tiny as it is, Lugar de Baixo is the only spot on Madeira that could be classified as a freshwater marshland. It is no more than a small seaside pond with a few reeds – the kind of place you wouldn't pay much attention to if it were anywhere on mainland Europe.

But this is Madeira and stray migrants are beggars, not choosers. For them, Lugar de Baixo is like a magnet. Vagrants that turn up, mostly in spring and autumn include shorebirds like Black-winged Stilt, Dunlin, Black-tailed Godwit, Redshank, Snipe and Ringed Plover. Common Waxbill is a resident in the reeds and

CROSSBILL GUIDES • MADEIRA

the site is the only place on the island where Coot breeds. You may see Moorhen as well.

Lugar de Baixo came into existence in 1804 with a bang when part of the cliff collapsed and blocked the flow of the nearby stream. Now the marsh is separated by a dam of rocks, from which you overlook the marsh. On the rocks, there are masses of Madeira Wall Lizards.

To get to Lugar de Baixo, follow the main road from Ribeira Brava to Ponta do Sol. There are two large tunnels on this section. Directly after exiting the second tunnel, park on the right side of the road, near the restaurants. Take the footbridge to the other side of the road and there's the marsh, right by the ocean.

B – Cabo Girão and Fajã dos Padres

Cabo Girão is one of Madeira's prime tourist attractions. At an altitude of 560 m, this colossal cliff is one of the highest sea capes in the world, offering amazing views of the coastline and the pebble beach and fajã under your feet. Recently a glass-floored platform was installed making this the highest 'skywalk' in Europe. The much photographed fajã below was formerly only accessible by boat. Only recently a cable system was installed to take the farmers to and from their fields. From the platform, you may see Kestrel, Plain Swift and Buzzard.

The Cabo Girão is a hotspot for rare cliff flora, but from the platform you'll see very little of that. With one exception: there is a rare, yellow-flowered mustard that grows right beneath the glass floor: *Sinapidendron angustifolium*. This species only occurs on a few Madeiran sea cliffs; in fact the entire genus of *Sinapidendron* is endemic to Madeira.

C – Seawatching from Funchal

West of the city centre of Funchal there are several vantage points that are ideal for scanning the ocean for seabirds, whales and dolphins. The best is Ponta da Cruz, the headland that protrudes into the ocean just west of the harbour. Spend some time here (preferably with a telescope) and you should be able to see lots of seabirds. The best time is between May and September.

The view down from Cabo Girão. With a drop of 560 metres, this is one of the world's highest sea cliffs.

Typically, the birds that fly east in the morning and west in the afternoon breed on the Desertas. Hundreds of Cory´s Shearwaters pass by, large numbers of Bulwer´s Petrels can be seen and there is a good chance of Desertas or Zino´s Petrel. Manx and Macaronesian Shearwater (all in the summer season), and whales are also regular. As the sea floor drops steeply near the coast, Common and Bottlenose Dolphin sometimes swim close to the shore. An advantage of the waters around Ponta da Cruz is that the sea is calmer than on the north side of the island. The downside is the light – during the day you're looking straight into the sun. Mornings and late afternoons are therefore best for seawatching here.

To get to Ponta da Cruz, follow the main road (*Estrada Monumental*) out of Funchal and pick up the signs *Ponta da Cruz*. Park at the car park at the end of the road and look for a vantage point next to the statue. You can also walk about 3 km westwards along the touristic Lido promenade, enjoy the gardens along the route, and find a suitable point near Ponta da Cruz car park.

D – Rocha Alta

The richness and importance of the original thermophyllous (drought-adapted) scrubland of southern Madeira has only recently been recognised. Formerly seen as a degraded form of laurel forest, ecologists now consider this is an original Madeiran ecosystem with its own unique flora and fauna. The original thermophyllous scrubland is extremely rare nowadays – tucked away in a few inaccessible sites that were never attractive to commercial uses nor invaded by alien species. You'll mostly find these remaining snippets in otherwise rather mundane locations – hardly the sort of place a tourist office would rave about.

One such site is Rocha Alta. It was only recently added to the Natura 2000 network. It is a steep sea slope with cliffs, right on the rather busy *Rua Conda Carvalhal*. On the slopes there is an original coastal grassland with wild Madeira Olive Trees and Spear-leaved Spurges. On the cliffs, scan for delightful wildflowers like both houseleeks, the rare Pinnate Lavender* (*Lavandula pinnata*; endemic to Madeira and the Canaries) and Small Pride of Madeira* (*Echium nervosum*). The star species however is the beautiful Golden Musschia* (*Musschia aurea*), a rare endemic of some coastal and a few inland cliffs of Madeira.

To get to Rocha Alta coming along the motorway from Funchal, take exit 14 (*S Gonçalo*) and turn right to São Gonçalo. Continue for 800 metres

until on your left, you see a viewpoint by the sea – *Mirdadouro do Pináculo*. Park here, which is easiest if you turn at the restaurant a little further on. The aforementioned wildflowers can be found around the viewpoint – the Musschia grows on the bare cliff that faces the road opposite of the viewpoint.
Note that the Dragon Tree Garden *Nucleo da Dragoeiras das Neves* is very close to this spot. See page 209 for details.

E – Quinta do Palheiro

  Quinta do Palheiro or Blandy's Garden lies just to the northeast of Funchal and is another of the island's famous botanical gardens. Since given protected status in the 1980s, Trocaz Pigeons, once largely restricted to the island's laurel forests, have been increasingly seen in semi-urban settings around Funchal. Small numbers are now resident in this garden and along its margins with a local golf course which gives an unrivalled opportunity to see and photograph them at close quarters.

Trocaz Pigeon on the lawn of Quinta do Palheiro. This often elusive bird is seen in these gardens with relative ease.

F – Miradouro do Curral das Freiras

  The *Curral das Freiras* or Corral of the Nuns is a secluded, deep valley in the mountains above Funchal. According to legend, the nuns of Funchal hid here from raiding pirates in the 16th century. In another account, the village is said to be founded by nuns from Funchal in the late 15th century. In any case, what remains today is a small village in an extreme landscape – a deep valley tucked away beneath the Areeiro massif. The village developed in isolation. It wasn't until 1959 that the first road to Curral das Freiras was constructed. Today you can drive it up to the pass where a large restaurant is situated at one of the most spectacular viewpoints on the whole of Madeira. From there you can walk the way down over the old road into the valley, which geologically is the result of erosion of ash and soft rocks that piled up here after some violent eruptions.
To reach the *Miradouro do Curral das Freiras* from Funchal go west and take exit 10 to Freiras, follow the ER107 and turn left just before a tunnel to Eira do Serrado. You can also visit the village by car through a new tunnel of the VE6.

ADDITIONAL SITES

G – Funchal ecological park

The Funchal Ecological Park was created in 1994. It is a protected area in the mountains north of the city on the road to Pico do Areeiro. Access is easy and there are picnic areas and walking trails going up the mountain slopes. Part of the Ecological Park was destroyed by the 2010 fires and programs to recover the natural vegetation started soon after. Educational programmes are run to make people aware of the value of Madeira's natural heritage.

For the naturalist visitor, the part close to the road (near the warden's house) is worth a (picnic) stop if you are passing by. Even though you're on the south slope, you are right in the laurel forest zone, and (planted) laurel forest species are right in the side of the trail, such as Madeira Marguerite (*Argyranthemum pinnatifidum*), Honey Spurge, Pride of Madeira, Tree Sow-thistle* (*Sonchus fruticosus*) and Black Parsley* (*Melanoselinum decipiens*). The slopes are gentle and flowery so in good weather, there can be many butterflies present. It is a good place to look for Madeira Brimstone and Madeiran Speckled Wood, amongst others.

To get there from Funchal, follow the signs *Monte* and keep on the ER103. Once in the forest, you will see a building in a hairpin bend, which is the reception centre of the Ecological Park.

H – Pico do Areeiro

Even if you are not planning on doing any serious hiking in the mountains, you can't miss out on a visit to the Pico do Areeiro. You can drive all of the way up to the top of this most spectacular of the Madeiran mountains, thanks to the large, moon-shaped military radio station. The station cannot be visited, but there is a restaurant, gift shop and an interesting exhibition on the endemic Zino's Petrel which breeds in the nearby mountains.

Pico do Areeiro

Apart from the views (which alone warrant a visit), there are several things to do. Around the peak itself, right by the restaurant, butterflies are 'hilltopping' – a typical behaviour of some butterfly species to follow hills upslope to the top, where they gather to find a mate. Pico do Areeiro is such a peak, which means that butterfly concentrations are often (but not always) higher. Both Red Admiral and the Macaronesian endemic Canary Red

Admiral are frequent, as are Clouded Yellow, Small Copper and Queen of Spain Fritillary. In summer, Madeiran Graylings are plentiful.

In May and June, there are a few Madeira Early-purple Orchids* (*Orchis scopulorum*) and Madeiran Thrift* (*Armeria maderense*) around. You'll see masses more of those (and other plant species) as you walk along the spectacular ridge over to the next viewpoint (see point one of route 12). All the while, Plain Swifts fly low over the crests, offering fine views.

Before arriving on the Pico, you pass through some, by Madeiran standards, rather gentle slopes with flowery grasslands. This is one of the island's better sites for butterflies, especially in summer. A good spot to look is around the *Poço da Neve* (around 500 m from the top), which is in itself an interesting historical site. The igloo-shaped snow pit (as *Poço da Neve* literally translates) was used to store snow in in the winter months. Compacted to form ice, it was brought down in summer to cool perishable food.

I – Ponta Garajau

Ponta Garajau is a small cape with high cliffs above the sea. The *Cristo Rei* statue on its top can be seen from far and wide and the site enjoys good views of the coast to the east and west and over the ocean. This is a good spot for observing feeding Plain Swifts breeding in the cliffs and for the much rarer Pallid Swift. Sometimes they are joined by the swallows and martins that visit the island. Berthelot´s Pipit and (in winter) Spectacled Warbler live on the dry slopes and the endemic coastal plant Golden Musschia* (*Musschia aurea*) grows in a wall of the road that goes down to the shore. Other native cliff plants include Spear-leaved Spurge, Willow-leaved Globularia and the rare *Andryala crithmifolia*. The sea below, protected as a Nature Reserve, is very rich in underwater life and offers good opportunities for diving.

A night visit to Ponta Garajau has interesting things to offer. Barn Owl and Leisler´s Bat visit the place in search for food and are relatively easy to see. Cory´s

The statue of Cristo Rei at Garajau.

ADDITIONAL SITES

Shearwaters breed in the inaccessible slopes and visit their nests when it is dark. During the nightly visits to their nest burrows, the shearwaters produce the weirdest sounds – deep, harsh, rasping and sobbing screams and man-like wails like *kaaa-ough* or *kooo-hoigh* can be heard from some distance (if this doesn't make sense, google the Cory´s shearwater call and imagine hearing this in the night – it is amazing). *Cagarra* is the Portuguese name of the Cory´s Shearwater, referring to its nocturnal sounds and Garajau means 'seabirds' in Madeiran dialect. A few Madeiran Storm-petrels also breed in the cliffs. They make softer sounds, their flight call is a repeated phrase sounding like 'a finger rubbed hard on a wet window'.

Another night-time attraction we found at Garajau was in the unlikeliest of places, the public toilets. Two species of gecko, Moorish and Tropical House Gecko, hunt for insects on its walls.
Ponta Garajau is a little east of Funchal. Take exit 15 on the VR1 and follow the signs *P. Garajau* and later *Cristo Rei*. Just before entering the car park near Christ Statue a small road signed Restaurante Praia goes down to the shore in westerly direction. Take the cable car down or walk the 800 m to the beach adjacent to the cliff. From the Cristo Rei statue there is a small path runs down the ridge.
Off the beach are some of the better places for snorkelling on Madeira (see page 207).

Beautiful animals are sometimes found in odd spots – a Tropical House Gecko hunting for insects on the window of Garajau's public toilets is a case in point.

J – Fajã da Nogueira

From the bottom of the Fajã da Nogueira valley you can see the *Balcões* and the dense laurel forest on the steep slopes above you (Ribeiro Frio, route 6). The sensation of being at the bottom is radically different from being at the top! The river is fed by numerous side streams that carry a lot of water in winter but are often dry in summer.
A gravel road leads to the electric power plant. This is a good and easy spot to search for the local flora and fauna. Make stops to scan the mighty slopes for Trocaz Pigeons. Grey Wagtails breed near the water and woodland birds like Blackcap, Blackbird, Robin and Madeira Firecrest also live here.
To get there from Ribeiro Frio follow the ER103 to Faial for about 7 km. A sign just before an old stone bridge indicates *Central Fajã da Nogueira*. Enter and park your car to start the about 4 km walk to the *Central*.

ADDITIONAL SITES

K – Seixal and Chão da Ribeira valley

The picturesque village of Seixal is sandwiched between high cliffs and the ocean. It is not built on a fajã as are so many other coastal villages, but on a young lava flow. The irregular surface of the coal-black lava is the result of the rapid loss of gas during the outflow.

At the edge of the lava there is a natural black beach and a *piscina natural*, but it is altogether less elaborate and fancy than the one at Porto Moniz.

High above the village lies the Seixal or Chão da Ribeira valley, which is highly recommended. It is, in contrast to the other Madeiran valleys wide and U-shaped – the result of a thick flow of lava that bulldozed its way down the valley creating its distinctive profile.

The Chão da Ribeira valley is a lovely, traditional area, with old houses and small farming plots at the base and laurel forest on the slopes. The woodland edges and bramble thickets around the village are excellent spots to search for Madeiran Speckled Woods and Madeira Brimstones. After passing the last houses, you can park and walk a few hundred metres to where the river enters the forest. This area is good for staking out Trocaz Pigeons that breed nearby. In autumn they also come down to feed in the fields (which is not appreciated by the farmers).

A short walk along the river is easy and will bring you to a narrow gorge, lined with some big trees. A steep and difficult hike, which we wouldn't recommend to anyone but the most dedicated hiker, starts here. Near the river though, look around to find Madeira Firecrest, Madeira Chaffinch, Grey Wagtail and other birds. Grey Herons are often around, attracted to the fish in the nearby trout farm.

The road towards the secluded valley of Chão da Ribeira.

L – Porto Moniz

Situated on the far western tip by the ocean, slightly bigger than nearby villages and with a number of tourist attractions, Porto Moniz is an agreeable

ADDITIONAL SITES

village – touristy enough not to be dull, small enough to retain some of its charm. The village's most eye-catching feature is its *piscina natural* – natural tidal pools filled by the ocean during high tides. The coarse lava edges have been smoothed to make a walkway, making access easy. This is not only superb bathing, it is also a great spot to see sea life of the intertidal zone. Porto Moniz has a large tidal bath and a smaller one with more sea life, just beneath the conspicuous islet off the coast. The latter is known as the *Ilhéu Mole* or Soft Island, as it consists of a volcanic cone covered by soft, yellowish tuff stone, which contrasts sharply with the black lava on the coast. Like in Seixal, the coarse black lava in Porto Moniz is the result of recent eruptions. The edge of the lava stream lies in the sea where irregular dark lava pools have been formed. The lava stream coagulated in the cold water, stopping the flow just in front of the *Ilhéu Mole*, which thus has a different volcanic origin.

During migration periods, Porto Moniz is the best seawatching spot of Madeira. High numbers of pelagic birds pass by in spring and autumn. Other than coast hugging species like Common Tern and Yellow-legged Gull, the most obvious species are Cory´s, Manx and (much rarer) Macaronesian Shearwaters and Bulwer´s Petrel. Desertas and Zino´s Petrel are less frequently seen. After the breeding season, Gannet, Great and Sooty Shearwaters and Great, Arctic and Pomarine Skuas pass by. Rarities from southern oceans have been seen too, such as Brown Booby. During our preparatory trip we even saw a South Polar Skua!

In summer and autumn whales and dolphins can be seen almost daily, the most regular being Sperm, Sei and Bryde´s Whale and Atlantic Spotted and Bottlenose Dolphins. Loggerhead Sea Turtle is also seen occasionally. Results of seabird and sea mammal counts are featured on the Dutch website **www.trektellen.nl**.

The boulevard is the best place for seawatching and we advise to use a telescope. An alternative is booking a room with balcony and ocean views so you can start watching from breakfast.

Do not forget to check out the small harbour. Also the Fort Saint John the Baptist, built in 1730, deserves a visit. Today it houses the small but pretty Madeira Sea Aquarium (open daily 10.00 to 18.00 pm; € 7.00).

The tidal pools of Porto Moniz.

ADDITIONAL SITES

M – Levada de Ribeiro Janela

High above Madeira's largest river, the Ribeiro Janela, runs the levada that goes by the same name. It traverses the largest single stretch of old laurel forest on the island and is for that reason alone worth the walk. The slope of this walk is gentle and in the end it meets the mythical Ribeiro Janela. Why mythical? Well, although it is the island's longest river, it runs through a completely inaccessible valley. The only way to get to it (apart from where it enters the ocean; see route 9), is walking this trail. However, it is a 13 kms walk before you come to the stream. The length of this trail alone makes it a hard walk to do in its entirety (but of course, no-one forces you to go all the way).

On the second part of the walk there are many tunnels (one of which is 2.5 kms long) which have waterfalls inside. It is impossible to stay dry there, so come prepared with waterproofs and torch! All in all an adventurous and beautiful walk.

To get to the starting point of the route, follow the direction of Funchal from Porto Moniz. After a number of hairpins, you come to a roundabout, from where you follow the sign to Ribeira da Janela.

There are plenty of tunnels on your walk along the Levada de Ribeiro Janela.

N – The crest route – from Encumeadas to Pico Ruivo

This high altitude route is the less busy alternative to the walk from Pico do Areeiro to Pico Ruivo (route 12). For many hikers who come to Madeira frequently, this is therefore the more attractive of the high mountain walks.

Like the Pico do Areeiro walk, this is a long, single direction route. It crosses the eastern mountains from east to west, starting at Encumeadas (starting point of route 11) and ending at Achadas da Teixeira (starting point of route 13). Or vice versa of course. This walk is too long to go back and forth in a single day, so it is best to arrange to be picked up when you've completed the walk. The crest route follows the north-south divide of the island and changes sides a couple of time, offering views to both the south and the north slopes. Apart from the views, the flora is amazingly rich. Among the birdlife, it is the Spectacled Warbler (in breeding season) that is the most attractive species.

EXCURSIONS

Excursions

The great wide ocean with its whales, dolphins and seabirds, the hidden, untamed gorges and the deserted islands – the Madeira Archipelago abounds in places that are hard, if not impossible to reach without local help.
Fortunately, there are plenty of choices for booking excursions with experts that take you to these spots. This section of the book is dedicated to these guided excursions. They vary from trips of 2.5 hour for € 30.00 meant for the general public to exclusive 5 day journeys that cost an arm and a leg. But first some general remarks.
There are many companies offering whale-watching trips, canyoning, sea-kayaking and trips to the Desertas islands. More aimed at the dedicated birdwatcher are the specialist trips on both the land and the ocean. The most exclusive of them all is a multiple day trip to the Selvagens Islands.
All these companies are to be found in the docks of Funchal (part of route 1, see map on page 119) and it won't take you much effort to book one there and then. Even a faint hint of interest will trigger the sales staff into action offering you their leaflets. It's up to you to decide whether to accept their offer or to (try to) shake them off. The latter becomes harder the longer you linger. How to make your choice?
The first thing to realise when seeking out your excursion is that many of these companies aim at a general audience. Madeira attracts a wide range of tourists sympathetic to nature and wildlife. A typical whale-watching tour for example will be a mix of actual whalewatching, an informative talk about sea life and a swim in the sea afterwards. By no means do we mean to disparage these trips (it is a great experience and views are generally excellent), but don't expect to find yourself in the selective company of men and women draped in optics.

Sailing to the Desertas Islands.

EXCURSIONS

There are very few companies that cater specifically to naturalists, bird-watchers and wildlife photographers. These are **www.venturadomar.com**, **www.madeirawindbirds.com** and **www.birdsandcompany.com**. Our experience is limited to Venturadomar, the oldest of these companies, run by knowledgeable marine biologists (who still do research on cetaceans) and have helped in editing the relevant chapters of this book. They offer pelagic birdwatching trips, birdwatching trips on the island and multiple day trips to the Selvagens and have a shop in the Funchal harbour too.

Preparations for an excursion on the ocean

Madeira's generally warm and sunny conditions promise pleasant voyage across the sea. Realise, however, that on the water, it is always much colder and windier than on land. How much depends not only on the day, but also on the kind of trip you're embarking on.

The conditions on a short dolphin-watching trip that stays on the leeward side of Madeira are not very different from those in Funchal, but the trips that venture out further or cross over to the Desertas catch the full force of the wind. The wind chill there can be considerable, so make sure to bring, like in the mountains, several layers of clothing topped off with something windproof. Also ask for advice about clothing when you book your excursion.

Other things not to forget are sunglasses and sunscreen. If you are susceptible to sea-sickness, make sure take your medication before setting out (as most manufacturers suggest) and that you have pills with you to avoid nausea.

1 – Whale and dolphin watching

  A trip to Madeira just isn't complete without a trip out to sea to see whales and dolphins. Year round, cetaceans (the collective name for whales and dolphins) are present in the Madeiran waters, especially in the calm waters on the south side of the island, which is where all companies head for. Although sightings can never be guaranteed, the trips have an incredible success rate for seeing dolphins, while whales are often seen in the summer months. Seeing three or four species in a single tour is not exceptional. Add to this the presence of seabirds and the distinct possibility of seeing sea turtles and you understand why this is such an exciting excursion.

The Madeiran companies often work together in locating the animals. That is, if it isn't the other way round – Common, Spotted and Bottlenose Dolphins often speed towards a boat and follow the bow, playing around

EXCURSIONS

or using the floaters (on catamarans) to scratch their backs. And can you blame them? What else can they use to get rid of an itch?! The views at such moments are superb. Photographers be warned – bring a standard or wide-angle lens as well. We've seen photographers standing in confusion with utterly useless telephoto lenses as their partners took great shots with their mobile phones of the dolphins jumping in and out of the water at an arm's length!

As far as we can tell, no harm is done by whale-watching, but nonetheless, there is a strict code, enforced by Portuguese law, that a single boat must leave a pod of dolphins or whales after ten minutes. Again in our experience and to the best of our knowledge, the companies strictly abide by this rule. Nevertheless, if you have the feeling the company you're with is breaking rules or ethical codes, ask the staff about their policy and report misconduct if needed.

Most whalewatching trips start in Funchal harbour and stay close to the coast, exploring the waters between, roughly, Garajau and Cabo Girão. In 2018, the prices were around € 15.– to € 40.– for a 2.5-4 hour trip. A single trip usually brings along several dozens of visitors.

There is often more to see than dolphins on a dolphin watching trip. One of the frequently seen 'extras' is the Loggerhead Turtle.

2 – Trip to the Desertas islands

From afar, the three islands that together form the Desertas appear impossibly steep and rough mountain crests that stick out of the ocean like a broken saw. When the boat

EXCURSIONS

approaches and you can see them from up close, they turn out to be just as forbidding and dramatic. It isn't until you are very near that you discover the sliver of level land near a secluded bay where you can land.

All three islands of the Desertas, including the surrounding ocean, are nature reserves. They are home to one of the world's last populations of Monk Seals (see page 92), the endemic Desertas Petrel and the large, endemic Desertas Tarantula (*Hogna ingens*; see page 113).

The warden's house – the only habitation on the Desertas. This is where you land during your excursion to the islands.

An excursion to the Desertas is another highlight of your wildlife holiday, although your expectations on seeing the above rarities shouldn't be too high – the spider lives in an inaccessible area, the seal is only occasionally encountered and even if seen the petrel is virtually impossible to distinguish from Zino's on the ocean. What remains is nevertheless a spectacular trip over the ocean with great chances to see seabirds, whales, dolphins and sea turtles, plus a short walk on the small coastal plain in the middle of the central island, Deserta Grande. Between June and August, you have on the island the rare chance of seeing sea birds like Cory's Shearwater and Bulwer's Petrel on their nest! During the crossing you'll see large numbers of them on the ocean.

Even more spectacular is spending a night on the Desertas during the breeding season, where, away from light pollution and the rumble of human civilization, you are submerged in what must be one of nature's most wondrous sounds – thousands of Cory's Shearwaters and hundreds of Bulwer's Petrels and Madeiran Storm-petrels are calling as they come ashore. Words fail to describe that experience.

On your Desertas trip look out for:

In and directly outside of the Funchal harbour, look for coastal birds: Yellow-legged and Black-headed Gull, Common Tern and Roseate Tern. Manx Shearwater is also a frequent bird.

After about 20 minutes the ship reaches the pelagic zone where the ocean is more than 1,000 m deep. Search here for the shearwaters, petrels and

EXCURSIONS

storm-petrels – all Madeiran species are possible. Large congregations of seabirds often point to the presence of a pod of dolphins or whales (and vice versa). In autumn and winter, Gannets and skuas may be present. All of the 29 species of cetaceans could be seen, the most frequent being Sperm, Bryde´s and Short-finned Pilot Whale and Atlantic Spotted, Common, Striped and Bottlenose Dolphins. A turtle may show up at any moment. The most abundant is the Loggerhead. You may also be surprised by some flying fish moving low over the waves and disappearing in the water.

Close to the Desertas, scan for the shy Monk Seal, which is most often seen to the south side of the Deserta Grande island, where their breeding caves are. In the water of the secluded bay where the boat lands, there are many fish.

The small area of flat land on Deserta Grande is the result of the collapse of part of the mountain a little over a century ago. Here is the warden's house (the only house on the islands) and a short trail that you'll follow with your guide. Berthelot's Pipit and Canaries are easy to see here, as well as the Desertas subspecies of the Madeira Wall Lizard.

Manx Shearwater (top) and Bulwer's Petrel (bottom).

3 – Pelagic birdwatching tour

Watching seabirds from a coastal headland is a great pastime but observing them from a boat is infinitely more exciting. During a pelagic birdwatching trip, you go out about 15 nautical miles, which is far enough to be able to encounter the truly pelagic birds like storm-petrels. There, a pellet of frozen fish remains is released which slowly dissolves in the ocean.

And then you wait.

As the 'chum' (this type of 'feeding the birds' is called chumming) dissolves and the odour spreads, seabirds pick up on it and start flocking in. At least that's the theory. In practice, it is always different but some of the 'goodies' are practically always seen. On our pelagic trip, we saw four species of storm-petrels (European, Madeiran, Wilson's and White-faced)! Check with the company for recent sightings.

An advantage of the sea south of Madeira is that, due to prevailing northerly winds, the sea is usually not too rough. The less wind, the less movement the boat makes and the easier it is to see the birds. Too little wind, however, makes it harder for the birds to pick up the smell, so it remains a delicate balance between mutually exclusive advantages.

On your tour you will be accompanied by experienced bird guides, who'll try to show you the petrels and shearwaters as well. Undoubtedly, of all the sea trips, this is your best choice for seeing and photographing seabirds. Even though billed as a birding trip, the guides won't shy away from making a brief stop if a Sperm Whale pops up or a pod of dolphins joins the boat. In other words, they are whale-watching guides too and know where the animals are.

Desertas Petrel

Trips are typically 4-6 hours and you'll go out with a small and fast RIB (rigid-inflatable boat). Make sure you have proper clothing to protect against wind and cold and keep in mind that a toilet stop is not an option.

4 – Zino´s Petrel night excursion

The Zino's Petrel is a very rare seabird that roams the oceans of the world, except in the breeding season, when, astonishingly, all of the 70-odd pairs return to Madeira to breed on the steep slopes of the Pico do Areeiro.

A night trip to their breeding grounds is a unique experience. Many excursions are called unique (in that sense none of them is), but this one really is something else. Up on the peak, high above the clouds and under the massive starry skies, you stand in absolute silence, until you start to hear the spooky calls of the Zino's Petrel.

The locals thought that those eerie sounds were the suffering souls of the dead shepherds who died in the mountains. It wasn't until the

ornithologist Francis Zino put two and two together and found out that the folklore related to the calls of a seabird (see page 102).

The Zino's Petrel night excursions can be booked between May to August. The trip only takes place when weather conditions are right (not too windy and no clouds). It is nevertheless bound to be cold (so come prepared) and you'll need a torch. The excursion involves some hiking in the dark in precipitous terrain (hence you shouldn't try this on your own) but is doable if you are in good condition.

5 – Land birdwatching

With this guide in hand, you don't really need to book an organised excursion to see Madeira's land birds, but it is certainly easy and informative to put yourselves in the hands of capable local birders. Birdwatching trips on Madeira take a half or a whole day and will aim at finding the harder-to-find species like Trocaz Pigeon, Roseate Tern and Spectacled Warbler, but will also give you time to observe the commoner ones like Madeira Firecrest, Canary and Plain Swift.

Time is spent in the mountains, the laurel forest and the coastal zone. No extensive walking or other physically challenging activities are involved in the birdwatching trip, so anyone can participate.

EXCURSIONS

6 – Five day cruise to the Selvagens islands

It is hard if not impossible to find a more remote and difficult-to-reach destination than the small Selvagens archipelago, which lies some 300 kms south of Madeira. These uninhabited islands (there is only a warden's house and occasionally there are some researchers) can only be reached on a boat trip from Madeira on a round trip which will take five days. The islands and the surrounding ocean form a reserve and only the nature tour organisation Venturodomar is licensed to organise trips to the Selvagens from Madeira. Even for them, it is not an annual event – yes, a journey to the Selvagens is that exclusive!

Even though chances are very small that you'll find yourself on such a trip, we nevertheless wanted to describe the possibility as it is as close as you'll get to a journey of discovery – even for the people organising the trip, the adventure is real and the experience exceptional.

The cruise takes five days and costs is € 1,100 (all inclusive, based on a trip of around 7 passengers) and it is wise to book well in advance. The trip is only possible when weather conditions allow it, between June and the middle of September.

Landing on Selvagem Grande (top). Madeira Firecrest (facing page). White-faced Storm-petrel (bottom).

PRACTICAL PART

TOURIST INFORMATION & OBSERVATION TIPS

Travel and accomodation

Travelling to Madeira and Porto Santo
The most popular way to travel to Madeira is by air. Madeira's main airport, named after the local football hero Cristiano Ronaldo, receives a steady flow of aircrafts from all over Europe. Tour operators offer package deals (flight plus hotel), sometimes with discounts, making for bargain prices. The downside is a lack of flexibility over the location and length of your stay. However, Madeira is a relatively small island, so this is not as critical as it might be elsewhere.

Porto Santo also has an airport, but with few international flights. Porto Santo is better reached by ferry (see page 169).

Very recently, a new car ferry line opened between Portimão in the Algarve and Funchal. The trip takes 24 hours and prices are reasonable (between € 85 and € 200 depending on your preferred level of comfort, and € 125 for a small car). Also very recent is the ferry from Funchal to Santa Cruz on Tenerife and Las Palmas on Gran Canaria. For more information: **www.madeira-ferry.pt/en**

Travelling on Madeira
A hire car is by far the easiest way to travel around. The motorways Vía Rápida VR1 and VR2 connect towns and villages near the coast and is definitely the quickest way to cross the island. Roads that go into the interior are good but sometimes steep and with many turns. There are no toll roads.

You can hire your car at the airport and in all towns and larger villages. Just to be certain however, we recommend hiring your car in advance via your travel agent or the internet.

The alternative to car hire is the bus service. This is definitely the cheapest means of transport and gets you to many places, but it is less convenient, not very fast and to make good use of them, you need to be familiar with bus timetables. Consult **www.horariosdofunchal.pt**. The cable cars provide quick and easy access to various sites, look at **www.telefericodofunchal.com** for the one in Funchal. The larger hotels also offer excursions and guided hikes into the interior of the island, which include a transfer by coach or taxi.

Taxis are yellow with a blue stripe and have official rates, which you can ask the driver to show you. Taxis are widely used for transport from hotel to the airport and to the start (or end) of levada walks. Ask the reception at your hotel to book a taxi or, alternatively, hail a taxi in the street, go to a taxi stand or book one on the internet – **www.taximadeira.com**.

Accommodation

The choice of your hotel and where to stay on the island depends on your personal choice. If you hire a car, all routes in this book are easily reached from anywhere on the island that is not too far from the main *Via rápida* (VR) coastal road. That way you don't need to divide your time between two locations – one hotel can serve as a base for all your trips on the island.

If you don't drive, Funchal is arguably the best place to stay, because it is at the centre of the bus network.

A possible exception is a visit to Porto Santo. It is worth considering spending one night there, so you can take your time exploring the island.

There is a distinct difference between the south and north side of Madeira. Overall, the south is busier, not only in terms of tourism, but also because most Madeirans live here and there is a lot of rather intense and unattractive agriculture, mainly west of Funchal in the form of banana plantations. This also means that the provision of services is greater and there is just more going on than in the north. Also, in the south there are more places to swim, the sun shines more often and it is more convenient if you plan on doing whale watching trips visiting Porto Santo.

Funchal is, despite its size, a charming town and has a wide range of hotels from rather inexpensive (and somewhat run down) mostly west of the old city centre to top end hotels with swimming pools in the vibrant tourism epicentre of São Martinho. The south-east of the island has the best weather and some attractive towns, like Machico.

The north arguably has more charm. Santana and nearby villages are authentic and quiet. Rural holiday homes are often in a spectacular setting and offer the perfect base for walks in the forests. The weather is the downside here. If you choose accommodation further up in the hills, you must be prepared for thick clouds and occasional rain, while knowing that on the other side of the island, people are walking around in shorts and T-shirts or sunning themselves by the pool.

Package deals: In spite of the general lack of beaches on the island, Madeira is popular as a sun and leisure destination. Therefore, package deals of flight and hotel are almost the rule if you book through a travel agency. Be careful as the hotels they offer are sometimes uninspiring. They often stress the ocean views, but that doesn't mean very much. It is hard to pick a spot on Madeira where the ocean isn't visible in the distance. The upside of package deals is that last minute prices can be

very low. Some final advice: pay special attention to the immediate surroundings of your hotel – a park or large garden attracts birds and wildlife and offers a potential for great sightings even from your hotel room.
Choosing your own hotel: there are beautiful, traditional guest houses called *Casa do Campo*, but there are very few of them. Most are situated on the sunny south side of the island and prices are usually reasonable. It is a different way to discover Madeira and brings you closer to local culture and to nature. On Porto Santo it is easy to find a privately owned holiday home or apartment.
Camp sites: camping is not the first thing that comes to mind when thinking about Madeira. It is possible though! There are two camp sites, one near Funchal and one near Porto Moniz and also Porto Santo has a *Parque de Campismo*, located near the long sunny beach.

Shops – opening hours
Small shops are open from Monday to Friday between 09.00 and 19.00, usually with a break for lunch from 13.00 to 15.00. On Saturdays they only open in the morning, between 09.00 and 13.00. Large supermarkets and shopping centres are open 7 days a week from 09.00 to 22.00 or later. The usual opening hours for banks and post offices are 09.00 until 13.00 and from 14.00 to 19.00, Monday to Friday. Some pharmacies stay open for 24 hours.
Bars where locals have breakfast open at 07.00 and some stay open until midnight. Most locals have a warm dish for lunch, usually between 13.00 and 15.00. The *prato do día* (dish of the day) is cheap and filling, with rice, potatoes, vegetables and meat or fish. Dinner is served from 19.00, but of course in tourist areas you can get a meal all day.

Safety issues

Both in terms of general security and natural hazards there is little to fear on Madeira. However, do keep the following in mind.
Theft: Crime is low on Madeira. The level of street crime that plagues some areas in the Mediterranean is completely unknown on Madeira. Nevertheless, the island is a major tourism destination and that alone should be a reason to be a little more alert. Try not to leave valuables in your car and certainly not in plain view.
Dangerous animals: no dangerous or poisonous animals occur on Madeira.
Climate: prepare for all kinds of weather! The laurel forest zone can be drearily damp or rain sodden, so bring a waterproof (and a jumper to put under it). Close to the coast, the wind can be very strong and high up in the mountains, you may have both. You may want to take a change of clothes with you in the car or rucksack.

If the sun is shining, it is warm and bright, so take sunglasses, a cap or hat and sun screen when in the sunny south of Madeira, above the clouds in the mountains or on Porto Santo. If you go out to sea, dress warmer than you think you might need, take a wind and showerproof jacket at least and do not forget your sun screen. Remember too to take any medication for seasickness before you set off.

Preparations for walking

The hiking on Madeira is superb! The spectacular rough and green slopes are laced with trails and the good news is that many of them are quite easy to walk – all thanks to the levadas for which more or less level walkways were constructed. Every now and then, these channels run through tunnels, which make your walk only more exciting.

You'll need to come prepared though. Fog and rain can make it quite cold on the slopes, especially in winter. Temperature difference can be very great between the south and north slopes. Before going out, check the weather forecast and choose the best days for walking in mountains or the laurel forests. Always take a waterproof with you, even if rain is not forecast. Water always drops from the trees and in the tunnels and some trails lead underneath small waterfalls. Parts of the trails are slippery pretty much throughout the year and you will encounter puddles in the tunnels, so put on good and waterproof walking shoes or boots.

The weather in the high mountains is unpredictable. When walking here, don't forget to pack the sunscreen and hat. Also note that there are not many levadas in the high mountains, so the trails tend to be more demanding.

Do not forget a torch for the tunnels, and of course a bottle of water, a small first aid pack and enough food for a long walk. Some trails are very narrow, others go up steep hillsides and are not good for those who have fear of heights. On the other hand, most if not all of levada trails (certainly those in this book) are lined with solid fencing where the slopes are steep, so trails are not particularly dangerous. The walking routes are marked with signs, so it is almost impossible to get lost.

Responsible tourism

Rambling and wildlife tourism on Madeira is booming. This makes the laurel forests, the spectacular cliffs, the cetaceans and sea turtles a valuable resource which, following an economic rationale, deserves protection. In principle, that is good news. Even if people don't recognise the intrinsic value of nature, one can make a case for the importance of conservation purely on commercial grounds. The interests of economic development and the preservation of nature align – at least to some extent.

On the island, you'll find wildlife walks and boat trips being advertised everywhere, but regulations to avoid damage to the environment are not so eagerly promoted.

Regulations that impede the touristic development are an inconvenient necessity. But a necessity nonetheless. Here are some tips to minimise the negative impact and maximise the positive effects of your visit.

Obviously, as a visitor to the nature reserves and other attractive areas of Madeira, you've an obligation to behave considerately and respectfully. Littering, picking flowers and disturbing wildlife are the obvious 'no-nos' when travelling here (or anywhere else). Note that the vegetation on Madeira is especially fragile. In busy places, like Rabaçal, Pico do Areeiro and Ponta da São Lourenço, don't stray from the trails. Many plants (and animals) here are extremely rare and therefore easily damaged or destroyed.

Ecotourism code of conduct

We appeal to every naturalist, birdwatcher and photographer to abide by this code of conduct in the interests of birds, wildlife and their environment.

- Learn patterns of animal behaviour – know when not to interfere with an animal's life cycle.
- Acquaint yourself with the fragility of the ecosystem – stay on trails to lessen your impact.
- When out in the field, use good judgement – treat the wildlife, plants and places as if you were their guest.
- Treat other observers and photographers courteously – ask before joining others already in an area.
- Keep distance to the birds to avoid stressing or exposing them to danger, exercise restraint and caution during observation, photography, sound recording or filming. Use appropriate lenses to photograph wild animals – if an animal shows stress, move back and use a longer lens.
- Keep well back from burrows, nests, colonies, roosts, display areas and important feeding sites. Do not handle birds, chicks or eggs unless for recognised research activities.
- Before advertising the presence of a rare species of plant or animal, evaluate the potential for disturbance, its surroundings and other people in the area, and proceed only if access can be controlled, disturbance minimized, and, where applicable, permission has been obtained from private land-owners. Unless officially publicised, the sites of rare nesting birds should be divulged only to the proper conservation authorities.
- Do not enter private property without the owner's explicit permission.
- Tactfully inform others if you observe them engaging in inappropriate or harmful behaviour – many people unknowingly endanger themselves and animals. If this doesn't help, report inappropriate behaviour to proper authorities.
- Be a role model – educate others by your actions; enhance their understanding.
- Support the protection of important bird habitat.

Coastal lagoons and freshwater ponds are important resting spots for migrant birds. When you go out birding, keep in mind that as these sites are small, birds are easily disturbed. Don't get too close.

The food you choose to buy is another way to take responsibility. A lot of food is imported from the mainland – either by boat or, if it is fresh, by plane. As far as possible choose foods produced on the islands, in particular the fresh goods like vegetables and fish (see below). This reduces the pollution that comes with transportation. Tap water is safe all over the islands, so there is no need to buy bottled water. Instead, bring a refillable bottle.

Be picky when choosing the company that takes you whale or bird watching. The noticeboards on kiosks on the quay of Funchal clearly show which are the more serious operators with ties to conservation organisations and research. In general, show that you care about the environmental policies of the company you choose. This is an incentive for those companies and for the government to take conservation seriously. Last but not least, visit exhibitions and information desks of nature conservation organisations (such as the Zino's Petrel exhibition on Pico do Areeiro) and donate to their causes.

Food

Typical Madeira food includes a lot of local fish and exotic fruits, often originating from Brazil, but grown on Madeira. It is a visual feast to go to the market in Funchal and walk along the fruit and vegetable stalls where you can buy and try this rich bounty.

The fishmarket is equally interesting. The different species of fish and seafoods are explained on big information boards on the walls.

We could write an extensive chapter on the Madeira food, but we will limit ourselves in listing the Madeiran specialities.

Bolo do Caco is a sweet Madeiran bread, made with sweet potatoes, flour, salt, and water, flattened and baked in the oven. Usually it is served hot with garlic and herb butter as an appetizer before the main dish.

The Prego is the Madeiran sandwich you can find in almost every café and snack bar. There are many variations, basically it is a Bolo do Caco with meat, lettuce, cheese, egg and whatever else they put in it. It looks somewhat like a hamburger.

Caldo Verde is a green soup, made of potatoes, onions, shredded kale and topped with a piece of sausage.

Açorda, a dish originally from the Algarve, consists of bread, olive oil, vinegar, garlic topped by a poached egg.

Lapas are limpets, the shellfish that live on the shoreline, attached to cliffs and boulders. Lapas are collected by the locals at low tide who sell them to the restaurants, where they are grilled with garlic butter to make a marvellous dish – the Madeiran version of the French escargots.

Among the fresh fish, **Espada** is the most famous Madeiran speciality. Espada is Portuguese for black scabbard fish or black swordfish, an impressive 'monster' of the deep sea (see page 37). It is caught only in few places in the world. It is worth seeing this impressive fish on ice in the fish market before ordering them in the restaurant. You will be delighted with its flavour. The fillets are seasoned with garlic, lemon juice, salt, and pepper. Accompanied by baked bananas gives it a tropical flavour.

Pargo is a sea bream. Most are caught on the west coast (it gave its name to Punta do Pargo). Pargo is grilled with olive oil and is delicious.

Bacalhau, codfish, is a cheap fish that can be prepared in many ways. It is very popular in Portugal. On Madeira they say there is a recipe for every day of the year. Traditionally, Madeiran cuisine is focused on the sea. Among the meat dishes, it is the **espetada** that is typical of Madeira. An espetada is a skewer with pieces of meat which is barbecued over a wood fire.

For dessert, try the **Bolo de Mel**, which is the traditional Madeiran cake (not to be confused with the English 'Madeira Cake', a sponge cake which was traditionally served with Madeira wine). Originally it was made with cane sugar syrup, and has been a part of the Madeiran cuisine since the introduction of the sugar cane. Today it is made with honey and can be bought almost everywhere. It remains edible for five years, so it is a perfect product to take home!

Do not forget the Madeira wine (see also page 59). Try it in the restaurant or buy a bottle in the shop.

It is hard to say to what extent any of these fine dishes are environmentally friendly, come from a sustainable catch or are 'organic'. Products with the official label 'organic', are about as rare as the Madeiran Wood Pigeon. This doesn't necessarily mean that all these products are environmentally unfriendly, merely that there are no labels. Our best advice is to stick with local products and to steer clear from those products that you know from your experience at home may not be very environmentally friendly (e.g. overfished, raised at great cost to the environment, etc).

Planning your trip

When to go
Madeira's climate shows relatively little seasonal change and the vegetation is ever-green. This makes the island a wonderful destination year-round. Nevertheless, there is a clear peak in the flowering season, the time in which most butterflies are out and the period in which most birds are present. That 'peak period' extends from May to early October.

The winter season (December to February) is the coolest season. Away from the (south) coast, it is chilly. The laurel forests are even wetter and foggier than normal and with few tourists around, they invite long contemplative walks. Since most birds on Madeira are residents, there are only a few birds that you'll miss in the winter time. The Plain Swift is absent and the sea birds are missing most of the specialities that make Madeira such an attractive destination in summer. There are a few wildflowers about, some of which have the winter season as their principle flowering period (e.g. the orchid Two-leaved Gennaria). Butterflies are generally scarce but in the gardens on the south slope, the more common Madeiran species can still be found.

In March and April, nature switches into spring mode. This is the period in which the wildflowers of the dry lowlands (Porto Santo, Ponta São Lourenço) are at their best. The Plain Swifts and Cory's Shearwaters arrive and since migration on the African coast is in full swing, an increasing number of vagrant birds are seen on the island. Mid-May to late June is spectacular. At this time, the high mountains turn into a visual feat of wildflowers, one that soon shifts to the flowers of the laurel forest. The seabird colonies are filling up with Bulwer's Petrels, shearwaters, storm-petrels and the Zino's and Desertas Petrels are returning. The winter cetaceans are replaced by the summer species.

Consider July as a transitional month. There are still many wildflowers, particularly in the laurel forests and high mountains, but some of the spring species have clearly gone over, while late summer ones are not yet or just beginning to bloom. Some butterflies, in particular Madeira Grayling, start to fly in this season and continue to be present until the beginning of autumn.

Come August, Madeira experiences what can be considered a second spring. A relatively large number of spectacular wildflowers start to bloom: Lily-of-the-Valley Tree, Foxglove Tree, Wollaston's and Golden Musschia, Madeiran Lady's-tresses are among the most spectacular wildflowers of the islands and they flower in this period. The numbers of seabirds are spectacular and this is also one of the best periods to see the larger species of whales.

From mid September to mid October, many of the aforementioned wildflowers are still in bloom and the birdlife is enriched with many migrants, including seabirds that can be seen from capes and vantage points from land.

From late October onwards, the quiet winter season starts again.

Additional information

Recommended reading

Many, but not all, field guides that cover Europe also include Madeira. If you don't want to pack your suitcase full with field guides, you may consider buying the new (2018) *Wildlife of Madeira and the Canary Islands* by John Bowler (Wildguides, ISBN 9781400889266).

- **Flora** For an island that is known as the flower island, wildflower guides are disappointingly scarce. Only the *Flora of Madeira* by J.R. Press and M.J. Short (Natural History Museum, ISBN 9781784270490) is a good, if dry and academic, source of information. It is a key with line drawings of the endemic species. It is an expensive book that we didn't find on the island but had to order online, well in advance. Locally there are a few flower guides, all of which focus more on the introduced species than on the native ones and none of them are very good.
  The superb online flora atlas of Portugal **www.flora-on.pt** is only just beginning to add Madeiran species to the site. If the team behind this website continues their excellent work, this could be a great reference in the future.
- **Marine mammals** In 2004, the Museu da Baleia published the excellent book *Cetáceos no Arquipélago da Madeira*. News, info, sightings and trip reports regarding dolphins and whales are publishes on **www.madeirawhales.com**. You also can report your own sightings.
- **Birds** The definitive European field guide is *Collins Bird Guide* by Lars Svensson (Harper Collins; ISBN-13: 9780007268146). It includes the Madeira endemics.
  In addition, you can buy Birds of the Atlantic Islands by Tony Clarke (Helm Guides; ISBN 9780713660234 Pub. 2006). It describes all the birds of the Macaronesian Islands, including all its vagrants. The latter group takes up two thirds of the book, which makes it less useful as a field guide but it is of interest as a reference guide.
  A less bulky and more recent (2011) but equally useful alternative guide to Clarke's book is the *Field Guide to the birds of Macaronesia* by Eduardo Garcia-del-Rey (Lynx ISBN; 9788496553712) which has the advantage having distribution maps (although these are more useful to visitors to the Canaries).
  Where to watch birds in the Madeira archipelago by Cláudia Delgado (SPEA; 9789729901898) and *A Birdwatchers' Guide to Portugal, the Azores & Madeira Archipelagos* By Colm Moore, Gonçalo Elias and Helder Costa (Prion; 9781871104134) offer information on where to watch birds (although these books offer little extra in addition to this guidebook).
  On the internet, there is quite a lot of information that can be consulted. Birds of the archipelagos of Madeira and the Selvagens II – new records and checklist

update (1995-2010) can be found on **www.researchgate.net**. A breeding bird atlas based on 2 x 2 km squares was published in 2004 as Birds of the Archipelago of Madeira and can be found on *www.atlasdasaves.netmadeira.com*. Information on seabirds, sea mammals and more can be found on **madeira.seawatching.net**. Trip reports of birdwatchers can be found on **www.cloudbirders.com**.

General information for naturalists and hikers There are many hiking guides for Madeira. They are all roughly similar in layout and have a considerable overlap in routes. Check Sunflower guides, Cicerone guides, Rother or Trailblazer and choose your preferred walking guide.

A great source of information (although one with considerable overlap with this book) is *Madeira natural history in a nutshell* by Peter Sziemer (ISBN 9789729177316). It is in English and although the language is a bit peculiar, it offers information on landscapes, species and geology. We could not buy it on the island but had to order it online.

The *Serviço de Parque Natural da Madeira* publish some outstanding leaflets on-line in English on some of the archipelago's reserves. The titles are *Ponta de São Lourenço, As Ilhas Desertas* and *As Ilhas Selvagens*. They can be consulted on **is-suu.com/parquenaturalmadeira/docs**.

The official tourist website is **www.visitmadeira.pt**.

Ecotourist companies

Several ecotourism companies work on the island, offering excursions for birds and butterfly watching, pelagic trips for birds, dolphins and whales, levada walks and more. This is a great way to experience the parts of the island (and the sea!) that are hard to visit by yourself. For more information, see page 186.

Maps

A good map is a must to get around on the island. If possible buy one before you go in your local specialist bookshop (if you have one) or online. In our opinion, the *Kompass guide* is the best (1:50,000), but ask if new maps are available. Whichever map you choose, make sure it is detailed enough to display all the hiking trails as well as a clear indication of elevation and slope.

A good alternative to a paper map is an app. Make sure you choose one on which you don't need internet connection, such as the free **maps.me**.

Observation tips

Tips for exploring the laurel forest
The laurel forest is the most exceptional and beautiful of the terrestrial habitats of Madeira. Besides the stunning landscape, the flora and fauna of the laurel forest is very rich. Here are some tips to get the best out of your visit to the laurel forest.
The most special atmosphere in the laurel forest is when there is fog. The air of mystery that comes with the limited, indistinct horizons and the deep green mosses, ferns and liverworts is amazing. For landscape photography, these are also the most rewarding moments (when sunny, the forest becomes a riot of bright spots that destroys all the depth in your photo). Usually, the fog builds up during the day and the transition period when the first wisps are forming is superb. Generally, this means that you should be well into the forest in mid morning.
The most beautiful laurel forest walks are quite popular with hikers, so it is another reason to start early to beat the crowds.
If you are looking for wildflowers, the levada sides and rocky areas are the best. In addition, the gorges and waterfalls have special plants you won't easily find elsewhere. This is also where the rarest plants of Madeira grow. These are also the most inaccessible places and we strongly advise against trying to enter these gorges if there is no trail. Apart from the sensitivity of these environments, exploring these steep places is seriously dangerous! Some of the rarest wildflowers of the laurel forests can be admired in the small botanical gardens in the middle of the laurel forest at Ribeiro Frio and Queimadas. Go and see them there!
The sought-after birds of the laurel forest – Madeira Firecrest and Trocaz Pigeon – are not hard to see. To observe them well, though, they each require a different strategy. For the Firecrest, go for a hike and wherever you hear the high-pitched vocalisations of a 'crest' (mostly near tall heaths) stop and look for movement. You'll see them, sooner rather than later – restless but not shy, like all crests. The Trocaz Pigeon is a stake-out bird. Go to a good vantage point (the *Balcões* for example; route 6) and scan until it flies by. The Trocaz Pigeon is a bird of the canopy which spends most of its time in the foliage high up in laurel trees. It is mostly seen flying from tree to tree (hence the vantage point) and with luck you can see it perched when it lands on a branch.

Tips for watching seabirds
Most seabird species are hard to spot, even in such a good place as Madeira. The best plan is to go out at sea with an organised trip for watching seabirds (see Ecotourist companies on page 187). They know where the birds (and sea mammals) are and sometimes throw fish remains and fish oil (chum) onto the ocean to attract the birds (see page 190). The ferry crossing to Porto Santo can also be rewarding.

Most seabirds stay away from the shore as much as possible. Vantage points that stick out into the ocean give you your best chance of seeing them, particularly during strong onshore winds, as numbers concentrate as they fly round the land. This is the case not only during the annual migration periods but also on a daily basis, as the birds 'commute' from the breeding grounds to the feeding waters. The best time of day for seawatching from the shore is in the morning and in the evening (the first few hours after sunrise and the final hours before sunset). If you choose your vantage point and time of day, take the light conditions into account.

Seabirds are not easy to identify, not in the least because they may be very distant and views are often fleeting, so pick a time and location when the light's behind you. Headlands such as Cabo Girão and Ponta do Pargo may seem like good vantage points, but they are too high up, which makes it difficult to pick out the birds. The best vantage points, such as Porto Moniz (site L on page 183) and Ponta da Cruz (site C on page 177) are at lower elevations; high enough so that birds are not hidden in the troughs of waves but low enough so that they occasionally rise above the horizon. However, despite its height, Garajau (site I on page 181) can be worth a try.

Once you've figured all of this out, it is a matter of scanning and waiting. A high-powered telescope on a stable tripod is better than hand-held binoculars. You may also be lucky enough to find a good seat in a bar at one of the vantage points.

Swimming

Admit it – even for the most hardcore naturalist a dip in the ocean looks tempting after a long, tiring walk on a hot day. Just to cool off and to not feel the constant

SWIMMING ON MADEIRA

pull of gravity on your feet. If it's not for you, then it's your family who'll enjoy an hour or two in the water.
Rugged Madeira has only a few good bathing sites on its coast and here they are:

1 - **Praia da Prainha** is one of the very few natural sand beaches on Madeira. It is little visited and wonderfully natural. See route 2 (point 7) for directions.
2 - **Praia da Ribeira Natal**, **Caniçal** is a rough pebble beach near the snorkelling centre of Caniçal (see page 124, also for directions).
3 - **Praia da Machico** is the only beach with Saharan sand, especially designed to accommodate beach lovers. It is small and the water is tranquil thanks to a breakwater. The beach is right next to the river mouth in downtown Machico.
4 - **Ponta Garajau Beach** is excellent for both swimming and snorkelling.
5 - There are various pebble and stone beaches between **Madalena do Mar** and **Ponta do Sol**. They are quite exposed, but on some you can swim. Follow the ER 101 / VE3 to find them.
6 - **Porto Moniz** with its famous tidal sea-bathing pools is definitely worth visiting (see site L on page 183).
7 - The small black beach and tidal pools of **Seixal** are a simpler and quieter version of those of Porto Moniz (see site K on page 183).
8 - Clearly the longest and best beach of the archipelago is not on Madeira but on **Porto Santo** (see page 171).

Snorkelling

Snorkelling in Madeira's seas is excellent. The sea life is rich and the waters are clear. The zenith of a snorkelling experience is a swim with dolphins or sea turtles.

There are two ways to go snorkelling – by yourself from one of the pebble beaches, or on an organised excursion. The latter will take you to the best places and is arguably safer, especially for beginners. Also, if you don't have your own equipment, you can hire it. The downsides are obviously that it is costlier and you are less free in where and when to go. Some companies offer a swim (or dive, for those who have a certification) between dolphins. You go out with a ship to a pod of dolphins and join them in the water. Seeing these agile animals dart through the water from beneath the surface is beautiful – quite a different experience than seeing the animals jump out of the water from a ship.

Being the rugged island that Madeira is, good snorkelling spots from the land are few, but there are several. What you need is an accessible beach in a tranquil part of the coast, which is nearly always on the south side of the island. The best places are Ponta Garajau Beach, the snorkelling centre just west of Caniçal and Praia da Prainha. See map and list above for details of their locations.

The diving companies that offer both snorkelling and diving trips are Explora Madeira Diving Centre (**www.exploramadeira.com**) and Madeira Divepoint (**www.madeiradivepoint.com**), both in Funchal. Mero Diving Centre (**www.merodivingcenter.com**) is situated in Garajau, Azul Diving Centre (**www.azuldiving.com**) in Canical, and Manta Diving Centre (**www.mantadiving.com**) in Caniço de Baixo.

On Porto Santo, snorkelling is excellent too. According to client reviews, the company Porto Santo Free Snorkelling Tour has an excellent track record in viewing submarine wildlife, in particular octopuses.

Gardens and Natural History Museums

Madeira abounds in interesting museums and gardens. A few of them (*Jardim Municipal do Funchal, Santa Catarina, Monte Palace Tropical Garden* and the *Jardim Botanico*) are described in route 1, while the semi-natural laurel forest parks (*parques florestales*) are part of route 6 and 14. We won't discuss those again in this chapter, but focus on some other interesting museums instead.

1 - Whale museum of Caniçal

The whale museum is devoted to the history of whaling on Madeira. The latter ceased as recently as 1982 and many whalers donated their whaling equipment to the museum. The collection contains many items and photographs of whaling on Madeira. The centre piece is a life-size replica of a Sperm Whale.

Open Tuesdays to Sundays from 10:00 to 12:00 and from 13:00 to 18:00.
www.museudabaleia.org

2 - Museum A Cidade do Açúcar

This museum is dedicated to the history of the sugar cane on Madeira.

Open: Monday to Friday from 9:00 to 17:30

Address: Praça Colombo n° 5; Funchal

Tel: +351 291 236 910

3 - Funchal Natural History Museum and Aquarium

The *Museu de História Natural* is situated in a historical eighteenth century building in Funchal. It shows an interesting collection of more than 41,000 fish, birds, mammals, marine

MUSEUMS ON MADEIRA

reptiles, invertebrates, plants as well as marine fossils, rocks and minerals from the Madeira archipelago. An aquarium is located on the ground floor where the coastal marine fauna of Madeira is represented. Here you have an excellent opportunity to get to know more about the underwater life of the Archipelago.
Open: Tuesday to Sunday from 10.00 to 18.00.
Address: Rua da Mouraria 31, Funchal; Tel.: +351 291 229 761

4 - Christopher Columbus House Museum
Christopher Columbus lived on Porto Santo at various periods in his life and was well enough established to marry the governor's daughter. The house he lived in is now a museum, devoted not only to his life on the island, but to the colonial history of Porto Santo and Madeira.
Open: Mondays and Wednesdays to Saturdays from 10:00 to 12:30 and from 14:00 to 15:30 / Sundays: 10:00 to 13:00.
Address: Travessa da Sacristia 2 e 4, Porto Santo

5 - Parque Temático
The farms in the hills above the north-Madeiran village of Santana have a special architecture with thatched houses known as *palhaças*. You can see them in the open-air museum *Parque Temático de Santana*. This popular 'theme park' has much more to offer: There is artisanal food and bread baking, you can see handicraft in action, there is an exhibition space with changing topics usually regarding the rural life of Madeira. All is set in a lush and flowery garden and with a playground for children.
Open: all year from 10:00 to 19:00 except on Christmas day
Address: Fonte da Pedra, Santana6; **www.parquetematicodamadeira.pt**

6 - Grutas de São Vicente Caves
Volcanic eruptions on Madeira some 890,000 years ago created a unique cave system just south of São Vicente. This is your unique chance to stand inside a lava tube – the channel through which thousands of cubic metres of liquid lava once rushed. Next to the caves is an information centre on volcanism, where you can book a guided visit to the cave where you can also experience a 'light and music show'.
Open: every day between 10:00 and 18:00 except Christmas (10:00 to 18:00).
Address: Sitio do Pé do Passo, São Vicente; **www.grutasecentrodovulcanismosaovicente.com/en/**

7 - Nucleo da dragoeiras das Neves
The small nature conservation centre of *Nucleo de Dragoeiras das Neves* protects a group of magnificent dragon trees – the most monumental ones on the island. They are the centrepiece of a beautiful garden with native plants of the warm lowland scrub. You can take a guided tour through the garden.
Open: Monday to Friday between 9:00 and 12:30, and between 14:00 and 17:30.
Address: Caminho da Portada, São Gonçalo 9060-245, Funchal.

Birdwatching list

The following bird list includes all breeding and wintering birds and regular passage migrants. Numbers between the brackets (...) refer to the routes from page 118 onwards. With fuller coverage of this relatively underwatched island, some rarer species may yet turn out to be regular if very scarce visitors in suitable conditions.

Shearwaters, petrels and storm-petrels This group of pelagic birds usually stay well off the coast (14, sites C and L on page 177 and 183, excursions on the ocean – see page 190). The best season to see them is April to October. Cory's Shearwater is the most abundant and can also easily be seen from the coast. Numbers of Manx and Macaronesian Shearwaters are much lower. Great, Balearic and Sooty Shearwater are seen on migration only. Bulwer´s Petrel is common, numbers of Zino´s Petrel and Desertas Petrel are low. Madeiran Storm-petrel is uncommon and numbers of White-faced Storm-petrel, Wilson´s, European and Leach's Storm-petrel are usually low.

Gannets and cormorants Northern Gannet is regular and most common on the ocean in winter (14, sites C and L on page 177 and 183, excursions on the ocean – see page 190). Great Cormorant is an irregular visitor.

Herons, egrets, storks, ibises and spoonbills Little Egret and Grey Heron don't breed but are present year round, visiting pools, reservoirs and river mouths (2, 3, 15). They are particularly fond of fish rearing pens, such as at São Lourenço (3). Low numbers of Purple Heron and Cattle Egret are seen during migration periods while Spoonbill and Glossy Ibis are occasionally recorded. They may occur in rivers or wetlands (2, 9, 15, site A on page 176).

Ducks Feral Muscovy Ducks are the most common ducks on Madeira. They are bred in freshwater ponds and river mouths (9, site A on page 176) where they seriously degrade the habitat for other birds. The Mallard is rare but still the most frequent wild duck on Madeira. Small numbers breed in ponds and reservoirs and on the golf course of Porto Santo (15). Escaped Mandarin Duck have bred in several reservoirs in Porto Santo. Teal is a rare winter visitor. Some northern European ducks such as Gadwall and American ducks such as Green-winged Teal are seen occasionally.

Birds of prey The Sparrowhawk is a breeding resident of forested areas on Madeira and Porto Santo (6, 7, 8, 9, site J on page 182). It is widespread but occurs in low numbers with more pairs on higher altitudes in the laurel forests. Due to its forest dwelling habits it is not easy to see. The Buzzard is a common breeding bird on Madeira and Porto Santo from the coast up to high in the mountains. Buzzards can be encountered in many places (2, 4, 7, 10, 12, 15, 16). The Kestrel is the commonest raptor in the archipelago and easy to spot on all routes.

Partridges, rails, crakes and coots The introduced Red-legged Partridge occurs in open land on Madeira and Porto Santo. (3, 5, 10, 12, 15, 16). The Quail is a rare and decreasing resident breeder on Madeira (3, 5) and Porto Santo (14), more frequent on the latter island. The Moorhen and Coot, both recent colonists, are scarce residents of Madeira and Porto Santo (2 (only Moorhen), 15 and site A on page 176).

Waders Kentish Plover is a resident but rare breeder on Porto Santo (15). Woodcock is a resident breeder in the moist forests of Madeira (e.g. 7, 9). Both are hard to spot. Many other wader species occur on the coast on migration or during winter, usually in small numbers and many more are irregular or vagrants. The most regular visitors (mainly passage/winter) are Ringed Plover, Redshank, Greenshank, Whimbrel and Common Sandpiper plus, less frequently, Dunlin, Ruff, Snipe and Curlew. In winter the coasts hold good numbers of Sanderling and Turnstone (scarcer in other months). Good routes for these birds are 1, 2, 3, 4, 15 and site A on page 176).

Gulls and terns Atlantic Yellow-legged Gull is an abundant breeding bird on all islands. Black-headed and Lesser Black-backed Gulls are regular winter and passage visitors, as are Arctic, Pomarine and Great Skuas. Common Tern breeds and can be found all along the coast. Route 1 and 4 are best to see the rare Roseate Tern, which breeds in low numbers on islets off the coast.

Doves and pigeons Rock Dove or Feral Pigeon is widespread on Madeira, Porto Santo and Desertas. The population of the Trocaz Pigeon on Madeira is increasing and is now fairly common in the laurel forests. It can be seen on all laurel forest routes, but the best places are the *Balcões* at Ribeiro Frio (6), Ribeira da Janela (9) and Blandy Garden (site E on page 179). Just wait and scan the canopy until you see some birds in flight.

Turtle Dove is a migrant and a very rare (perhaps extinct) breeding bird on Madeira. The Collared Dove has recently colonized Porto Santo (15) and Madeira (2, site L on page 183).

Parakeets Escaped Rose-ringed Parakeet live in the Funchal area.

Owls The Barn Owl is a widespread but uncommon breeding bird on Madeira and Porto Santo in agricultural areas, towns and villages (1, site I on page 181). Short-eared Owl is seen on passage and in winter.

Swifts The Plain Swift breeds on Madeira from sea level up to the highest mountain peaks and on small rocky islands surrounding it (e.g. 1, 3, 9, 10, 12). It is common all around the islands and easy to spot in summer. Pallid Swift is a rare breeder of Madeira, present from February to October. It can be seen near the coast and at intermediate altitudes, good areas are Funchal (1), Ponta do Garajau (I), Ribeira Brava (A) and Ponta do Pargo (5). Common Swift is seen in small numbers on passage.

Bee-eaters, rollers and hoopoes Hoopoe is a rare breeding resident on Madeira (2, 3) and a common resident on Porto Santo (15) where it can be seen anywhere and especially on the golf course. Small numbers of Bee-eaters and Rollers are seen during the migration periods.

Larks Skylark is a migrant and winter visitor in low numbers (e.g. 5, 10, 15).

Martins and swallows Swallow and House Martin are regularly seen during migration in small numbers. Other members of the family are rare.

Pipits and wagtails The Berthelot´s Pipit is a locally common resident on Madeira of open dry habitats (2, 3, 10, 13, 15 and 16, also on the Desertas). The Grey Wagtail is a fairly common resident and breeding bird on Madeira. It lives wherever there is fresh water, from the coast to the high mountains and even can be seen in Funchal (1, 2, 4, 9; sites J and K on pages 182-183). The White Wagtail is a winter bird and passage migrant.

Thrushes, chats, wheatears, redstarts and allies Blackbirds and Robins are common breeding residents of woodlands and gardens all over Madeira. Robins on Porto Santo are probably migrants. Redstart, Black Redstart and Wheatear are regularly seen on migration. Redwing and Fieldfare are rare visitors in exceptional winters. Mistle Thrush is also rare but may have bred.

Warblers The Spectacled Warbler is a scarce and localised resident on Madeira. It breeds in open areas with pastures, grasslands and bushes (3, 10, 12, 13, 15). The Blackcap is widespread on Madeira in gardens and forests, especially common at lower altitudes and present up to about 1000 m. Chiffchaff is a scarce and irregular visitor. Other warblers have occurred but are all exceptional or vagrants.

The Madeira Firecrest breeds on Madeira in the laurel forests and other woodlands and large gardens, with the highest densities in areas covered with Tree Heath (1, 6, 7, 8, 9,10 11 and 14).

Flycatchers Both Spotted and Pied Flycatcher are regularly seen during migration.

Shrikes and orioles Golden Oriole and Woodchat Shrike visit the islands during migration.

Starlings and sparrows The Spanish Sparrow breeds in the south of Madeira (2, very rare) and on Porto Santo (15, common). Rock Sparrow is a resident breeder in the eastern point of Madeira (3) and on Porto Santo (15, 16). The Starling is a winter bird that is in some years fairly numerous.

Finches The Madeira Chaffinch is common (and tame!) in forests of middle and higher altitudes (6, 7, 8, 9, 11, 12, 13). In the winter it visits rural areas. The Canary has a wide distribution on Madeira, Porto Santo and Desertas. It can be seen in villages, bushy and grassy areas and forms flocks of up to dozens of birds (1, 2, 3, 4, 5, 9, 10, 15). The Goldfinch is more common on Porto Santo than on Madeira (1, 2, 15). The Common Linnet is a resident breeder on Madeira (4; rare) and Porto Santo (15, 16). Small numbers of Greenfinch breed in cultivated areas and gardens on Madeira. Unexpectedly, Siskin bred on Madeira in 2002 north of Funchal near Montado do Pereiro and in subsequent years more pairs have been found.

Exotics. The Common Waxbill sustains a stable population on Madeira. It breeds near the coast and can be seen in river mouth with reeds in villages (2, site A on page 176).

ACKNOWLEDGEMENTS

It took many pleasurable hours in the field to make this book. But that wasn't enough. Nor was the equally enjoyable time that we spent with our noses in books and on the internet, browsing for sources and information. The help we had from experts, both local and not-so-local, was vital to create to book in front of you.

We are indebted to Miguel Pinto da Silva Menezes de Sequeira, botanist from the University of Madeira, for his insights in the vegetation, flora and natural history of the island. Felipe Silva and Luis Diaz gave us important information on bird-life and cetaceans of Madeira. Madeira-traveller Klaas van Dort helped us in compiling the final route list from our own 'long-list', while Frank Verslype checked several of the routes and Chris van Swaaij researched some of the good butterfly and dragonfly sites. Long-standing Crossbill Guides author and entomologist Albert Vliegenthart wrote the chapters on the insects, while Crossbill-member and botanist Kim Lotterman checked the botanical information. We warmly thank John Cantelo and Brian Clews for their careful editing work.

Finally, as with all our guides, good photography is very important for our books. And although Madeira is such a dramatic island that it is easy to make wonderful photos, it is actually quite hard to come by photos of some of the rare or shy species, not to mention the ones that live far out on the ocean. We thank all photographers for sharing their great shots with us. Furthermore, we greatly appreciate Chris Winter and Nicole Nijhuis sharing with us their Madeira experiences and stories of the Selvagens expedition they undertook in 2005. It has been an important base of our Selvagens Islands description.

Dirk Hilbers and Kees Woutersen
Crossbill Guides Foundation – March 2019

PICTURE CREDITS

In the references that follow, the numbers refer to the pages and the letters to the position on the page (t=top, c=centre, b=bottom, with l and r indicating left and right).

Crossbill Guides / Hilbers, Dirk: cover, 4 (1st, 3rd and 4th), 5 (2nd and 4th), 10, 13, 14, 16, 17, 20, 21, 22, 23 (all photos), 24, 26, 28, 31 (b), 33, 36, 38 (t), 42, 43, 44 (t, b), 45, 46 (t), 47, 48 (t, b), 50, 51 (t), 52, 54, 57 (t, b), 58 (t), 59, 62,63 (t), 64, 66, 68, 70, 75 (c), 76 (b), 78 (1st, 2nd, 3rd), 79 (t), 80 (1st), 81 (2nd, 4th), 82 (3rd, 4th), 83 (1st, 4th), 87, 96 (b), 99 (t, c, b), 102, 104, 107 (t, b), 109 (t), 110 (t), 114, 115 (t), 116, 119 (t, b), 120 (b), 123 (t), 125 (b), 126 (t, b), 128 (t, b), 129, 133, 135 (t, b), 136, 137, 140 (b), 142 (t, b), 143, 145, 146, 147, 149 (t, b), 150 (t, b), 153, 156 (b), 159, 160 (t, c, b), 161, 163 (t, b), 166, 167, 170, 171, 172 (t), 174 (t+b), 175, 180, 183, 186, 188 (t), 189, 190 (b), 192, 193 (b), 194
Crossbill Guides / Woutersen, Kees: 4 (2nd), 5 (1st and 3th), 15, 29 (r), 39 (t), 41, 46 (b), 58 (b), 60, 61, 73 (r), 78 (b), 86, 112 (b), 113, 121 (t, b), 124, 125 (t), 131, 139 (t, b), 169, 176 (b), 177, 181, 182, 184, 185
Gérard: 156 (t)
Nijhuis, Nicole: cover, 18, 19, 38 (b), 91, 92 (t, b), 98, 101, 106, 115 (b), 120 (t), 172, 118 (b), 190 (t), 193
Sonius, Petra: 30, 157 (t)
de Vries, Kees: 39 (b), 191
van Vugt, Rogier: cover, 53 (t, b), 64 (t), 73 (l), 76 (t), 79 (2nd, 3rd, 4th), 80 (2nd, 3rd, 4th), 81 (1st, 3rd), 82 (1st), 84 (t, b), 140, 154 (b), 157 (b), 164 (t, c, b)
van Swaaij, Chris: 108 (t)
Uriarte, Pilar: 37, 132
Saxifraga / Prius, Ben: 112 (t)
Saxifraga / Vastenhouw, Bart: 109 (b)
Silva, Felipe: 95, 103, 123 (b), 176 (t), 179
Vlot, Jorris: 29, 94, , 154,
Van der Wielen, Pierre: 51 (b), 90
Zut, Miranda: 31 (t), 63 (b), 75 (t, b), 82 (2nd), 83 (2nd, 3rd), 88, 89, 96 (t), 108 (b), 110 (b), 151
Wikimedia Commons CC 4.0 – Patrice78500: 85

SPECIES LIST & TRANSLATION

215

The following list comprises all species mentioned in this guidebook and gives their scientific, German and Dutch names. It is not a complete checklist of the species of Madeira. Some names have an asterisk (*) behind them, indicating an unofficial name. See page 7 for more details.

Flora

English	Scientific	German	Dutch
Acacia, Black Wattle	Acacia mearnsii	Schwarzholz-Akazie	Zwarte acacia*
Agapanthus	Agapanthus praecox	Südafrikanische Schmucklilie*	Afrikaanse lelie
Aichryson, Glabrous	Aichryson divaricatum	Madeira-Aichryson*	Madeira-steenlook*
Aichryson, Hairy	Aichryson villosum	Behaartes Aichryson*	Harig steenlook*
Andryala, Downy*	Andryala glandulosa	Drüsige Wolldistel	Madeira-wolsla*
Asphodel, Hollow-stemmed	Asphodelus fistulosus	Röhriger Affodill	Holle affodil*
Balm, Canary	Cedronella canariensis	Kanaren-Zitronenstrauch	Cedronella
Bean-caper, Desfontaines*	Zygophyllum fontanesii	Desfontaines-Jochblatt	Zygophyllum*
Beech, European	Fagus sylvatica	Buche	Beuk
Bilberry	Vaccinium myrtillis	Heidelbeere	Blauwe bosbes
Bindweed, Massoni's	Convolvulus massonii	Madeira Winde	Madeira-winde*
Blueberry, Madeiran	Vaccinium padifolium	Madeira Heidelbeere	Madeira-bosbes
Bracken	Pteridium aquilinum	Adlerfarn	Adelaarsvaren
Brookweed	Samolus valerandi	Salz-Bunge	Waterpunge
Broom, Common	Cytisus scoparius	Besenginster	Gewone brem
Bush-madder, Noble*	Phyllis nobla	Edle Phyllis	Struikmeekrap*
Butcher's-broom, Climbing	Semele androgyna	Zwittrige Semele	Klimmende muizendoorn*
Butcher's-broom, Madeira	Ruscus streptophyllus	Madeira Mäusedorn	Madeira muizendoorn*
Buttercup, Canary	Ranunculus cortusifolius	Kanaren-Hahnenfuss	Canarische boterbloem
Campion, Sea	Silene uniflora	Klippen-Leimkraut	Zeesilene*
Canary-grass, Bulbous	Phalaris aquatica	Wasser-Glanzgras	Knolrietgras*
Caterpillar Plant	Scorpiurus muricatus	Stachlicher Skorpionsschwanz	Schorpioenstaart
Chestnut, Sweet	Castanea sativa	Edelkastanie	Tamme kastanje
Coral-necklace	Illecebrum verticillatum	Knorpelkraut	Grondster
Crane's-bill, Anemone-leaved*	Geranium palmatum	Anemonenblättriger Storchschnabel	Anemoonbladige ooievaarsbek*
Cypress, Monterey	Cupressus macrocarpa	Monterey-Zypresse	Montereycipres
Elder, Madeiran	Sambucus lanceolata	Madeira-Holunder	Madeira-vlier*
Fern, Chain	Woodwardia radicans	Wurzelnder Kettenfarn	Woodwardia
Fern, Deer's-tongue*	Elaphoglossum semicylindricum	Kleine Hirschzunge*	Hertentongvaren*
Fern, Disc-leaved*	Adiantum reniforme	Talerfarn	Schijfvaren*
Fern, Filmy	Hymenophyllum tunbrigense	Englischer Hautfarn	Platte vliesvaren
Fern, Hard	Blechnum spicant	Rippenfarn	Dubbelloof

TOURIST INFORMATION & OBSERVATION TIPS

Fern, Hare's-foot	Davallia canariensis	Kanaren-Davallia	Davallia*
Fern, Japanese Holly	Cyrtomium falcatum	Sichelfarn	IJzervaren
Fern, Killarney	Vandenboschia speciosa	Prächtige Dünnfarn	Prachtvaren*
Fern, Madeiran Sickle*	Polystichum falcinellum	Madeira-Schildfarn*	Madeira naaldvaren*
Fern, Maidenhair	Adiantum capillus-veneris	Venushaarfarn	Venushaar
Fern, Tasmanian Tree	Dicksonia antarctica	Australischer Taschenfarn	Tasmaanse boomvaren
Figwort, Madeira*	Scrophularia hirta	Madeira Braunwurz	Madeira-helmkruid*
Fleabane, Mexican	Erigeron karvinskianus	Mexikanisches Berufkraut	Muurfijnstraal
Flower, Bird of Paradise	Strelitzia reginae	Paradiesvogelblume	Paradijsvogelbloem
Forget-me-not, Changing	Myosotis discolor	Buntes Vergissmeinnicht	Veelkleurig vergeet-mij-nietje
Foxglove, Purple	Digitalis purpurea	Roter Fingerhut	Gewoon vingerhoedskruid
Gennaria, Two-leaved	Gennaria diphylla	Zweiblättriger Grünstendel	Tweehartenorchis
Globularia, Willow-leaved	Globularia salicina	Weidenartige Kugelblume	Wilgbladige kogelbloem*
Gorse, European	Ulex europaeus	Stechginster	Gaspeldoorn
Hare's-ear, Willow-leaved*	Bupleurum salicifolium	Weidenblättriges Hasenohr	Wilgbladig goudscherm*
Hawkweed, Madeira*	Tolpis macrorhiza	Madeira-Pippau	Madeira-schijnhavikskruid*
Heath, Besom	Erica platycodon	Besen-Heide	Bezemdophei
Heath, Madeiran	Erica maderensis	Madeira-Glockenheide	Madeira hei*
Heath, Sea	Frankenia laevis	Glatte Frankenie	Zeehei*
Heath, Tree	Erica arborea	Baum-Heide	Boomhei
Heath, White Sea*	Frankenia pulverulenta	Seeheide	Witte zeehei*
Heberdenia	Heberdenia excelsa	Heberdenie	Heberstruik*
Herb-Robert, Giant*	Geranium maderense	Madeira Storchschnabel	Madeira-ooievaarsbek
Houseleek, Disc*	Aeonium glandulosum	Madeira-Aeonium*	Madeira huislook*
Houseleek, Viscid*	Aeonium glutinosum	Klebriges Aeonium*	Kleverige huislook*
Iceplant	Mesembryanthemum crystallinum	Kristall-Mittagsblume	IJsplantje
Jacaranda	Jacaranda mimosifolia	Palisanderholzbaum	Jacaranda
Jasmine, Wild	Jasminum odoratissimum	Wohlriechender Jasmin	Welriekende jasmijn
Juniper, Madeiran	Juniperus cedrus	Zedern-Wacholder	Madeira-jeneverbes*
Lady's-tresses, Madeiran	Goodyera macrophylla	Madeira-Netzblatt	Madeira-dennenorchis
Laurel, Barbusano*	Apollonias barbujana	Barbusano	Barbusano laurier*
Laurel, Canary	Laurus novocanariensis	Kanaren-Lorbeer	Canarische laurier
Laurel, Stink	Ocotea foetens	Stinklorbeer	Stinklaurier*
Lavender, Pinnate*	Lavandula pinnata	Gefiederter Lavendel	Veerbladige lavendel*
Leek, Three-cornered	Allium triquetum	Dreikantiger Lauch	Driekantig look
Lichen, Red Beard	Usnea rubicunda	Rote Bartflechte	Rood baardmos
Lily, Ginger	Hedychium gardnerianum	Zieringwer	Siergember
Lobelia, Heath	Lobelia urens	Land-Lobelie	Brandlobelia
Mahogany, Madeira	Persea indica	Indische Persea	Indische laurier*
Marguerite, Madeira*	Argyranthemum pinnatifidum	Madeira-Kanarenmargerite	Madeira-margriet*
Marguerite, Mandon's	Argyranthemum p. ssp succulentum	Sukkulente Kanarenmargerite*	Dikbladige margriet*

Milkweed	Gomphocarpus fruticosus	Baumwoll-Seidenpflanze	Afrikaanse zijdeplant*
Moneywort, Madeiran	Sibthorpia peregrina	Madeira-Sibthorpie*	Schijnhondsdraf*
Mountain-Tea, Porto Sancto*	Sideritis candicans	Weissliches Gliedkraut	Madeira ijzerkruid*
Musschia, Desertas*	Musschia isambertoi	Isamberto´s Riesenglockenblume	Isamberto's madeiraklokje*
Musschia, Golden*	Musschia aurea	Madeira-Riesenglockenblume	Madeiraklokje*
Musschia, Wollaston's*	Musschia wollastonii	Wollaston´s Riesenglockenblume	Wollaston's madeiraklokje*
Myrtle, Bog	Myrica gale	Gagel	Wilde gagel
Myrtle, Candleberry	Myrica / Morella faya	Makaronesischer Gagelbaum	Canarische gagel*
Navelwort	Umbilicus rupestris	Felsen-Nabelkraut	Muurnavel
Oak, Pedunculate	Quercus robur	Stiel-Eiche	Zomereik
Orchid, Dense-flowered	Neotinea maculata	Gefleckte Waldwurz	Nonnetjesorchis
Orchid, Madeira Marsh*	Dactylorhiza foliosa	Madeira-Knabenkraut	Madeira-rietorchis*
Orchid, Madeiran Early-purple*	Orchis scopulorum	Felsen-Knabenkraut	Madeira-mannetjesorchis*
Parsley, Black*	Melanoselinum decipiens	Schwarze Petersilie	Zwarte peterselie*
Pericallis, Eared*	Pericallis aurita	Madeira-Cinerarie	Madeira pericallis*
Picconia	Picconia excelsa	Picconia	Picconia
Pine, Maritime	Pinus pinaster	Strandkiefer	Zeeden
Plantain, Ascherson's*	Plantago aschersonii	Kanaren-Krähenfuss-wegerich*	Canarische hertshoornweegbree*
Plantain, Shrubby*	Plantago arborescens	Bonsai-Wegerich*	Bonsaiweegbree*
Polypody, Macaronesian	Polypodium macaronesicum	Makaronesischer Tüpfelfarn	Eilandeikvaren*
Pride of Madeira	Echium candicans	Madeira-Natternkopf	Madeira slangenkruid*
Pride of Madeira, Small*	Echium nervosum	Prächtiger Natternkopf	Prachtslangenkruid*
Red-cedar, Japanese	Cryptomeria japonica	Sicheltanne	Japanse ceder
Savoury, Madeira	Micromeria thymoides	Veränderliche Bergminze	Madeira-bonenkruid*
Saxifrage, Madeira*	Saxifraga maderensis	Madeira-Steinbrech*	Madeira steenbreek*
Saxifrage, Porto Santo*	Saxifraga portosanctana	Porto-Santo-Steinbrech*	Porto Santo steenbreek*
Seakale, Shrubby	Crambe fruticosa	Madeira-Meerkohl*	Madeira bolletjeskool*
Sea-lavender, Lowe's*	Limonium lowei	Lowe-Strandflieder*	Lowes lamsoor*
Selaginella	Selaginella denticulata	Gezähnter Moosfarn	Mediterrane selaginella*
Sideroxylon	Sideroxylon mirmulans	Sideroxylon	Sideroxylon
Smilax, Canary	Smilax canariensis	Kanaren-Stechwinde	Canarische steekwinde
Snakeroot, Sticky	Ageratina adenophora	Wasserdost, Drüsiger	Knopaster*
Sow-thistle, Madeiran*	Sonchus ustulatus	Brand-Gänsedistel*	Aangebrande melkdistel*
Sow-thistle, Pinnate*	Sonchus pinnatus	Stiel-Gänsedistel*	Gesteelde melkdistel*
Sow-thistle, Tree*	Sonchus fruticosus	Löwenzahnbaum	Reuzenmelkdistel*
Spleenwort, Maidenhair	Asplenium trichomanes	Braunstieliger Streifenfarn	Steenbreekvaren
Spurge, Fish-stunning	See Spear-leaved Spurge		
Spurge, Honey	Euphorbia mellifera	Honiggebende Wolfsmilch	Honingwolfsmelk*
Spurge, Spear-leaved*	Euphorbia piscatoria	Speerblättrige Wolfsmilch*	Speerbladige wolfsmelk*
Squill, Madeiran	Scilla madeirensis	Madeira-Blaustern	Raketsterhyacint*
St. John's-wort, Trailing	Hypericum humifusum	Niederliegendes Johanniskraut	Liggend hertshooi

English	Scientific	German	Dutch
St. John's-wort, Canary	Hypericum canariense	Kanaren-Johanniskraut	Canarisch hertshooi*
St. John's-wort, Large-leaved*	Hypericum grandifolium	Grossblättriges Johanniskraut	Grootbladig hertshooi*
Stock, Madeira Sea*	Matthiola maderensis	Madeira Levkoje	Madeira-violier*
Stonecrop, Mealy*	Sedum farinosum	Mehlige Fetthenne	Melig vetkruid
Sycamore	Acer pseudoplatanus	Berg-Ahorn	Gewone esdoorn
Tail, Peacock	Padina pavonia	Trichteralge	Trechteralg
Thistle, Broad-leaved*	Cirsium latifolium	Lorbeerwald-Kratzdistel*	Laurierbosdistel*
Thistle, Willow-leaved Carline *	Carlina salicifolia	Weidenblättrige Eberwurz	Wilgbladige driedistel*
Thrift, Madeiran*	Armeria maderense	Madeira Grasnelke	Madeira Engels gras*
Thyme, Madeira*	Thymus micans	Madeira-Thymian*	Madeira-tijm*
Tree, African Tulip	Spathodea campanulata	Afrikanischer Tulpenbaum	Afrikaanse tulpenboom
Tree, Blue Gum	Eucalyptus globulus	Blauer Eukalyptus	Blauwe gomboom
Tree, Dragon	Dracaena draco	Drachenbaum	Drakenbloedboom
Tree, Lily-of-the-valley	Clethra arborea	Immergrüne Scheineller	Lelietje-van-dalen-boom
Tree, London Plane	Platanus x hispanica	Ahornblättrige Platane	Gewone plataan
Tree, Madeira Foxglove*	Isoplexis sceptrum	Madeirische Fingerhut	Madeira-vingerhoedskruid*
Tree, Madeira Olive	Olea maderensis	Madeira-Ölbaum	Madeira-olijfboom*
Trefoil, Pitch	Bituminaria bituminosa	Asphaltklee	Pekklaver
Trefoil, Silvery*	Lotus glaucus	Silber-Hornklee*	Zilveren rolklaver*
Valerian, Annual	Centranthus calcitrapae	Fussangel-Spornblume	Dwergspoorbloem*
Violet, Common Dog	Viola riviniana	Hain-Veilchen	Bleeksporig bosviooltje
Violet, Madeira*	Viola paradoxa	Madeira-Veilchen	Madeira-viooltje*
Violet, Sweet	Viola odorata	Duft-Veilchen	Maarts viooltje
Viper's-buglosses	Echium spec.	Natternkopf	Slangenkruid
Wallflower, Shrubby	Erysimum bicolor	Zweifarbiger Schöterich	Tweekleurige muurbloem*
Walnut	Juglans regia	Echte Walnuss	Okkernoot/Walnoot
Willow, Canary	Salix canariensis	Kanaren-Weide	Canarische wilg
Wormwood, Madeira*	Artemisia argentea	Madeira-Beifuss	Madeira-bijvoet*
Wrack, Bladder	Fucus vesiculosus	Blasentang	Blaaswier

Mammals

English	Scientific	German	Dutch
Bat, Grey Long-eared	Plecotus austriacus	Graues Langohr	Grijze grootoorvleermuis
Bat, Leisler's	See Lesser Noctule		
Dolphin, (Atlantic) Spotted	Stenella frontalis	Zügeldelfin	Atlantische gevlekte dolfijn
Dolphin, (Atlantic) Striped	Stenella coeruleoalba	Streifendelfin	Gestreepte dolfijn
Dolphin, Bottlenose	Tursiops truncatus	Grosstümmler	Tuimelaar
Dolphin, Common	Delphinus delphis	Gemeiner Delfin	Gewone dolfijn
Dolphin, Risso´s	Grampus griseus	Rundkopfdelfin	Gramper, Grijze dolfijn
Dolphin, Rough-toothed	Steno bredanensis	Rauzahndelfin	Snaveldolfijn
Mouse, House	Mus musculus	Hausmaus	Huismuis
Noctule, Lesser	Nyctalus leisleri	Kleinabendsegler	Bosvleermuis

Orca	*Orcinus orca*	Schwertwal	Orca
Pipistrelle, Madeira	*Pipistrellus maderensis*	Madeira-Zwergfledermaus	Madeira dwergvleermuis
Rabbit	*Oryctolagus cuniculus*	Wildkaninchen	Konijn
Rat, Black	*Rattus rattus*	Hausratte	Zwarte rat
Rat, Brown	*Rattus norvegicus*	Wanderratte	Bruine rat
Seal, Monk	*Monachus monachus*	Mittelmeer-Mönchsrobbe	Mediterrane monniksrob
Whale, Bryde's	*Balaenoptera brydei*	Brydewal	Brydevinvis
Whale, Cuvier's Beaked	*Ziphius cavirostris*	Cuvier-Schnabelwal	Dolfijn van Cuvier
Whale, False Killer	*Pseudorca crassidens*	Kleiner Schwertwal	Zwarte zwaardwalvis
Whale, Fin	*Balaenoptera physalus*	Finnwall	Gewone vinvis
Whale, Killer	See Orca		
Whale, Minke	*Balaenoptera acutorostrata*	Zwergwal	Dwergvinvis
Whale, Sei	*Balaenoptera borealis*	Seiwal	Noordse vinvis
Whale, Short-finned Pilot	*Globicephala macrorhynchus*	Kurzflossen-Grindwal	Indische griend
Whale, Sperm	*Physeter macrocephalus*	Pottwall	Potvis

Birds

English	Scientific	German	Dutch
Bee-eater	*Merops apiaster*	Bienenfresser	Bijeneter
Blackbird	*Turdus merula*	Amsel	Merel
Blackcap	*Sylvia atricapilla*	Mönchsgrasmücke	Zwartkop
Booby, Brown	*Sula leucogaster*	Weissbauchtölpel	Bruine gent
Buzzard	*Buteo buteo*	Mäusebussard	Buizerd
Canary	*Serinus canaria*	Kanarengirlitz	Kanarie
Chaffinch, Madeira	*Fringilla coelebs maderensis*	Madeira-Buchfink	Madeiravink
Chiffchaff	*Phylloscopus collybita*	Zilpzalp	Tjiftjaf
Coot	*Fulica atra*	Blässhuhn	Meerkoet
Cormorant, Great	*Phalacrocorax carbo*	Kormoran	Aalscholver
Curlew	*Numenius arquata*	Grosser Brachvogel	Wulp
Dove, Collared	*Streptopelia decaocto*	Türkentaube	Turkse tortel
Dove, Rock	*Columba livia*	Felsentaube	Rotsduif
Dove, Turtle	*Streptopelia turtur*	Turteltaube	Tortelduif
Duck, Mandarin	*Aix galericulata*	Mandarinente	Mandarijneend
Duck, Muscovy	*Cairina moschata*	Moschusente	Muskuseend
Dunlin	*Calidris alpina*	Alpenstrandläufer	Bonte strandloper
Egret, Cattle	*Bubulcus ibis*	Kuhreiher	Koereiger
Egret, Little	*Egretta garzetta*	Seidenreiher	Kleine zilverreiger
Firecrest, Madeira	*Regulus madeirensis*	Madeiragoldhähnchen	Madeiragoudhaan
Flycatcher, Pied	*Ficedula hypoleuca*	Trauerschnäpper	Bonte vliegenvanger
Flycatcher, Spotted	*Muscicapa striata*	Grauschnäpper	Grauwe vliegenvanger
Gadwall	*Anas strepera*	Schnatterente	Krakeend
Gannet, Northern	*Morus bassanus*	Basstölpel	Jan van Gent
Godwit, Black-tailed	*Limosa limosa*	Uferschnepfe	Grutto
Goldfinch	*Carduelis carduelis*	Distelfink	Putter

Goshawk	*Accipiter gentilis*	Habicht	Havik
Greenfinch	*Carduelis chloris*	Grünling	Groenling
Greenshank	*Tringa nebularia*	Grünschenkel	Groenpootruiter
Gull, Atlantic Yellow-legged	*Larus michahellis*	Weisskopfmöwe	Geelpootmeeuw
Gull, Black-headed	*Chroicocephalus ridibundus*	Lachmöwe	Kokmeeuw
Gull, Lesser Black-backed	*Larus fuscus*	Heringsmöwe	Kleine mantelmeeuw
Heron, Grey	*Ardea cinerea*	Graureiher	Blauwe reiger
Heron, Purple	*Ardea purpurea*	Purpurreiher	Purperreiger
Hoopoe	*Upupa epops*	Wiedehopf	Hop
Ibis, Glossy	*Plegadis falcinellus*	Braunsichler	Zwarte ibis
Kestrel	*Falco tinnunculus*	Turmfalke	Torenvalk
Kittiwake	*Rissa tridactyla*	Dreizehenmöwe	Drieteenmeeuw
Linnet, Common	*Carduelis cannabina*	Bluthänfling	Kneu
Mallard	*Anas platyrhynchos*	Stockente	Wilde eend
Martin, House	*Delichon urbicum*	Mehlschwalbe	Huiszwaluw
Martin, Sand	*Riparia riparia*	Uferschwalbe	Oeverzwaluw
Moorhen	*Gallinula chloropus*	Teichhuhn	Waterhoen
Oriole, Golden	*Oriolus oriolus*	Pirol	Wielewaal
Osprey	*Pandion haliaetus*	Fischadler	Visarend
Owl, Barn	*Tyto alba*	Schleiereule	Kerkuil
Owl, Madeiran Scops	*Otus mauli*	Madeira-Zwergohreule	Madeira-dwergooruil
Owl, Short-eared	*Asio flammeus*	Sumpfohreule	Velduil
Parakeet, Rose-ringed	*Psittacula krameri*	Halsbandsittich	Halsbandparkiet
Partridge, Red-legged	*Alectoris rufa*	Rothuhn	Rode patrijs
Petrel, Bulwer's	*Bulweria bulwerii*	Bulwersturmvogel	Bulwers stormvogel
Petrel, Desertas	*Pterodroma deserta*	Desertas-Sturmvogel	Desertasstormvogel / Gon-gon
Petrel, Fea's	*Pterodroma feae*	Kapverden-Sturmvogel	Kaapverdische stormvogel
Petrel, Soft-plumaged	*Pterodroma mollis*	Weichfedersturmvogel	Donsstormvogel
Petrel, Zino´s	*Pterodroma madeira*	Madeira-Sturmvogel	Freira
Pigeon, Feral	*Columba livia f. domestica*	Stadttaube	Stadsduif
Pigeon, Madeira Wood	*Columba palumbus maderensis*	Madeira-Ringeltaube	Madeira houtduif
Pigeon, Trocaz	*Columba trocaz*	Silberhalstaube	Trocazduif
Pigeon, Wood	*Columba palumbus*	Ringeltaube	Houtduif
Pipit, Berthelot´s	*Anthus berthelotii*	Kanarenpieper	Berthelots pieper
Plover, Kentish	*Charadrius alexandrinus*	Seeregenpfeifer	Strandplevier
Plover, Little Ringed	*Charadrius dubius*	Flussregenpfeifer	Kleine plevier
Plover, Ringed	*Charadrius hiaticula*	Sandregenpfeifer	Bontbekplevier
Quail	*Coturnix coturnix*	Wachtel	Kwartel
Redshank	*Tringa totanus*	Rotschenkel	Tureluur
Redstart	*Phoenicurus phoenicurus*	Gartenrotschwanz	Gekraagde roodstaart
Redstart, Black	*Phoenicurus ochruros*	Hausrotschwanz	Zwarte roodstaart
Redwing	*Turdus iliacus*	Rotdrossel	Koperwiek
Robin	*Erithacus rubecula*	Rotkehlchen	Roodborst
Roller	*Coracias garrulus*	Blauracke	Scharrelaar
Ruff	*Philomachus pugnax*	Kampfläufer	Kemphaan

English	Scientific	German	Dutch
Sanderling	*Calidris alba*	Sanderling	Drieteenstrandloper
Sandpiper, Common	*Actitis hypoleucos*	Flussuferläufer	Oeverloper
Sandpiper, Spotted	*Actitis macularius*	Drosseluferläufer	Amerikaanse oeverloper
Shearwater, Balearic	*Puffinus mauretanicus*	Balearen-Sturmtaucher	Vale pijlstormvogel
Shearwater, Macaronesian	*Puffinus baroli*	Makaronesischer Sturmtaucher	Kleine pijlstormvogel
Shearwater, Cory´s	*Calonectris borealis*	Gelbschnabel-Sturmtaucher	Kuhls pijlstormvogel
Shearwater, Great	*Puffinus gravis*	Grosser Sturmtaucher	Grote pijlstormvogel
Shearwater, Manx	*Puffinus puffinus*	Schwarzschnabel-Sturmtaucher	Noordse pijlstormvogel
Shearwater, Sooty	*Puffinus griseus*	Dunkler Sturmtaucher	Grauwe pijlstormvogel
Shrike, Woodchat	*Lanius senator*	Rotkopfwürger	Roodkopklauwier
Siskin	*Carduelis spinus*	Erlenzeisig	Sijs
Skua, Arctic	*Stercorarius parasiticus*	Schmarotzerraubmöwe	Kleine Jager
Skua, Great	*Stercorarius skua*	Skua	Grote jager
Skua, Pomarine	*Stercorarius pomarinus*	Spatelraubmöwe	Middelste jager
Skua, South Polar	*Stercorarius maccormicki*	Antarktikskua	Zuidpooljager
Skylark	*Alauda arvensis*	Feldlerche	Veldleeuwerik
Snipe, Common	*Gallinago gallinago*	Bekassine	Watersnip
Sparrow, Rock	*Petronia petronia*	Steinsperling	Rotsmus
Sparrow, Spanish	*Passer hispaniolensis*	Weidensperling	Spaanse mus
Sparrowhawk	*Accipiter nisus*	Sperber	Sperwer
Spoonbill	*Platalea leucorodia*	Löffler	Lepelaar
Starling	*Sturnus vulgaris*	Star	Spreeuw
Stilt, Black-winged	*Himantopus himantopus*	Stelzenläufer	Steltkluut
Stint, Little	*Calidris minuta*	Zwergstrandläufer	Kleine strandloper
Storm-petrel, European	*Hydrobates pelagicus*	Sturmschwalbe	Stormvogeltje
Storm-petrel, Leach's	*Oceanodroma leucorhoa*	Wellenläufer	Vaal stormvogeltje
Storm-petrel, Madeiran	*Oceanodroma castro*	Madeirawellenläufer	Madeirastormvogeltje
Storm-petrel, White-faced	*Pelagodroma marina*	Weissgesicht-Sturmschwalbe	Bont stormvogeltje
Storm-petrel, Wilson´s	*Oceanites oceanicus*	Buntfuss-Sturmschwalbe	Wilsons stormvogeltje
Swallow	*Hirundo rustica*	Rauchschwalbe	Boerenzwaluw
Swallow, Red-rumped	*Cecropsis daurica*	Rötelschwalbe	Roodstuitzwaluw
Swift, Common	*Apus apus*	Mauersegler	Gierzwaluw
Swift, Pallid	*Apus pallidus*	Fahlsegler	Vale gierzwaluw
Swift, Plain	*Apus unicolor*	Einfarbsegler	Madeiragierzwaluw
Teal	*Anas crecca*	Krickente	Wintertaling
Teal, Green-winged	*Anas carolinensis*	Carolinakrickente	Amerikaanse wintertaling
Tern, Common	*Sterna hirundo*	Flussseeschwalbe	Visdief
Tern, Roseate	*Sterna dougallii*	Rosenseeschwalbe	Dougall's stern
Tern, Sandwich	*Thalasseus sandvicensis*	Brandseeschwalbe	Grote stern
Turnstone	*Arenaria interpres*	Steinwälzer	Steenloper
Wagtail, Grey	*Motacilla cinerea*	Gebirgsstelze	Grote gele kwikstaart
Wagtail, White	*Motacilla alba*	Bachstelze	Witte kwikstaart
Warbler, Spectacled	*Sylvia conspicillata*	Brillengrasmücke	Brilgrasmus
Waxbill, Common	*Estrilda astrild*	Wellenastrild	Sint-Helenafazantje

English	Scientific	German	Dutch
Wheatear	Oenanthe oenanthe	Steinschmätzer	Tapuit
Whimbrel	Numenius phaeopus	Regenbrachvogel	Regenwulp
Whinchat	Saxicola rubetra	Braunkehlchen	Paapje
Whitethroat	Sylvia communis	Dorngrasmücke	Grasmus
Woodcock	Scolopax rusticola	Waldschnepfe	Houtsnip

Reptiles and Amphibians

English	Scientific	German	Dutch
Frog, Iberian Water	Pelophylax perezi	Iberischer Wasserfrosch	Iberische meerkikker
Frog, Stripeless Tree	Hyla meridionalis	Mittelmeer-Laubfrosch	Mediterrane boomkikker
Gecko, Moorish	Tarentola mauritanica	Maurischer Gecko	Muurgekko
Gecko, Selvagens Island	Tarentola bischoffi	Selvagens-Mauergecko*	Selvagens-muurgekko*
Gecko, Tropical House	Hemidactylus mabouia	Afrikanisches Hausgecko	Huisgekko
Lizard, Madeira Wall	Teira dugesii	Madeira-Eidechse	Madeirahagedis
Lizard, Tenerife	Gallotia galloti	Kanareneidechse	Canarische Hagedis
Slider, Red-eared	Trachemys scripta	Rotwangen-Schmuckschildkröte	Roodwangschildpad
Snake, Flower Pot	Indotyphlops braminus	Blumentopfschlange	Gewone wormslang
Turtle, Green Sea	Chelonia mydas	Grüne Meeresschildkröte	Soepschildpad
Turtle, Hawksbill Sea	Eretmochelys imbricata	Echte Karettschildkröte	Karetschildpad
Turtle, Kemp's Ridley Sea	Lepidochelys kempii	Atlantik-Bastardschildkröte	Kemps zeeschildpad
Turtle, Leatherback Sea	Dermochelys coriacea	Lederschildkröte	Lederschildpad
Turtle, Loggerhead Sea	Caretta caretta	Unechte Karettschildkröte	Dikkopschildpad

Invertebrates

English	Scientific	German	Dutch
Admiral, (Common) Red	Vanessa atalanta	Admiral	Atalanta
Admiral, Canary Red	Vanessa vulcania	Kanarischer Admiral	Canarische atalanta
Anemone, Snakelocks	Anemonia sulcata	Wachsrose	Wasroos
Barnacle, Poli's Stellate	Chthamalus stellatus	Sternseepocke	Sterzeepok
Blue, Lang´s Short-tailed	Leptotes pirithous	Kleiner Wander-Bläuling	Klein tijgerblauwtje
Blue, Long-tailed	Lampides boeticus	Grosser Wander-Bläuling	Tijgerblauwtje
Bluetail, Small	Ischnura pumilio	Kleine Pechlibelle	Tengere grasjuffer
Bollworm, Cotton	Helicoverpa armigera	Baumwoll-Kapseleule	Katoendaguil
Brimstone, Madeira	Gonepteryx maderensis	Madeira-Zitronenfalter	Madeiracleopatra
Bush-cricket, Madeiran Steppe	Montana barretii	Madeira Beissschrecke*	Madeira-sabelsprinkhaan*
Cleopatra, Madeiran	See Madeira Brimstone		
Copper, Small	Lycaena phlaeas	Kleiner Feuerfalter	Kleine vuurvlinder
Crab, Sally Lightfoot	Percnon gibbesi	Felsenkrabbe	Gibbesi krab
Darter, Island	Sympetrum nigrifemur	Madeira-Heidelibelle	Eilandheidelibel
Darter, Red-Veined	Sympetrum fonscolombii	Frühe Heidelibelle	Zwervende heidelibel
Dogwhelk	Nucella lapillus	Nordische Purpurschnecke	Purperslak

English	Scientific	German	Dutch
Emperor, Blue	Anax imperator	Grosse Königslibelle	Grote keizerlibel
Emperor, Lesser	Anax parthenope	Kleine Königslibelle	Zuidelijke keizerlibel
Emperor, Vagrant	Anax ephippiger	Schabrackenlibelle	Zadellibel
Fritillary, Queen of Spain	Issoria lathonia	Kleiner Perlmutterfalter	Kleine parelmoervlinder
Grasshopper, Handsome Cross	Oedaleus decorus	Kreuzschrecke	Kruissprinkhaan*
Grasshopper, Madeira Pincer	Calliptamus madeira	Madeira Schönschrecke*	Madeira-rosevleugel*
Grayling, Madeiran	Hipparchia maderensis	Madeira-Samtfalter	Madeiraheivlinder
Hawk-moth, Hummingbird	Macroglossum stellatarum	Taubenschwänzchen	Kolibrievlinder
Hawk-moth, Madeiran Spurge*	Hyles tithymali gecki	Madeira-Wolfsmilchschwärmer	Madeira- Madeiran Wolfsmelkpijlstaart*
Herald	Scoliopteryx libatrix	Zackeneule	Roesje
Lady, Painted	Vanessa cardui	Distelfalter	Distelvlinder
Limpet, China	Patella ulyssiponensis	Lissabon-Napfschnecke	Ruwe schaalhoren
Man-o-War, Portuguese	Physalia physalis	Portugiesische Galeere	Portugees oorlogschip
Migrant, African	Catopsilia florella	Afrikanischer Einwanderer	Gele trekvlinder
Monarch	Danaus plexippus	Monarchfalter	Monarchvlinder
Shades, Angle	Phlogophora meticulosa	Achateule	Agaatvlinder
Shell, Top	Monodonta edulis	Kreiselschnecke	Tolschelp*
Shrimp, Rockpool	Palaemon elegans	Kleine Felsengarnele	Gewone steurgarnaal
Speckled, Crimson	Utetheisa pulchella	Harlekinbär	Prachtbeer
Tarantula, Desertas*	Hogna ingens	Deserta-Tarantel	Desertas-tarantula*
Tiger, False Plain	Hypolimnas misippus	Scheinmonarch*	Valse monarchvlinder
Tiger, Plain	Danaus chrysippus	Afrikanischer Monarch	Kleine monarchvlinder
Twin-spot, Golden	Chrysodeixis chalcites	Tomaten-Goldeule	Turkse uil
Wartbiter, Southern	Decticus albifrons	Südlicher Warzenbeisser	Zuidelijke wrattenbijter
White, Bath	Pontia daplidice	Reseda Falter	Resedawitje
White, Madeira Large	Pieris brassicae wollastoni	Madeira-Kohlweissling	Madeirakoolwitje
White, Small	Pieris rapae	Kleiner Kohlweissling	Klein koolwitje
Wood, Common Speckled	Pararge aegeria	Waldbrettspiel	Bont zandoogje
Wood, Madeiran Speckled	Pararge xiphia	Madeira-Waldbrettspiel	Madeira bont zandoogje
Yellow, Clouded	Colias crocea	Postillion	Oranje luzernevlinder

Fish

English	Scientific	German	Dutch
Fish, Black Scabbard	Aphanopus carbo	Schwarzer Degenfisch	Zwarte haarstaartvis

CROSSBILL GUIDES
IF YOU WANT TO SEE MORE

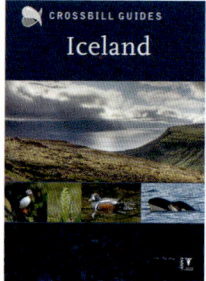 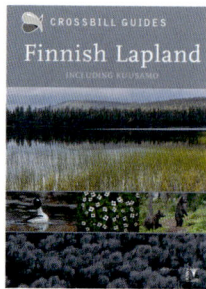 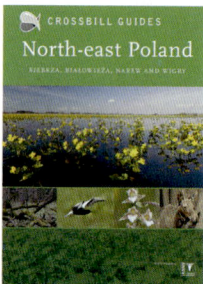 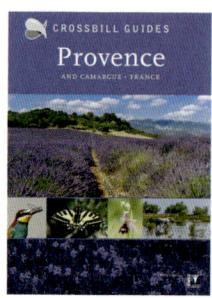
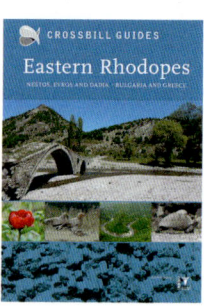 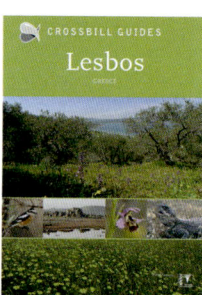 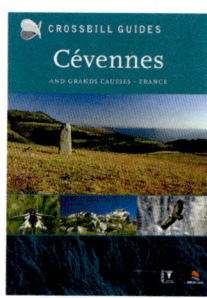 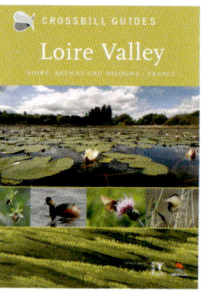
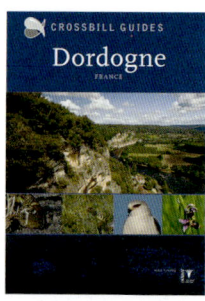 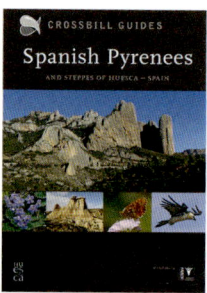  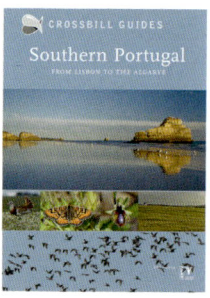
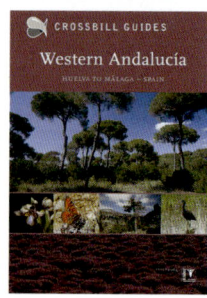 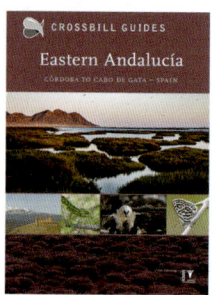 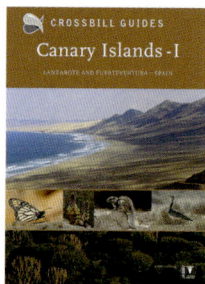 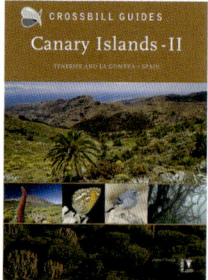

More titles are in preparation. Check our website for further details and updates.
WWW.CROSSBILLGUIDES.ORG